Prepare with The Power of Classroom Practice

Register for **MyEducationLab** today at www.myeducationlab.com

What is MyEducationLab?

MyEducationLab is easy to use and integrate into this book.

Wherever you see the MyEducationLab logo in the margins or elsewhere in the text, follow the simple instructions to access the videos, strategies, cases, and artifacts associated with these assignments, activities, and learning units on MyEducationLab. MyEducationLab is organized topically to enhance the coverage of the core concepts discussed in the chapters of your book. For each topic on the course you will find most or all of the following resources:

Students:

- Take **Practice Tests** for each chapter of your text.
  - Completion of each practice test generates a **study plan** that is unique to you.
  - The study plan links to text excerpts, activities with feedback, and videos and other media that can help you master concepts covered in your text.

- Complete **Assignments and Activities** to apply text content to real classroom situations.

- Explore the **Building Teaching Skills and Dispositions** exercises to practice and strengthen the skills that are essential to teaching.

MyEducationLab offers:

- Authentic **classroom video** shows real teachers and students interacting, and helps prepare you for the classroom.

- **Case studies** offer real-life perspectives on common issues and challenges faced in the classroom.

- Authentic student and teacher **classroom artifacts** provide you with the actual types of materials encountered every day by teachers.

CONNECTION TO NATIONAL STANDARDS: Now it is easier than ever to see how coursework is connected to national standards. Each topic on MyEducationLab lists intended learning outcomes connected to the appropriate national standards. And all of the Assignments and Activities and all of the Building Teaching Skills and Dispositions in MyEducationLab are mapped to the appropriate national standards and learning outcomes.

ASSIGNMENTS AND ACTIVITIES: Designed to save instructors preparation time and enhance student understanding, these assignable exercises show concepts in action (through video, cases, and/or student and teacher artifacts). They help students synthesize and apply concepts and strategies they read about in the book.

BUILDING TEACHING SKILLS AND DISPOSITIONS

These learning units help students practice and strengthen skills that are essential to quality teaching. Students are presented with the core skill or concept and then given an opportunity to practice their understanding of this concept multiple times by watching video footage (or interacting with other media) and then critically analyzing the strategy or skill presented.

STUDY PLAN

A MyEducationLab Study Plan is a multiple choice assessment tied to chapter objectives and supported by study material. A well-designed Study Plan offers multiple opportunities to fully master required course content as identified by the objectives in each chapter:

- **Chapter Objectives** identify the learning outcomes for the chapter and give students targets to shoot for as they read and study.
- **Multiple Choice Assessments** assess mastery of the content. These assessments are mapped to chapter objectives, and students can take the multiple choice quiz as many times as they want. Not only do these quizzes provide overall scores for each objective, but they also explain why responses to particular items are correct or incorrect.
- **Study Material: Review, Practice and Enrichment** give students a deeper understanding of what they do and do not know related to chapter content. This material includes text excerpts, activities that include hints and feedback, and interactive multi-media exercises built around videos, simulations, cases, or classroom artifacts.
- **Flashcards** help students study the definitions of the key terms within each chapter.

GENERAL RESOURCES ON YOUR MYEDUCATIONLAB COURSE

The Resources section on MyEducationLab is designed to help students pass their licensure exams, put together effective portfolios and lesson plans, prepare for and navigate the first year of their teaching careers, and understand key educational standards, policies, and laws. This section includes:

- **Licensure Exams:** Contains guidelines for passing the Praxis exam. **The Practice Test Exam** includes practice multiple-choice questions, case study questions, and video case studies with sample questions.
- **Lesson Plan Builder:** Helps students create and share lesson plans.
- **Licensure and Standards:** Provides links to state licensure standards and national standards.
- **Beginning Your Career:** Educate Offers tips, advice, and valuable information on:
  - o Resume Writing and Interviewing: Expert advice on how to write impressive resumes and prepare for job interviews.
  - o Your First Year of Teaching: Practical tips on setting up a classroom, managing student behavior, and planning for instruction and assessment.
  - o Law and Public Policies: Includes specific directives and requirements educators need to understand under the No Child Left Behind Act and the Individuals with Disabilities Education Improvement Act of 2004.

What if I need help?

We've got you covered 24/7.
There is a wealth of helpful information on the site, under "Tours and Training "and" Support."
Technical support is available 24 hours a day, seven days a week, at http://247pearsoned.custhelp.com.

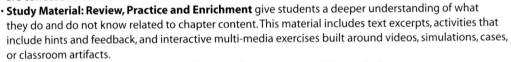

Visit **www.myeducationlab.com** for a demonstration of this exciting new online teaching resource.

ACTION RESEARCH

A Guide for the Teacher Researcher

FOURTH EDITION

Geoffrey E. Mills
Southern Oregon University

Boston Columbus Indianapolis New York San Francisco Upper Saddle River
Amsterdam Cape Town Dubai London Madrid Milan Munich Paris Montreal Toronto
Delhi Mexico City Sao Paulo Sydney Hong Kong Seoul Singapore Taipei Tokyo

Editor-in-Chief: Paul Smith
Editorial Assistant: Matthew Buchholz
Development Editor: Christina Robb
Vice President, Director of Marketing: Quinn Perkson
Marketing Manager: Jared Brueckner
Production Editor: Gregory Erb
Editorial Production Service: NK Graphics/Tonnya Norwood
Manufacturing Buyer: Megan Cochran
Electronic Composition: NK Graphics
Interior Design: NK Graphics/Michel Newkirk
Cover Designer: Linda Knowles

For related titles and support materials, visit our online catalog at www.pearsonhighered.com.

Between the time website information is gathered and then published, it is not unusual for some sites to have closed. Also, the transcription of URLs can result in typographical errors. The publisher would appreciate notification where these errors occur so that they may be corrected in subsequent editions.

Library of Congress Cataloging-in-Publication Data

Mills, Geoffrey E.
  Action research: a guide for the teacher researcher/Geoffrey E. Mills.—4th ed.
    p. cm.
  Includes bibliographical references and index.
  ISBN-13: 978-0-13-700314-3
  ISBN-10: 0-13-700314-5 (pbk.)
  1. Action research in education—United States—Handbooks, manuals, etc.
2. Teaching—United States—Handbooks, manuals, etc. I. Title.
  LB1028.24.M55 2010
  370.7'2—dc22   2009034973

Printed in the United States of America
10 9 8 7 6 5 4 3 2 1   RRD-VA   14 13 12 11 10

www.pearsonhighered.com

ISBN-10: 0-13-700314-5
ISBN-13: 978-0-13-700314-3

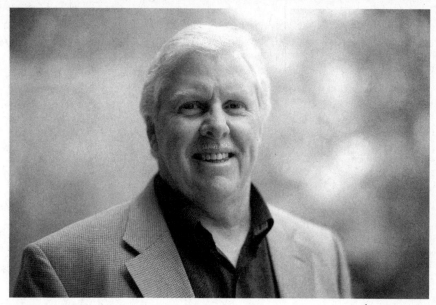
Photograph courtesy of Rory Finney Photography

About the Author

A native of Australia, Geoff moved to the United States in 1986 to undertake doctoral studies at the University of Oregon. After completing his PhD in 1988, Geoff accepted his first teaching position at Southern Oregon State College (now Southern Oregon University). After 12 years of teaching, Geoff moved in to university administration and is now in his tenth year as Dean and Professor of Education in the School of Education at Southern Oregon University.

Geoff has traveled extensively and given invited action research presentations in Australia, New Zealand, Greenland, United Kingdom, Canada, and many states in the United States. In addition to *Action Research: A Guide for the Teacher Researcher*, 4e, Geoff is also the only active author of *Educational Research: Competencies for Analysis and Applications* (2009) (with L. R. Gay and P. Airasian), now in its 9th edition.

For Ernie Mills, Audrey Mills, Dr. Milton H. Brown, and Catherine S. Brown—
Your love, support, and spirit live with me always.

Brief Contents

Contents

Preface

New to This Edition

The fourth edition of *Action Research* has been revised in response to expert reviewer feedback. The fourth edition includes:

Balanced Coverage of Quantitative Data Collection and Analysis Techniques
- Additional coverage of mixed methods research has been added throughout the book.

A Focus on Producing Critical Consumers of Action Research
- A new chapter, "Evaluating Action Research" (Chapter 9), helps students become critical consumers of research.
- Included in Chapter 9 is an article from an action research journal that is analyzed using the new criteria for evaluating action research.
- Appendix A, "Action Research in Action," contains an extended example and evaluation of an action research case study.

An Expanded Coverage of Ethics
- Chapter 2, "Ethics," provides an expanded discussion of ethical guidelines and provides guidance for seeking and obtaining Institutional Review Board (IRB) approval.

Integration to the MyEducationLab for Action Research Website
- The fourth edition of *Action Research* includes margin note integration with MyEducationLab for Action Research, a dynamic online learning environment that provides students with the opportunity to build a better understanding of action research through engagement with real products from the research process.

The Role of Action Research in Effecting Educational Change

Action research has the potential to be a powerful agent of educational change. Action research helps to develop teachers and administrators with professional attitudes, who embrace action, progress, and reform rather than stability and mediocrity. In addition, the action research process fosters a democratic approach to decision making while, at the same time, empowering individual teachers through participation in a collaborative, socially responsive research activity.

Commitment to action research positions teachers and administrators as learners rather than experts. Those committed to action research will willingly undertake continued professional development because they believe that there is a gap between the real world of their daily teaching practices and their vision of an ideal one.

Incorporating action research into preservice teacher education programs and professional development programs for inservice teachers will help make action research an ongoing component of a professional teacher's practice. Such action will ultimately help teachers incorporate action research alongside other critical components of teaching, such as curriculum development, authentic assessment strategies, classroom management strategies, teaching strategies, and caring for children. Such actions will encourage teachers to embrace change.

It is my hope that this book will, in some small part, help us keep moving forward, even in difficult times. Action research is an invitation to learn, a means to tackle tough questions that face us individually and collectively as teachers, and a method for questioning our daily taken-for-granted assumptions as a way to find hope for the future.

Conceptual Framework and Organization of the Text

This book has evolved over a number of years based on my experience of doing and teaching action research. During this time I have had the opportunity to work with some outstanding university faculty, classroom teachers, and principals who were committed to looking systematically at the effects of their programs on children's lives. This book's organization has grown out of these experiences and has been field tested by numerous students and colleagues.

Each chapter opens with an action research vignette that illustrates the content that will follow. These vignettes, most of which have been written by teachers and principals with whom I have worked, show readers what action research looks like in practice and who does it. The order of these chapters roughly matches the action research process, an approach that I have found successful when teaching action research.

Contents of This New Edition

Chapter 1, "Understanding Action Research," defines action research and provides historical and theoretical contexts for the rest of the book. The chapter also reviews various models of action research and concludes with the four-step process (identifying an area of focus, collecting data, analyzing and interpreting data, and developing an action plan) and the dialectic model on which this book is based. The remaining chapters mirror these steps.

Chapter 2, "Ethics," provides an expanded discussion of ethical guidelines and poses an ethical dilemma vignette to spark teacher researchers' thinking about how best to resolve ethical dilemmas if and when they arise. This chapter also provides guidance for seeking and obtaining Institutional Review Board (IRB) approval.

Chapter 3, "Deciding on an Area of Focus," provides guidelines for selecting an area of focus, along with step-by-step directions for how to do a literature review using many online resources as well as traditional university library resources. The chapter provides an expanded discussion of how to write a literature review and culminates with an action research plan that provides a practical guide for moving teacher researchers through the action research process.

Chapter 4, "Data Collection Techniques," offers a comprehensive discussion of qualitative data collection that covers the "3 Es" of qualitative data collection: experiencing, enquiring, and examining. It also provides a comprehensive discussion of quantitative data collection techniques that covers collecting data from teacher-made tests, standardized tests, and attitude scales. A section on triangulation covers how to work with multiple sources of data.

Chapter 5, "Data Collection Considerations: Validity, Reliability, and Generalizibility," addresses important data collection considerations to ensure that the data collected will be "trustworthy."

Chapter 6, "Data Analysis and Interpretation," describes selected techniques of data analysis and data interpretation and distinguishes between the goals of the two processes.

Included in this chapter is an expanded discussion of data analysis and interpretation with examples of each for qualitative and quantitative data sources.

Chapter 7, "Action Planning for Educational Change," helps teacher researchers take action using a helpful Steps to Action Chart. The chapter also discusses potential obstacles to change and suggests strategies for overcoming these obstacles.

Chapter 8, "Writing Up Action Research," provides practical guidelines for writing up action research and ways that teacher researchers can "get the word out." A reprinted action research article with marginal notations gives researchers an example of the general structure and components of written action research. A self-evaluation rubric helps teacher researchers make sure their write-up is ready for publication. There is also a discussion of using the *Publication Manual of the American Psychological Association* (6th ed.) during the writing process.

Finally, Chapter 9, "Evaluating Action Research," is new to this edition and focuses on analyzing and evaluating action research studies. Included in this edition is a new article from an online journal that is analyzed using the new criteria for evaluating action research publications.

Appendix A, "Action Research in Action," contains an extended example of action research through a case study of Curtis Elementary. This case study follows the process described throughout the book and includes an evaluation of the project on the basis of criteria for evaluating action research presented in Chapter 9. Appendix B, "Standard Deviation and Action Research," contains a brief discussion of standard deviation and how it can be applied to the analysis and interpretation of teacher research. Appendix C, "Displaying Data Visually," presents a variety of examples of visual displays of data—bar graphs, tables, and a concept map—from action research projects. Using these display techniques helps teachers "see" data for better analysis and more effective communication of their findings.

Features of the Text

The text's user-friendly format includes chapter objectives, Key Concepts boxes, Research in Action checklists, margin note integration to the MyEducationLab for Action Research website (described below), expanded chapter summaries, and questions for further thought. The text also includes many practical illustrations of the action research process that will help teacher researchers apply the process in their own school or classroom setting.

Discover the Student and Instructor Support for *Action Research*

PEARSON
myeducationlab

Go to the Assignments and Activities section of Topic #1, *Ethics*, in the MyEducationLab for your course and complete the activity titled "Understanding Ethical Standards." This activity provides an opportunity for you to learn more about the ethical guidelines for research developed by the U.S. National Institutes of Health and those of your institution.

MyEducationLab for Action Research

MyEducationLab for Action Research offers instructors and students a uniquely valuable teaching and learning tool that is also easy to use.

Wherever the MyEducationLab logo appears in the margins or elsewhere in the text, readers can follow the simple instructions to access the appropriate exercises and resources on MyEducationLab.

MyEducationLab is organized topically to enhance coverage of the core concepts discussed in this book. For each topic, readers will find most or all of the following resources:

- **Learning Outcomes** give students targets to shoot for as they read and study.
- **Assignments and Activities** can be assigned as homework or completed as in-class activities. Feedback for these exercises is available only to instructors.

- **Building Research Skills** exercises are included to give students the opportunity to build their research skills through focused exercises. Scaffolded feedback for these exercises is provided to students.

MyEducationLab for Action Research is easy to assign, which is essential to providing the greatest benefit to students. Visit **www.myeducationlab.com** for a demonstration of this exciting new online teaching resource.

Online PowerPoint® Slides

To enhance class lectures, Online PowerPoint® slides are available. To access the Online PowerPoint slides, go to **www.pearsonhighered.com/educator**. Enter the author, title, or ISBN, and click on this book. The PowerPoint® slides are available for download under the "Resources" tab.

Acknowledgments

I would like to thank the reviewers, who invested a great deal of time and provided critical feedback during the development of this book. These reviewers include Jennifer Esposito, Georgia State University; Jane B. Huffman, University of North Texas; Alice Merz, Indiana University-Purdue University, Fort Wayne; Lynne Walters, Texas A&M University.

I would also like to acknowledge the staff at Pearson, without whose guidance (and patience!) this book would not have become a reality. In particular, I thank Kevin Davis, Director of Media Solutions, for working with me on a fourth edition of the book so as to build on what we achieved with the previous editions. Although Kevin was promoted in the middle of this revision, I am fortunate that he stayed involved in the development of the book while undertaking his new responsibilities heading up the development of online learning for Pearson Education. After ten years of working with Kevin, the editorship of my books has been handed off to Paul Smith, who will have big shoes to fill! I would also like to thank Christie Robb, Development Editor, who worked diligently to ensure a quality, user-friendly text and patiently kept me on track in order to meet publication deadlines.

I would also like to extend my gratitude to the hundreds of students at Southern Oregon University who responded to various drafts of previous editions of this book and also endured my ramblings about the importance of being reflective practitioners and self-renewing professionals. Their insights into what makes a text user-friendly have been greatly appreciated and are reflected in the text. Similarly, I have had the pleasure of working with hundreds of teachers throughout Oregon who taught me what needed to be included in a "helpful" book.

Finally, I appreciate the support and encouragement of my wife, colleague, and best friend, Dr. Donna Mills (Southern Oregon University), who endured my mood swings and weekend writing commitments throughout this lengthy process. And I thank my son Jonathan, who gave up time with his dad and continually reminded me of three important things: (1) what it means to be a teacher and a learner, (2) that I must exercise every day so that I keep up with his energy and enthusiasm for life, and (3) that it's always the computer's fault when things don't work the way they are meant to! The writing of this fourth edition was tackled immediately following another long writing project, the ninth edition of *Educational Research: Competencies for Analysis and Applications* (Gay, Mills, and Airasian, 2009). My sincere thanks to Donna and Jonathan for their patience and support during the past two years.

—Geoff Mills

1

Understanding Action Research

This chapter introduces action research by providing an example of an action research project from a real teacher researcher, an exploration of the historical and theoretical foundations of action research, a discussion of the goals and justification for action research, and an explanation of the action research process.

After reading this chapter you should be able to:

1 Describe the goal of educational research and the different approaches researchers use.

2 Define action research.

3 Describe the origins of action research.

4 Identify the similarities and differences between critical and practical theories of action research.

5 Describe the goals of and rationale for action research.

6 Describe the justifications for action research and steps you can take to make it part of your daily teaching practice.

7 Describe the four stages of the action research process.

What Motivates Unmotivated Students?

DEBORAH SOUTH

Deborah South, a teacher in a rural Oregon high school, was a participant in an action research class. She shares the challenges she faced when, owing to a last-minute teaching assignment, she found herself working with a group of "unmotivated" students. Deborah's story illustrates the wide variety of factors that can influence students' learning and a teacher's willingness to critically examine her teaching methods and how they affected the children in her classroom. Although Deborah's interpretation of the results of her study did not validate her practice, it did provide data that Deborah and the school's principal could use to make changes to the existing curriculum for unmotivated students.

Teaching students who are unmotivated and apathetic can be a difficult challenge for any teacher to overcome. These students typically can be disruptive and negative and often require an extraordinary amount of teacher time to manage their behavior. My concern with teaching unmotivated students has existed almost since I began teaching 5 years ago. As an educator, one tries all kinds of possible strategies to encourage students to be successful. However, these strategies do not work with unmotivated students who are apathetic and exhibit unacceptable behavior. Eventually the patience runs out and, as ashamed as I am to admit it, I stop trying to find ways to reach these particular students. It soon becomes enough that they stay in their seats, be quiet, and do not disturb anyone.

However, last term my attitude was forced to change. I was given a study skills group of 20 of the lowest achieving eighth graders in the school. This new class consisted of 16 boys and 4 girls. My task was to somehow take these students and miraculously make them motivated, achieving students. I was trained in a study skills program before the term started and I thought that I was prepared: I had the students, I had the curriculum, and I had the help of an outstanding aide.

Within a week, I sensed we were in trouble. My 20 students often showed up with no supplies. Their behavior was atrocious. They called each other names, threw various items around the room, and walked around the classroom when they felt like it. Their attitudes toward me were negative. I became concerned about teaching these students. In part, I felt bad that they were so disillusioned with school and their future; I also felt bad because the thought of teaching in this environment every day for another 14 weeks made me wish summer vacation were here.

Given this situation, I decided to do some reading about how other teachers motivate unmotivated students and to formulate some ideas about the variables that contribute to a student's success in school. Variables I investigated included adult approval, peer influence, and success in such subjects as math, science, language arts, and social studies, as well as self-esteem and students' views of their academic abilities.

I collected the majority of the data through surveys, interviews, and report card/attendance records in an effort to answer the following questions:

- How does attendance affect student performance?
- How are students influenced by their friends in completing schoolwork?
- How do adults (parents, teachers) affect the success of students?
- What levels of self-esteem do these students have?

As a result of this investigation, I learned many things. For example, for this group of students attendance does not appear to be a factor—with the exception of one student, their school attendance was regular.

Not surprisingly, peer groups did affect student performance. Seventy-three percent of my students reported that their friends never encouraged doing homework or putting any effort into homework.

Another surprising result was the lack of impact of a teacher's approval on student achievement. Ninety-four percent of my students indicated that they never or seldom do their homework to receive teacher approval. Alternatively, 57 percent indicated that they often or always do their homework so that their families will be proud of them.

One of the most interesting findings of this study was the realization that most of my students misbehave out of frustration at their own lack of abilities. They are not being obnoxious to gain attention, but to divert attention from the fact that they do not know how to complete the assigned work.

When I looked at report cards and compared grades over three quarters, I noticed a trend. Between the first and second quarter, student performance had increased. That is, most students were doing better than they had during the first quarter. Between the second and third quarters, however, grades dropped dramatically. I tried to determine why that drop would occur, and the only common experience shared by these 20 students was the fact that they had been moved into my class at the beginning of the third quarter.

When I presented my project to the action research class during our end-of-term "celebration," I was convinced that the "cause" of the students' unmotivated behavior was my teaching. I had concluded through my data analysis and interpretation that the one experience these 20 children had in common was participation in my study skills class. This conclusion, however, was not readily accepted by my critical friends and colleagues in the action research class, who urged me to consider other interpretations of the data. For example, perhaps the critical mass of negativity present in one classroom provided the children with a catalyst to act out against the teacher. After all, this was the only class shared exclusively by these 20 students. Afterward, I shared the findings of my study with my school principal. As a result, she decided not to group these students together homogeneously for a study skills class the following year.

A s you can see, action research is a "wonderfully uncomfortable" (Lytle, 1997) place to be—once we start our journey of investigation, we have no way of knowing in advance where we will end up. Action research, like any other problem-solving process, is an ongoing creative activity that exposes us to surprises along the way. What appears to matter in the planning stages of an action research investigation may provide us with only a hint, a scratching of the surface, of what is really the focus for our investigations. How we deal with the uncertainty of the journey positions us as learners of our own craft, an attitude that is critical to our success. This book attempts to foster an openness in the spirit of inquiry guided by action research.

A Brief Overview of Educational Research

When you hear the words *scientific research*, you probably think of a scientist in a white lab coat (usually a balding, middle-aged man with a pocket full of pens!) mixing chemicals or doing experiments involving white mice. Traditional scientists, like the one pictured in this rather trite image, proceed with their research under the assumption that "all behaviors and events are orderly" and that all events "have discoverable causes" (Gay, Mills, & Airasian, 2009, pp. 5–6). This traditional belief that natural phenomena can be explained in an orderly way using empirical sciences is sometimes called **positivism**.

Human beings, however, are very complicated organisms, and compared with chemicals—and mice, for that matter—their behavior can be disorderly and fairly unpredictable. This presents a challenge to educational researchers, who are concerned with gaining insight into human behavior in educational environments such as schools and classrooms.

The goal of traditional educational research is "to explain, predict, and/or control educational phenomena" (Gay et al., 2009, p. 6). To do this, researchers try to manipulate and control certain **variables** (the factors that might affect the outcomes of a particular study) to test a **hypothesis** (a statement the researcher makes that predicts what will happen or explains what the outcome of the study will be). The word *control* is not used here in a negative sense; rather, it describes one of the characteristics of traditional, quantitatively-oriented research, in which the researcher must control the environment in order to be able to draw cause-effect relationship conclusions. This cannot occur unless the researcher is able to control the variables in the study that might affect a causal relationship.

For example, researchers might be interested in studying the effects of a certain phonics program (the independent variable) on the rate at which children learn to read (the dependent variable). The researchers may hypothesize using this phonics program will shorten the time it takes for students to learn to read. To confirm or reject this hypothesis, they might study the reading progress of one group of children who were taught using the phonics program (the **experimental group**) and compare it with the reading progress of another group of children (the **control group**) who were taught reading without the phonics program. Children would be randomly assigned to either the experimental or the control group as a way to reduce the differences that might exist in naturally occurring groups. At the end of the experiment, the researchers would compare the progress of each group and decide whether the hypothesis could be accepted or rejected with a predetermined level of **statistical significance** (for example, that the difference between the mean for the control group and the mean for the experimental group is large, compared with the standard error). Finally, the researchers would present the findings of the study at a conference and perhaps publish the results.

This process may sound very straightforward. In classroom and school settings, however, controlling all the factors that affect the outcomes of our teaching without disrupting the natural classroom environment can be difficult. For example, how do we know that the phonics program is the only variable affecting the rate at which students learn to read? Perhaps some students are being read to at home by their parents; perhaps one teacher is more effective than another; perhaps one group of students gets to read more exciting books than the other; perhaps one group of children has difficulty concentrating on their reading because they all skipped breakfast!

Action researchers acknowledge and embrace these complications as a natural part of classroom life and typically use research approaches that do not require them to randomly assign students in their classes to control and experimental groups. Teacher researchers studying their own practices also differ from traditional educational researchers (studying something other than their own practices) because they are committed to *taking action* and *effecting positive educational change* in their own classrooms and schools based on their findings. Traditional educational researchers may not be able to impact the subjects of their studies because they are outside of their locus of control. That is, traditional educational researchers can share the conclusions of their studies, but it is up to the subjects to determine whether or not they will take action on the findings. Another difference is that whereas educational research has historically been done by university professors, scholars, and graduate students on children, teachers, and principals, action researchers are often the schoolteachers and principals who were formerly the subjects of educational research. As such, they participate in their own inquiries, acting as both teacher and researcher at the same time. However, we should note that traditional educational researchers can also collaborate with teacher researchers in **collaborative action research** efforts. As Hendricks states, "The goal of this type of research is to utilize the expertise of the collaborators and to foster sustained dialogue among educational stakeholders in different settings" (2006, p. 10).

Research is also categorized by the methods the researchers use. Simply put, different research problems require different research approaches. These approaches to educational research are often classified as either quantitative or qualitative research. **Quantitative research** is the collection and analysis of numerical data to describe, explain, predict, or control phenomena of interest. However, a quantitative research approach entails more than just the use of numerical data. At the outset of a study, quantitative researchers state the hypotheses to be examined and specify the research procedures that will be used to carry out the study. They also maintain control over contextual factors that may interfere with the data collection and identify a sample of participants large enough to provide statistically meaningful data. Many quantitative researchers have little personal interaction with the participants they study because they frequently collect data using paper-and-pencil, noninteractive instruments. Underlying quantitative research methods is the philosophical belief or assumption that we inhabit a relatively stable, uniform, and coherent world that we can measure, understand, and generalize about. This view, adopted from the natural sciences, implies that the world and the laws that govern it are somewhat predictable and can be understood by scientific research and examination. In this quantitative perspective, claims about the world are not considered meaningful unless they can be verified through direct observation. By comparison, **qualitative research** uses narrative, descriptive approaches to data collection to understand the way things are and what the research means from the perspectives of the participants in the study. Qualitative approaches might include, for example, conducting face-to-face interviews, making observations, and video recording interactions. Key Concepts Box 1–1 provides a summary of action research.

Although quantitative and qualitative approaches need not be considered mutually exclusive, a study might incorporate both quantitative *and* qualitative techniques. Studies that combine the collection of quantitative and qualitative data in a single study are called **mixed-methods research designs**. Mixed-methods research designs combine quantitative and qualitative approaches by including both quantitative and qualitative data in a single study. The purpose of mixed-methods research is to build on the synergy and strength that exists between quantitative and qualitative research methods to understand a phenomenon more fully than is

KEY CONCEPTS BOX 1–1

A Summary of Action Research	
What?	Action research
Who?	Conducted by teachers and principals on children in their care.
Where?	In schools and classrooms.
How?	Using a variety of research designs to match the study's area of focus, including: qualitative methods to describe what is happening and to understand the effects of some educational intervention, quantitative methods to test hypotheses that rely on numerical analyses, and mixed-methods designs that combine quantitative and qualitative approaches to data collection in a single study.
Why?	To take action and effect positive educational change in the specific school environment that was studied.

possible using either method alone. Although this approach to research may appear obvious (i.e., of course we want a complete understanding of any phenomenon worthy of investigation), it requires a thorough understanding of both quantitative and qualitative research.

The area of focus or research question identified by the action researcher will determine the most appropriate approach (quantitative and/or qualitative) to use. While the majority of published action research studies use narrative, descriptive methods, some studies are more quantitatively oriented and use survey and quasi-experimental research designs. Therefore, while this book emphasizes the use of qualitative research designs, data collection, and data analysis, it also includes quantitative research designs, data collection, and analysis (using descriptive statistics).

Defining Action Research

Over the past decade, the typical "required" research course in many schools, colleges, and departments of teacher education has changed from a traditional survey class on research methods to a more practical research course that either focuses on or includes the topic of action research. But what is action research, and why has it captured the attention of teachers, administrators, and policy makers?

Action research is any systematic inquiry conducted by teacher researchers, principals, school counselors, or other stakeholders in the teaching/learning environment to gather information about how their particular schools operate, how they teach, and how well their students learn. This information is gathered with the goals of gaining insight, developing reflective practice, effecting positive changes in the school environment (and on educational practices in general), and improving student outcomes and the lives of those involved.

Action research is research done *by* teachers *for* themselves; it is not imposed on them by someone else. Action research engages teachers in a four-step process:

1. Identify an area of focus.
2. Collect data.
3. Analyze and interpret data.
4. Develop an action plan.

Before we elaborate on these four steps, however, we will explore the historical antecedents of action research and the theoretical foundations of current action research practices. As you read these descriptions, consider which philosophy best fits your beliefs about action research, teaching, and learning. Then consider how you might incorporate action research into your professional life.

Origins of Action Research

The history of action research has been well-documented and debated (cf. Adelman, 1993; Gunz, 1996; Kemmis, 1988; Noffke, 1994). Kurt Lewin (1890–1947) is often credited with coining the term *action research* around 1934. After a series of practical experiences in the early 1940s, he came to view action research as a process that "gives credence to the development of powers of reflective thought, discussion, decision and action by ordinary people participating in collective research on 'private troubles' that they have in common" (Adelman, 1993, p. 8).

The many "descendants" of early action researchers follow different schools of action research thought, including the American action research group, with its roots in the progressive education movement, particularly in the work of John Dewey (Noffke, 1994); the efforts in the United Kingdom toward curriculum reform and greater professionalism in teaching (Elliott, 1991); and Australian efforts located within a broad-ranging movement toward collaborative curriculum planning (Kemmis, 1988).

As is evident, the geographical locations and sociopolitical contexts in which action research efforts continue to evolve vary greatly. However, the primary focus of all these efforts, regardless of the context, is on enhancing the lives of students. As Noffke (1994) reminds us, reading the accounts of action research written by people housed in universities does little to illuminate the classroom experiences of teachers and what they hope to gain from participating in action research activities. Therefore, this book focuses on teachers examining issues related to the education of children and on partnering with teachers, administrators, counselors, and parents in the action research process.

Theoretical Foundations of Action Research

The theoretical perspectives and philosophies that inform the practices of today's teacher researchers are as varied as the historical roots for action research. The following sections briefly review the two main theories of action research: critical (or theory-based) and practical.

Critical Action Research

Critical action research is also known as emancipatory action research because of its goal of liberation through knowledge gathering. The term *critical action research* derives its name from the body of critical theory on which it is based, not because this type of action research is critical, as in "faultfinding" or "important," although it may certainly be both! The rationale for critical action research is provided by critical theory in the social sciences and humanities and by theories of postmodernism.

Critical theory in action research shares several fundamental purposes with critical theory in the social sciences and humanities (Kemmis, 1988). These similar interests or "commonalities of intent" include:

1. A shared interest in processes for enlightenment.
2. A shared interest in liberating individuals from the dictates of tradition, habit, and bureaucracy.
3. A commitment to participatory democratic processes for reform.

In addition to its roots in the critical theory of the social sciences and humanities, critical action research also draws heavily from a body of theory called **postmodernism**, which challenges the notions of truth and objectivity on which the traditional scientific method relies. Instead of claiming the incontrovertibility of fact, postmodernists argue that truth is relative, conditional, and situational, and that knowledge is always an outgrowth of previous experience. For example, historically there has been little or no connection between research and practice in education—an apparent failure of research to affect teaching. This is not news for teachers! Research has been viewed as something done *on* them, not *for* them. According to Kennedy (1997), the lack of influence of research on practice has been attributed to the following qualities of educational research:

- It is not persuasive and has lacked the qualities of being compelling to teachers.
- It has not been relevant to teachers' daily practices—it has lacked practicality.
- It has not been expressed in ways that are accessible to teachers.

The postmodern perspective addresses many of these concerns by advocating for research that challenges the *taken-for-granted assumptions* of daily classroom life and presenting *truths* that are relative, conditional, situational, and based on previous experience. So although research may provide insights into promising practices (from research conducted in *other* teachers' classrooms and schools), action research conducted in one's *own* classroom/school is more likely to be persuasive and relevant and to offer findings that are expressed in ways that are meaningful for teachers themselves.

Postmodern theory dissects and examines the mechanisms of knowledge production and questions many of the basic assumptions on which modern life is based. Thus, it inspires us "to examine the ordinary, everyday, taken-for-granted ways in which we organize and carry out our private, social, and professional activities" (Stringer, 1996, p. 156). Action research gives us a means by which we can undertake this examination and represent the classroom teachers' experiences that are contextually and politically constructed.

The values of critical action research dictate that all educational research should be socially responsive as well as:

1. Democratic—Enabling participation of people.
2. Participatory—Building a community of learners.
3. Empowering—Providing freedom from oppressive, debilitating conditions.
4. Life-enhancing—Enabling the expression of people's full human potential. (Stringer, 2004, p. 31)

Although this critical theory-based approach has been criticized by some for lack of practical feasibility (Hammersley, 1993), it is nonetheless important to consider because it provides a helpful heuristic, or problem-solving, approach for teachers who are committed to investigate through action research the taken-for-granted relationships and practices in their professional lives. Key Concepts Box 1–2 summarizes the most important components of a critical perspective of action research.

Practical Action Research

Practical action research places more emphasis on the "how-to" approach to the processes of action research and has a less "philosophical" bent. It assumes, to some degree, that individual teachers or teams of teachers are autonomous and can determine the nature of the investigation to be undertaken. It also assumes that teacher researchers are committed to continued professional development and school improvement and that teacher researchers want to systematically reflect on their practices. Finally, the practical action research perspective assumes that as decision makers, teacher researchers will choose their own areas of focus, determine their data collection techniques, analyze and interpret their data, and develop action plans based on their findings. These beliefs are summarized in Key Concepts Box 1–3.

Goals and Rationale for Action Research

Although the critical and practical theories of action research draw on vastly different worldviews, these two distinctly different philosophies are united by common goals that go a long way toward bridging whatever philosophical, historical, social, and regional variations exist.

Action research carried out according to both philosophies creates opportunities for all involved to improve the lives of children and to learn about the craft of teaching. All action

Components of a Critical Perspective of Action Research

KEY CONCEPT	EXAMPLE
Action research is participatory and democratic.	You have identified an area in your teaching that you believe can be improved (based on data from your students). You decide to investigate the impact of your intervention and to monitor whether it makes a difference.
Action research is socially responsive and takes place in context.	You are concerned that minority children (for example ESL [English as a Second Language] students) in your classroom are not being presented with curriculum and teaching strategies that are culturally sensitive. You decide to learn more about how best to teach ESL children and to implement some of these strategies.
Action research helps teacher researchers examine the everyday, taken-for-granted ways in which they carry out professional practice.	You have adopted a new mathematics problem-solving curriculum and decide to monitor its impact on student performance on open-ended problem-solving questions and students' attitudes toward mathematics in general.
Knowledge gained through action research can liberate students, teachers, and administrators and enhance learning, teaching, and policy making.	Your school has a high incidence of student absenteeism in spite of a newly adopted district-wide policy on absenteeism. You investigate the perceptions of colleagues, children, and parents toward absenteeism to more fully understand why the existing policy is not having the desired outcome. Based on what you learn, you implement a new policy and systematically monitor its impact on absenteeism levels and students' attitudes toward school.

researchers, regardless of their particular school of thought or theoretical position, are committed to a critical examination of classroom teaching principles and the effects teachers' actions have on the children in their care. The reality of classroom life is that teachers are constantly confronted with practical and critical challenges, and it is up to the individual action researcher to seek out approaches that provide both practical solutions and empowerment to address the critical social and cultural issues of classrooms today.

By now it should be evident that educational change that *enhances the lives of children* is a main goal of action research. But action research can also *enhance the lives of professionals*.

Osterman and Kottkamp (1993) provide a wonderful rationale for action research as a professional growth opportunity in their "credo for reflective practice":

1. Everyone needs professional growth opportunities.
2. All professionals want to improve.
3. All professionals can learn.
4. All professionals are capable of assuming responsibility for their own professional growth and development.
5. People need and want information about their own performance.
6. Collaboration enriches professional development. (p. 46)

Action research is largely about developing the *professional disposition* of teachers, that is, encouraging teachers to be continuous learners—in their classrooms and in their practice.

Components of a Practical Perspective of Action Research

KEY CONCEPT	EXAMPLE
Teacher researchers have decision-making authority.	Your school has adopted a school-based decision-making approach that provides teachers with the authority to make decisions that most directly impact teaching and learning. Given this decision-making authority, you decide as part of your continued professional development to investigate the effectiveness of a newly adopted science curriculum on students' process skills and attitudes.
Teacher researchers are committed to continued professional development and school improvement.	Based on the results of statewide assessment tests and classroom observations, the teachers and principal at your school determine that reading comprehension skills are weak. Collaboratively, the staff determines the focus for a school improvement effort and identifies the necessary professional development that will be offered to change the ways teachers teach reading.
Teacher researchers want to reflect on their practices.	You are a successful classroom teacher who regularly reflects on your daily teaching and what areas could be improved. You believe that part of being a professional teacher is the willingness to continually examine your teaching effectiveness.
Teacher researchers will use a systematic approach for reflecting on their practice.	Given a schoolwide reading comprehension focus, you have decided to monitor the effectiveness of a new reading curriculum and teaching strategies by video recording a reading lesson (once per month), administering reading comprehension "probes" (once per week), interviewing children in your classroom (once per term), and administering statewide assessment tests (at the end of the school year).
Teacher researchers will choose an area of focus, determine data collection techniques, analyze and interpret data, and develop action plans.	To continue the example above, you have focused on the effectiveness of a new reading curriculum and teaching strategies. You have decided to collect data using video recordings of lessons, regular "probes," interviews, and statewide assessment tests. During the year you try to interpret the data you are collecting and decide what these data suggest about the effectiveness of the new curriculum and teaching strategies. When all of the data have been collected and analyzed, you decide what action needs to be taken to refine, improve, or maintain the reading comprehension curriculum and teaching strategies.

Although action research is not a universal panacea for the intractability of educational reform, it is an important component of the professional disposition of teachers because it provides teachers with the opportunity to model for their students how knowledge is created.

Action research is also about incorporating into the daily teaching routine a *reflective stance*—the willingness to critically examine one's teaching in order to improve or enhance it. It is about a commitment to the principle that as a teacher one is always distanced from the ideal but is striving toward it anyway—it's the very nature of education! Action research significantly contributes to the professional stance that teachers adopt because it encourages them to examine the dynamics of their classrooms, ponder the actions and interactions of students, validate and challenge existing practices, and take risks in the process. When teachers gain new understandings about both their own and their students' behaviors through action research, they are empowered to:

- Make informed decisions about what to change and what not to change.
- Link prior knowledge to new information.

- Learn from experience (even failures).
- Ask questions and systematically find answers. (Fueyo & Koorland, 1997)

The goal of teachers to be professional problem solvers who are committed to improving both their own practice and student outcomes provides a powerful reason to practice action research.

Justifying Action Research: The Impact of Action Research on Practice

At the beginning of a course on action research, I often ask teachers to reflect on what they do in their schools and classrooms; that is, what are the assumptions they take for granted in their schools and what are the origins of those practices? Often the responses include the following:

In elementary grades, it is important to do the "skill" subjects in the morning and the "social" subjects in the afternoon because that is when young children can concentrate better and learn more.

The best way to do whole-group instruction with young children (grades K–3) is to have them sit on the "mat" in a circle. That way they are close to the teacher and pay more attention to what is being said.

In high schools the optimal time for a learning period is 43 minutes. Anything longer than that and the students get restless and lose concentration. Therefore, I think that the proposal for "block scheduling" is just an attempt to make us more like elementary school teachers.

If you simply share scoring guides with children, they will automatically do better on the test. There's no need to change instructional approaches.

In a science laboratory if children spend less time collecting data, they will develop a deeper understanding of the science concepts being taught.

Although these are real examples of just a few of the naive theories about teaching and learning that I have heard, they also indicate the gap that has existed between research and practice in the field of education. To what extent has teaching practice been informed by research? Is teaching informed by folklore? Do teachers acquire the culture of teaching through years of participation and observation, first as students and then as neophyte teachers? How did teachers get to be the way they are? Are some of the derogatory Hollywood portrayals of teachers and teaching (for example, as characterized in *Ferris Bueller's Day Off, Mr. Holland's Opus*, etc.) really warranted? What is it about research that makes teachers, in general, snicker at the thought that it can in some way improve practice? What is the potential for this discussion to put action into action research efforts?

According to Kennedy (1997), studies of the connection between research and practice and the apparent failure of research to affect teaching has provided the following insights:

- Teachers do not find research persuasive or authoritative.
- Research has not been relevant to practice and has not addressed teachers' questions.
- Research findings have not been expressed in ways that are comprehensible to teachers.
- The education system itself is unable to change or, conversely, it is inherently unstable and susceptible to fads.

Many teacher researchers may consider Kennedy's hypotheses to be statements of the obvious; however, these statements provide yet another rationale for why many teachers have chosen to be reflective practitioners: to address the intractability of the educational system. These hypotheses also speak to the desire to put action into ongoing action research efforts.

Action Research Is Persuasive and Authoritative

Research done by teachers for teachers involves collection of persuasive data. These data are persuasive because teachers are invested in the legitimacy of the data collection; that is, they have identified data sources that provide persuasive insights into the impact of an intervention on student outcomes. Similarly, the findings of action research and the actions recommended by these findings are authoritative for teacher researchers. In doing action research, teacher researchers have developed solutions to their own problems. Teachers—not outside "experts"—are the authorities on what works in their classrooms.

Action Research Is Relevant

The relevance of published research to the real world of teachers is perhaps the most common concern raised by teachers when asked about the practical applications of educational research—either the problems investigated by researchers are not the problems teachers really have or the schools or classrooms in which the research was conducted are vastly different from their own school environment. In reviewing the last two decades of research on schools and teaching, however, Kennedy (1997) cites the seminal works of Jackson's (1968) *Life in Classrooms* and Lortie's (1975) *Schoolteacher* as ways to illustrate the relevance of the findings of these studies. Kennedy's review (1997) found that classroom life was characterized by crowds, power, praise, and uncertainty:

> Crowds—Students are always grouped with 20 or 30 others, which means that they must wait in line, wait to be called on, and wait for help.
>
> Power—Teachers control most actions and events and decide what the group will do.
>
> Praise—Teachers give and withhold praise, so students know which of their classmates are favored by the teacher.
>
> Uncertainty—The presence of 20 to 30 children in a single classroom means there are many possibilities for an interruption in one's work.

Kennedy (1997) argues that one of the aims of research is to increase certainty by creating predictability within the classroom, because "Routines increase predictability and decrease anxiety for both teachers and students" (p. 6).

One of the outcomes of action research is that it satisfies the desire of all teachers to increase the predictability of what happens in their classrooms—in particular, to increase the likelihood that a given curriculum, instructional strategy, or use of technology will positively affect student outcomes. And although these desirable outcomes come at the initial expense of predictability—that is, they have emerged from the implementation of a *new* intervention or innovation—the findings of your action research inquiries will, over time, contribute to the predictability of your teaching environments.

Action Research Allows Teachers Access to Research Findings

Kennedy (1997) also hypothesizes that the apparent lack of connection between research and practice is due to teachers' poor access to research findings. This apparent lack of impact of research on teaching is, in part, credited to teachers' prior beliefs and values and the realization that teachers' practices cannot be changed simply by informing them of the results of a study. After all, if we reflect on how we currently teach and what we hold as sacred teaching practices, we are likely to find that our beliefs and values stem from how we were taught as children ("It worked for me and I'm successful. I'm a teacher.") and how we have had teaching modeled for us through our teaching apprenticeships (student teaching).

Simply informing teachers about research is unlikely to bring about change. Therein lies the beauty, power, and potential of action research to positively affect practice. As a teacher researcher, you challenge your taken-for-granted assumptions about teaching and learning. Your research findings are meaningful to you because *you* have identified the area of focus. *You* have been willing to challenge the conventional craft culture. In short, *your* willingness to reflect on and change your thinking about your teaching practices has led you to become a successful and productive member of the professional community.

Action Research Challenges the Intractability of Reform of the Educational System

Kennedy's (1997) final hypothesis is that the lack of connection between research and practice can be attributed to the educational system itself, not the research. Kennedy (1997) characterizes the American educational system as a system that:

- Has no consensus on goals and guiding principles.
- Has no central authority to settle disputes.
- Is continually bombarded with new fads and fancies.
- Provides limited evidence to support or refute any particular idea.
- Encourages reforms that run at cross-purposes to each other.
- Gives teachers less time than most other countries do to develop curricula and daily lessons.

Given this characterization, it is little wonder that the more things change, the more they stay the same! Again, action research gives teacher researchers the opportunity to embrace a problem-solving philosophy and practice as an integral part of the culture of their schools and their professional disposition, and to challenge the intractability of educational reform by making action research a part of the system, rather than just another fad.

Action Research Is Not a Fad

One insight that Kennedy does not address when discussing the apparent failure of research to affect teachers' practices is the belief of many classroom teachers that researchers tend to investigate trendy fads and are interested only in the curricular approach or instructional method *du jour*. Therefore, it is not surprising to hear critics of action research say: "Why bother? This is just another fad that, like other fads in education, will eventually pass if I can wait it out!" But action research is decidedly not a fad for one simple reason: *Good teachers have always systematically looked at the effects of their teaching on student learning.* They may not have called this practice action research, and they may not have thought their reflection was formal enough to be labeled research, but action research it was!

Making Action Research a Part of Daily Teaching Practices

The first step in making action research a part of daily teaching practices is to become familiar with the process and recognize how much action research is already a part of your daily life as a classroom teacher. Consider this analogy that reveals how similar the act of teaching is to the act of doing action research. In any individual lesson, you plan, implement, and evaluate your teaching, just as a teacher researcher does when undertaking action research. You develop a list of objectives (a focus area), implement the lesson, reflect on whether the children achieved the objectives through summative evaluation statements (data collection), spend time at the end of a lesson reflecting on what happened (data analysis and interpretation), and spend time at the end of the day considering how today's lesson will affect tomorrow's lesson (action planning). Like action research, the act of teaching is largely an intuitive process carried out idiosyncratically by both experienced and novice teachers.

I was recently reminded by a teacher enrolled in one of my action research classes that in my fervor and enthusiasm to illustrate data analysis and interpretation in practice (based on some of my own research), I had unwittingly made her feel that research was something that could realistically be done only by a full-time researcher who did not have a "real" job to contend with—namely, teaching twenty-eight very lively first graders! The teacher felt that action research was so difficult and time consuming that it was unreasonable to expect a mere mortal to undertake the activity. She felt as if she needed "Super Teacher" to burst into the classroom and take over business! Not so. If the process of action research cannot be done without adversely affecting the fundamental work of teaching, then it ought not to be done at all.

Throughout this text, we will explore practical, realistic ways that action research can become a normative part of the teaching-learning process. There will be an initial commitment of time and energy as one learns the process, but that time is an investment in enriching the education of students. If one is to realistically incorporate the process of action research into daily teaching practices, a few things need to happen:

- *Try the process and be convinced that the investment of time and energy is worth the outcomes.* First, undertake an action research project that is meaningful to you and addresses the needs of your students. Once the project is completed, you will see the contribution your new understanding of the subject will make to your teaching or your students' learning (or ideally, both!). Only then will you be fully confident that action research is a worthwhile investment of your time and energy. Your beliefs and attitudes about action research will be changed after you have tried it for yourself.
- *Know that action research is a process that can be undertaken without having a negative impact on your personal and professional life.* For example, action research, as it is described in this book, is not intended to be just "one more thing" for you to do. Teachers already have too much to do and not enough time in which to do it! The action research process advocated in this book is intended to provide you with a systematic framework that can be applied to your daily teaching routines. The investment of time as you learn how to do action research will be worth the outcomes. The process may also produce unexpected positive outcomes by providing opportunities for collaborative efforts with colleagues who share a common area of focus. This book provides strategies

Making Action Research a Part of Your Daily Teaching Practice

_____ Actually *try* the process to convince yourself that the investments of time and energy are worth the outcomes.

_____ Recognize that action research is a process that can be undertaken without negatively affecting your personal and professional life.

_____ Seek support from your professional colleagues.

you can use to develop your *reflective practice* utilizing many of the existing data sources in your classroom and school. It will provide you with a model that can be shared with like-minded colleagues who also are committed to improving the teaching-learning process in their classrooms.

- *Ask your professional colleagues for support with implementation.* Although such strategies as studying theory, observing demonstrations, and practicing with feedback enable most teachers to develop their skills to the point that they can use a model fluidly, skills development by itself does not ensure skills transfer. Relatively few persons who learn new approaches to teaching will integrate their skills into regular practice unless they receive coaching (Joyce, Hersh, & McKibben, 1983). That is why seeking support and guidance from other teacher researchers is critical to your success as an action researcher. These suggestions are summarized in Research in Action Checklist 1–1.

The Process of Action Research

Now that we have defined action research, described its historical and theoretical foundations, and explained why teachers do it, let's explore the process of action research. Many guidelines and models have been provided over the years for teacher researchers to follow, for example:

- Kurt Lewin (1952) described a "spiraling" cyclical process that included planning, execution, and reconnaissance.
- Stephen Kemmis (1988) created a well-known representation of the action research "spiral" (see Figure 1–1) that includes the essential characteristics of Lewin's model. Kemmis's model includes reconnaissance, planning, first action step, monitoring, reflecting, rethinking, and evaluation.
- Emily Calhoun (1994) described an Action Research Cycle (see Figure 1–2) that includes selecting an area or problem of collective interest, collecting data, organizing data, analyzing and interpreting data, and taking action.
- Gordon Wells (1994) described what he calls an Idealized Model of the Action Research Cycle (see Figure 1–3) that includes observing, interpreting, planning change, acting, and "the practitioner's personal theory" (p. 27), which informs and is informed by the action research cycle.
- Ernest Stringer (2004) described an Action Research Helix (see Figure 1–4) that includes looking, thinking, and acting as "phases of the research (are) repeated over time" (p. 10).

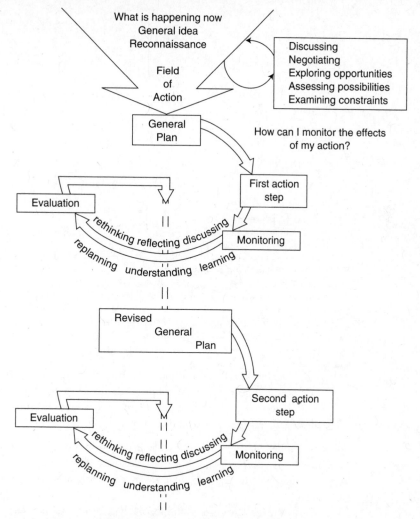

FIGURE 1–1 *A Representation of Lewin's Action Research Cycle*

Source: *Action Research in Retrospect and Prospect* (p. 29), by Stephen Kemmis, 1988, Victoria, Australia: Deakin University Press, distributor. Copyright 1988 Deakin University. Reprinted with permission. All rights reserved.

- John Creswell (2005) described action research as a dynamic, flexible process that involves the following steps: determining if action research is the best design to use, identifying a problem to study, locating resources to help address the problem, identifying necessary information, implementing the data collection, analyzing the data, developing a plan for action, and implementing the plan and reflecting on whether or not it makes a difference.
- Richard Sagor (2005) described a four-step process that includes clarifying vision, articulating theories, implementing action and collecting data, and reflecting and planning informed action (see Figure 1–5).

FIGURE 1–2   *The Action Research Cycle*

- Cher Hendricks (2006) described an action research process that follows the principle of "systematic inquiry based on ongoing reflection" (p. 9) that is heavily influenced by the work of Lawrence Stenhouse (1981) from the Center for Applied Research in Education at the University of East Anglia in England (see Figure 1–6).

All these models have enjoyed varying degrees of popularity, depending on the context in which they have been applied. For example, these action research models have been applied to agriculture, health care, social work, factory work, and community development in isolated areas.

Clearly, these action research models share some common elements: a sense of purpose based on a "problem" or "area of focus" (identification of an area of focus), observation or

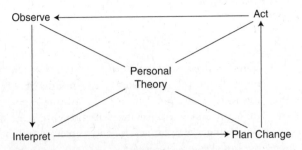

FIGURE 1–3   *An Idealized Model of the Action Research Cycle*

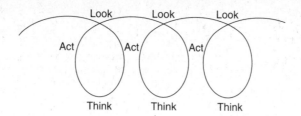

FIGURE 1–4 *Action Research Helix*

Source: *Action Research in Education* (p. 12), by Ernest Stringer, 2004, Upper Saddle River, NJ: Prentice Hall.

monitoring of practice (collection of data), synthesis of information gathered (analysis and interpretation of data), and some form of "action" that invariably "spirals" the researcher back into the process repeatedly (development of an action plan).

These shared elements are what we will focus on in this book. The following chapters will address in detail how to proceed with an action research process that includes the four elements mentioned above: **identifying an area of focus, collecting data, analyzing and interpreting data**, and **developing an action plan**. Key Concepts Box 1–4 illustrates the action research process used by Deborah South, described at the beginning of this chapter.

This four-step process, which I have termed the **Dialectic Action Research Spiral**, is illustrated in Figure 1–7. It provides teacher researchers with a practical guide and illustrates

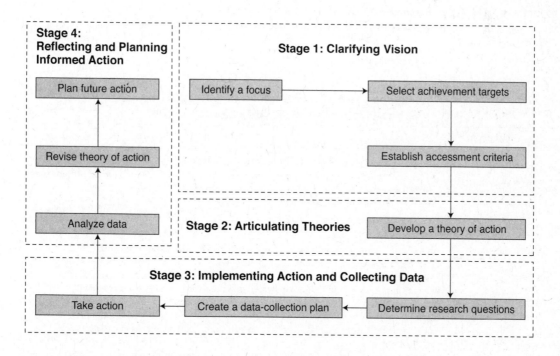

FIGURE 1–5 *The Action Research Cycle*

Source: *The Action Research Guidebook: A Four-Step Process for Educators and School Teams* (p. 7), by R. Sagor 2005, Thousand Oaks, CA: Corwin Press.

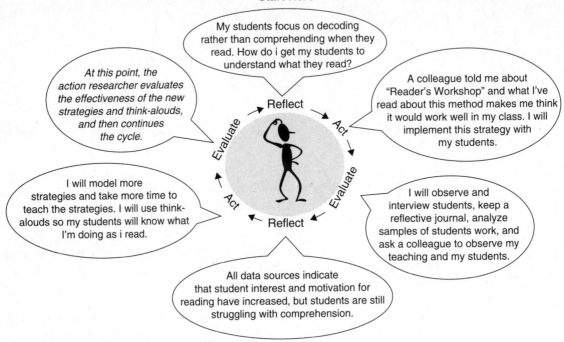

Start Here

My students focus on decoding rather than comprehending when they read. How do i get my students to understand what they read?

At this point, the action researcher evaluates the effectiveness of the new strategies and think-alouds, and then continues the cycle.

A colleague told me about "Reader's Workshop" and what I've read about this method makes me think it would work well in my class. I will implement this strategy with my students.

I will model more strategies and take more time to teach the strategies. I will use think-alouds so my students will know what I'm doing as i read.

I will observe and interview students, keep a reflective journal, analyze samples of students work, and ask a colleague to observe my teaching and my students.

All data sources indicate that student interest and motivation for reading have increased, but students are still struggling with comprehension.

FIGURE 1–6 *The Action Research Process*

Source: *Improving Schools through Action Research: A Comprehensive Guide for Educators* (p. 9), by Cher Hendricks, 2006, Boston, MA: Allyn and Bacon.

KEY CONCEPTS BOX 1–4

Steps in the Action Research Process Based on Deborah South's Example of "Unmotivated" Students

KEY CONCEPT	EXAMPLE
Identifying an area of focus	The purpose of this study was to describe the effects of a "study skills" curriculum on student outcomes. In particular, the study focused on the variables of student attendance, peer influence, adult influence, and students' self-esteem.
Collecting data	Data was collected through surveys, interviews, and report card/attendance records.
Analyzing and interpreting the data	Attendance did not appear to be an issue—children attended school regularly. Peer groups did affect performance. Students encouraged each other not to complete homework assignments. Teacher approval of student work appeared to have little effect on students' work habits, whereas about half of the children indicated that they were motivated to complete their homework to receive parental approval. On average, student grades had dropped dramatically during the term in which they were enrolled in the study skills class. Interpretation: The study skills class was having a negative impact on student outcomes, behavior, and attitudes.
Developing an action plan	It was determined that students would not be homogeneously grouped for a study skills class the following year because of a "critical mass of negativity" that appeared to emerge from the students as they fed off each other's lack of motivation. The study skills curriculum would continue to be used and monitored with a heterogeneous grouping of students.

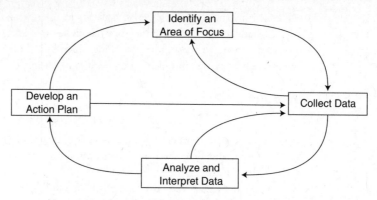

FIGURE 1–7 *The Dialectic Action Research Spiral*

how to proceed with inquiries. It is a model for research done *by* teachers and *for* teachers and students, not research done *on* them, and as such is a dynamic and responsive model that can be adapted to different contexts and purposes. It was designed to provide teacher researchers with "provocative and constructive ways" of thinking about their work (Wolcott, 1989, p. 137).

Summary

A Brief Overview of Educational Research

1. The goal of traditional educational research is "to explain, predict, and/or control educational phenomena" (Gay et al., 2009, p. 6). To do this, researchers try to manipulate and control certain variables (the factors that might affect the outcomes of a particular study) to test a hypothesis (a statement the researcher makes that predicts what will happen or explains what the outcome of the study will be).
2. Positivism is the belief that natural phenomena can be explained in an orderly way using empirical sciences.
3. At the end of an experiment, researchers would compare the progress of each group in the study and decide whether the hypothesis could be accepted or rejected with a predetermined level of statistical significance (for example, that the difference between the mean for the control group and the mean for the experimental group is large, compared with the standard error).
4. Collaborative action research utilizes the expertise of the collaborators and fosters sustained dialogue among educational stakeholders in different settings (Hendricks, 2006, p. 10).
5. Quantitative research focuses on controlling a small number of variables to determine cause-effect relationships and/or the strength of those relationships. This type of research uses numbers to quantify the cause-effect relationship.
6. Qualitative research uses narrative, descriptive approaches to data collection to understand the way things are and what the research means from the perspectives of the participants in the study. Qualitative approaches might include, for example, conducting face-to-face interviews, making observations, and video recording interactions.
7. Studies that combine the collection of quantitative and qualitative data in a single study are called mixed-methods research designs. The purpose of mixed-methods research is to build

on the synergy and strength that exists between quantitative and qualitative research methods to understand a phenomenon more fully than is possible using either method alone.

8. The area of focus or research question identified by the action researcher will determine the most appropriate approach (quantitative and/or qualitative) to use.

Defining Action Research

9. Action research is any systematic inquiry conducted by teacher researchers, principals, school counselors, or other stakeholders in the teaching/learning environment to gather information about how their particular schools operate, how they teach, and how well their students learn.

10. Action research engages teacher researchers in a four-step process (referred to in this text as the Dialectic Action Research Spiral):
    a. Identify an area of focus.
    b. Collect data.
    c. Analyze and interpret data.
    d. Develop an action plan.

Origins of Action Research

11. Kurt Lewin (1890–1947) is often credited with coining the term action research around 1934.

12. The many "descendants" of early action researchers follow different schools of action research thought, including the American action research group with its roots in the progressive education movement, particularly the work of John Dewey (Noffke, 1994); the efforts in the United Kingdom toward curriculum reform and greater professionalism in teaching (Elliott, 1991); and Australian efforts located within a broad-ranging movement toward collaborative curriculum planning (Kemmis, 1988).

Theoretical Foundations of Action Research

13. Critical action research is also known as emancipatory action research because of its goal of liberation through knowledge gathering. The term critical action research derives its name from the body of critical theory on which it is based, not because this type of action research is critical, as in "faultfinding" or "important," although it may certainly be both!

14. Postmodernism challenges the notions of truth and objectivity on which the traditional scientific method relies. Instead of claiming the incontrovertibility of fact, postmodernists argue that truth is relative, conditional, and situational, and that knowledge is always an outgrowth of previous experience.

15. The values of critical action research dictate that all educational research should be socially responsive as well as:
    a. Democratic
    b. Participatory
    c. Empowering
    d. Life-enhancing

16. Practical action research places more emphasis on the "how-to" approach to the processes of action research and has a less "philosophical" bent.

17. It assumes, to some degree, that individual teachers or teams of teachers are autonomous and can determine the nature of the investigation to be undertaken.

Goals and Rationale for Action Research

18. Action research carried out according to both philosophies creates opportunities for all involved to improve the lives of children and to learn about the craft of teaching. All action researchers, regardless of their particular school of thought or theoretical position, are committed to a critical examination of classroom teaching principles and the effects teachers' actions have on the children in their care.
19. The goal of teachers to be professional problem solvers who are committed to improving both their own practice and student outcomes provides a powerful reason to practice action research.
20. Action research is persuasive and authoritative.
21. Action research is relevant.
22. Action research allows teachers access to research findings.
23. Action research challenges the intractability of reform of the educational system.
24. Action research is not a fad.

Making Action Research a Part of Daily Teaching Practices

25. The first step in making action research a part of daily teaching practices is to become familiar with the process and recognize how much action research is already a part of your daily life as a classroom teacher.
26. Try the process and be convinced that the investment of time and energy is worth the outcomes.
27. Know that action research is a process that can be undertaken without having a negative impact on your personal and professional life.
28. Ask your professional colleagues for support with implementation.

The Process of Action Research

29. The Dialectic Action Research Spiral includes the following four elements:
    a. Identifying an area of focus.
    b. Collecting data.
    c. Analyzing and interpreting data.
    d. Developing an action plan.

Tasks

1. How would you describe the purpose(s) of action research?
2. How do the tenets of the critical perspective support the need for action research?
3. Suppose that the students in your class are not progressing in essay writing as you had hoped. Using the four steps in the action research process described in this chapter, sketch out briefly what you might do to systematically examine this issue.
4. Your school has received a large professional development grant focused on improving children's scores on a national reading test. You believe that your existing reading program is strong. What kind of action research study might you conduct to address the differences between your current reading program's outcomes and the concepts tested on the national test?

2

Ethics

This chapter describes the ethical issues that confront teacher researchers and suggests a series of ethical guidelines to help ensure that your research is conducted in an ethical manner.

After reading this chapter you should be able to:

1. Clarify ethical issues involved in conducting action research.

2. Recognize the challenges and procedures for obtaining Institutional Review Board (IRB) approval.

3. Recognize the ethical obligations that educational researchers have and describe the codes and procedures they follow to ensure they adhere to them.

The Use of Technology to Enhance Mathematics Achievement

CLEM ANNICE

Children learn at an early age the concept of light refraction. Peering into fishbowls, children see that the fish, rocks, plants, and toys appear larger than life, their movement, shape, and size distorted by the refraction of light. We have all been puzzled at some time in our lives by this illusion and the contradiction between what we see and what we get as we attempt to reach in and touch the inhabitants of the fishbowl. Can the same be said for the use of technology in mathematics reform? Is what we see in classrooms really what we get? Are students and teachers developing a functional and appropriate use of the technology, or are they just playing at the computer? Are teachers and students making connections between the use of technology for presenting models and the concepts that the models represent? How is the use of technology to enhance curriculum and instruction in mathematics affecting student outcomes in mathematics? It is this final question that drove the schoolwide action research project at Billabong Elementary School.

Billabong elementary school is a large K–7 school that has embraced the use of technology as a key component of its mathematics curriculum reform efforts. Visitors to the school—and there are many—are given tours. The teachers at Billabong Elementary consider that they "teach in a fishbowl," constantly on display to the outside world. In many ways, the school looks different from traditional schools, and visitors to the school are invited to look into classrooms through the large windows that provide them with snapshots into the inner sanctum of our classrooms.

The principal of Billabong Elementary is described by his teachers as a "visionary leader," and the school has a large collection of computer hardware and software because of the principal's grantwriting efforts. One key component of the principal's vision has been the introduction of technology to the school. In large part, this technology has been made possible through school-business partnerships that he has forged. The principal is committed to the use of technology at Billabong because of what he sees as the gap between the "real world" and the "school world"; he thinks that one way to bridge this gap is to embrace technology in an effort to prepare children for the 21st century.

As a site council responsible for guiding staff development efforts in the school, we decided to focus on the impact of our extensive investment in technology on student achievement in mathematics. In particular, we wanted to know:

1. If our use of technology was successfully meeting the National Council of Teachers of Mathematics (NCTM) Standards; and
2. How those Standards were being interpreted into classroom practice and student outcomes.

Our action research team decided that we would collect data by observing in each other's classrooms, interviewing teachers and children, analyzing mathematics test data, and comparing the mathematics curriculum taught in the school with the NCTM Standards. When we presented our project to the faculty, all of the teachers and the principal appeared to want to cooperate with the research team's requests for access to classrooms, curriculum materials, and so on. Our hope was to learn more about our technology intervention and how we might continue to evolve as a faculty in this area.

As you move through the halls at Billabong, there is a great deal to be seen—classrooms are open for the inquiring eye. Kindergarten through third-grade classrooms characteristically have six computers, as well as scanners, color printers, and networking with the school's library (thus having access to the extensive CD-ROM collection). The fourth- through seventh-grade classrooms have all of these resources and another six computers per classroom. In one class, all of the children are given an individual laptop computer to use for the year. Children can be seen using computers as part of their class assignments, busying themselves with creating HyperCard stacks for creative writing, "playing" math games, and so on. Math learning centers are evident, and each child is given varied opportunities to interact with a number of different math manipulatives: base 10 blocks, place value charts, construction materials, colored chips, tangrams, and geo-boards, to name a few.

However, what we saw from the inside of each other's classrooms was distinctly different from what we had seen from the outside "looking in." For example, in many of the classrooms children could be seen busily engaged with the computers playing math mazes. For the most part, however, children were engaged in low-level activities, and the purpose of the tasks was lost. Many of the children were engaged in "drill-and-kill" activities that had little relevance to their math learning. The computers had taken on the role of an electronic work sheet to keep children busy once they had completed other assigned math tasks.

Interviews with children were revealing. When we interviewed the children, we did so with a guarantee that their responses would be confidential and asked that they be honest with us—after all, our goal was to provide the best possible mathematics learning environment for them that we possibly could. Some children were brutally honest, telling in great detail the kinds of math activities some teachers used on the computers. Some activities were singled out by children as being a "waste of time," and others described some teachers as "not having a clue" about how the computers were really being used. Indeed, some of this information was confirmed by our own observations of classrooms where children had become profi-

cient at "scribbling" on the computer screen using the mouse and a graphics program and quickly returning to the "drill-and-kill" screen when the teacher approached.

While the computers were being heavily used, the appropriateness of their use was questionable. This was no more evident than in classrooms where the calculator function had been removed from the computers. As one teacher explained, "The children are unable to mentally compute, and their basic skills have deteriorated . . . so we can't have them using calculators until they master the basic skills!" There appeared to be consensus among the teachers that there was a direct relationship between providing children with access to computers and children's lack of ability to recall basic math facts.

The interviews with teachers revealed other problems. Many of the teachers knew very little about the NCTM Standards and continued to use their old "tried and proven" curriculum, in spite of a new textbook adoption promoted by the principal. In fact, some teachers were very unhappy about the textbook adoption because no teachers had been consulted in the process—the textbook had been selected by the principal who was a good friend of the author. In return for piloting the curriculum materials in the school, the principal secured free copies of the textbook.

Compared to other schools in the district, our children appeared to be doing below average on statewide assessments. This came as quite a surprise to some teachers who felt that their children were doing well in most math strands with the exception of open-ended problem-solving and algebraic relationships. In these teachers' views the problem was with the appropriateness of the tests, not the use of technology to enhance teaching and learning.

The findings of our schoolwide action research effort raised some difficult ethical dilemmas for the action research team:

1. What do we do with the data that provided a negative picture of individual teachers in the school? Do we share data on an individual basis with teachers who were singled out by students? What risks do we run in sharing this information? How can we promote professional development without hurting anyone?

2. What do we do with the data that indicated a great deal of dissatisfaction with how the principal had mandated the choice of curriculum? Do we risk alienating the teachers from the administration? Could some teachers be hurt professionally by action the principal might take?
3. How can we improve student achievement through the use of technology without hurting teachers (and the principal) in the process?

The action research team decided to adopt a "hold harmless" approach to dealing with the findings of the study. We shared the general findings of the study with teachers at a faculty meeting and invited teachers, on a voluntary basis, to meet with us to discuss the data for their classrooms. Similarly, we invited the principal to meet with us to discuss implications of the findings for future professional development opportunities.

This vignette provides an excellent illustration of the unpredictable events that can occur during the conduct of educational research. This vignette is not intended to frighten action researchers, but rather to provide an example of the kinds of challenges teacher researchers can face in conducting research in their own classroom and school. This chapter will help action researchers develop their own list of ethical guidelines so that they will act appropriately if and when confronted with a difficult ethical question. The chapter will also provide guidelines to help action researchers obtain Institutional Review Board (IRB) approval.

The Ethics of Research

All research studies involve ethical considerations. Therefore, all researchers must be aware of and attend to the ethical considerations related to their studies. In research, the ends do not justify the means, and researchers must not put their need to carry out their study above their responsibility to maintain the well-being of the study participants. Research studies are built on trust between the researcher and the participants, and researchers have a responsibility to maintain that trust, just as they expect participants to maintain it in the data they provide.

Many professional organizations have developed codes of ethical conduct for their members. Figure 2–1 presents the general principles of the American Psychological Association for the ethical conduct of researchers. Note that additional and much more specific ethical standards are grouped into the following eight categories: (1) general standards; (2) evaluation, assessment, or intervention; (3) advertising and other public statements; (4) therapy; (5) privacy and confidentiality; (6) teaching, training, supervision, research, and publishing; (7) forensic activities; and (8) resolving ethical issues. You may read the full text online at the American Psychological Association's Web site (www. apa.org/ethics/code.html). Most other professional organizations, such as the American Educational Research Association and the American Sociological Society, have similar codes for ethical research.

In 1974, the U.S. Congress put the force of law behind codes of ethical research and passed the **National Research Act of 1974**, which authorized the creation of the National Commission for the Protection of Human Subjects of Biomedical and Behavioral Research. This commission was

PRINCIPLE A: BENEFICENCE AND NONMALEFICENCE

Psychologists strive to benefit those with whom they work and take care to do no harm. In their professional actions, psychologists seek to safeguard the welfare and rights of those with whom they interact professionally and other affected persons, and the welfare of animal subjects of research. When conflicts occur among psychologists' obligations or concerns, they attempt to resolve these conflicts in a responsible fashion that avoids or minimizes harm. Because psychologists' scientific and professional judgments and actions may affect the lives of others, they are alert to and guard against personal, financial, social, organizational, or political factors that might lead to misuse of their influence. Psychologists strive to be aware of the possible effect of their own physical and mental health on their ability to help those with whom they work.

PRINCIPLE B: FIDELITY AND RESPONSIBILITY

Psychologists establish relationships of trust with those with whom they work. They are aware of their professional and scientific responsibilities to society and to the specific communities in which they work. Psychologists uphold professional standards of conduct, clarify their professional roles and obligations, accept appropriate responsibility for their behavior, and seek to manage conflicts of interest that could lead to exploitation or harm. Psychologists consult with, refer to, or cooperate with other professionals and institutions to the extent needed to serve the best interests of those with whom they work. They are concerned about the ethical compliance of their colleagues' scientific and professional conduct. Psychologists strive to contribute a portion of their professional time for little or no compensation or personal advantage.

PRINCIPLE C: INTEGRITY

Psychologists seek to promote accuracy, honesty, and truthfulness in the science, teaching, and practice of psychology. In these activities psychologists do not steal, cheat, or engage in fraud, subterfuge, or intentional misrepresentation of fact. Psychologists strive to keep their promises and to avoid unwise or unclear commitments. In situations in which deception may be ethically justifiable to maximize benefits and minimize harm, psychologists have a serious obligation to consider the need for, the possible consequences of, and their responsibility to correct any resulting mistrust or other harmful effects that arise from the use of such techniques.

PRINCIPLE D: JUSTICE

Psychologists recognize that fairness and justice entitle all persons to access to and benefit from the contributions of psychology and to equal quality in the processes, procedures, and services being conducted by psychologists. Psychologists exercise reasonable judgment and take precautions to ensure that their potential biases, the boundaries of their competence, and the limitations of their expertise do not lead to or condone unjust practices.

PRINCIPLE E: RESPECT FOR PEOPLE'S RIGHTS AND DIGNITY

Psychologists respect the dignity and worth of all people, and the rights of individuals to privacy, confidentiality, and self-determination. Psychologists are aware that special safeguards may be necessary to protect the rights and welfare of persons or communities whose vulnerabilities impair autonomous decision making. Psychologists are aware of and respect cultural, individual, and role differences, including those based on age, gender, gender identity, race, ethnicity, culture, national origin, religion, sexual orientation, disability, language, and socioeconomic status and consider these factors when working with members of such groups. Psychologists try to eliminate the effect on their work of biases based on those factors, and they do not knowingly participate in or condone activities of others based upon such prejudices.

FIGURE 2–1 *General Ethical Principles*

Source: From "Ethical Principles of Psychologists and Code of Conduct," by American Psychological Association, 2002, *American Psychologist, 57*, pp. 1060–1073. Copyright © 2002 by the American Psychological Association. Reprinted with permission.

charged with developing an ethical code and guidelines for researchers. The need for legal restrictions was graphically illustrated by a number of studies in which researchers lied to or put research participants in harm's way in order to carry out their studies. For example, in a study on the effects of group pressure (conducted some years ago) researchers lied to participants while they participated in and watched what they thought was actual electric shocking of other participants (Milgram, 1964). In another study, men known to be infected with syphilis were not treated for their illness because they were part of a control group in a comparative study (Jones, 1998). Incidents such as these prompted governmental regulations regarding research studies, and today, most universities, research centers, and medical centers adhere to ethical guidelines that prohibit such methods. Most universities have a review group, usually called the Human Subjects Review Committee (HSRC) or Institutional Review Board (IRB).

Institutional Review Boards and Action Researchers

Teacher researchers conducting action research as part of a university program of study face unique challenges associated with obtaining Institutional Review Board (IRB) approval and must meet standards that go beyond what most schools and school districts require as part of their own research protocols. IRBs are charged by universities to ensure the ethical conduct of research involving human subjects. The key issue for teacher researchers studying their own practices, and hence, collecting data primarily based on student outcomes, relates to the fact that they are not only acting as researchers, but also as the change agents who have the power and authority to bring about change in their classrooms. According to Nolen and Putten (2007), "These potentially conflicting roles can confound the individual's primary objective in the classroom or school: student learning" (p. 402). Given this potential conflict, Nolen and Putten raise a number of questions, the answers to which provide guidance for action researchers seeking to obtain IRB approval:

- At what point does teaching become research?
- Where does the accountability for this research lie?
- Are teachers properly trained to see the possible ethical pitfalls in such research?
- How are the rights and freedoms of the research participants (the students) protected?

Given the emancipatory nature of action research (and the definition of action research used in this text), it is clear that the answer to the first question is that teaching and research are intertwined. For action researchers studying their own practices and their impact on student outcomes, the inquiry lens of action research pervades the teaching process: teacher researchers are the data collection instruments constantly monitoring what is going on in their classrooms.

The accountability for this research lies not only with the teacher researcher, but in a university context, with the researcher's mentor/teacher, who must ensure that proposed action research studies are ethical in their conduct. As such, it is the responsibility of the university instructor to teach neophyte teacher researchers about the potential ethical pitfalls associated with classroom/school-based action research. It is the responsibility of the IRB to ensure that action researchers address potential ethical challenges in their written proposals, and (when called for) in supplementary oral presentations.

In many ways, the most complex issue action researchers face is how to safeguard the rights and freedoms of the students in the classrooms. How do teachers negotiate informed consent with students (and their parents)? Are students really in a position to opt out of any research their classroom teachers are conducting? Similarly, this question raises concerns about the role of power and authority in a classroom environment, and whether or not students can reasonably be expected to opt out of a study without being concerned about possible censure by the classroom teacher. It should be noted that these kinds of concerns are not new to action researchers or any other qualitatively oriented community-based researchers. IRBs (which are often populated by quantitatively oriented researchers) often struggle with social science research proposals that invariably focus on "insider" research, where the research process is inherently open-ended and intimate. Teachers are active participant observers of their classrooms, continually monitoring and adjusting their teaching based on formal and informal observations of their students. Nevertheless, IRBs have been condoning this kind of research for many years, and action researchers should not be intimidated by the prospect of answering important ethical questions, even if the accompanying frustration of "these quantitative researchers really don't understand what we do" threatens to sideline the research.

Given this context, I offer the following recommendations for action researchers wishing to obtain IRB approval (adapted from Nolen and Putten, 2007):

- Action researchers should provide IRBs with all the necessary university-based IRB requirements (which vary slightly from university to university).
- Action researchers should provide IRBs, school district administrators, and parents with data collection plans that clearly minimize data sources that could be construed as providing evidence that could be used in a coercive manner.
- Action researchers should provide IRBs, school district administrators, and parents with cover letters that explain their studies and include statements about the dual role of teacher and researcher and the sensitivity it takes to conduct research into one's own practice.
- Action researchers should provide IRBs, school district administrators, and parents with parental consent forms that clearly state how they will guarantee that students will be protected from harm, that is, that students will not be penalized for not participating in a study.
- Action researchers should include in all data collection instruments a final "yes or no" option such as "Please include my answers in the study," which unobtrusively allows the student to opt out of the study while appearing to participate.

It is the burden of the action researcher to provide the IRB with evidence that the proposed study clearly addresses issues of informed consent, protection from harm, student autonomy, and the potentially coercive nature of action research.

The National Research Act of 1974 was also designed to protect the privacy of students' educational records. Among its provisions is the specification that data that actually identify students may not be made available unless written permission is acquired from the students (if of age) or a parent or legal guardian. The consent must indicate what data may be disclosed, for what purposes, and to whom. If part of your study requires obtaining information from individual elementary students' record files, you would need to obtain written permission from each student's parent or guardian, not a blanket approval from the school principal or classroom teacher. Note that if you are interested in using only class averages (in which no individual student is identified), individual consent from the principal would likely suffice. However, if you calculate the class average from individual student records, individual permission would be necessary because you have access to individual records.

There are some exceptions that may not require written consent. For example, school personnel with a "legitimate educational interest" in a student would not need written consent to examine student records. In other cases, the researcher could request that a teacher or guidance counselor either remove names from students' records completely or replace them with a coded number or letter. The researcher can then use the records without knowing the names of the individual students. Again, this adherence to providing anonymity offers other instructional challenges for the teacher researcher who wishes to use formative and summative evaluation data to develop specific instructional interventions designed to meet students' needs.

It is also worth noting that some IRBs do not require IRB approval for action research conducted as part of a university course. Be sure to check with your instructor and/or IRB to determine if IRB approval is required at your university. Sometimes the determining factor in this decision relates to whether or not the outcomes of the proposed study will be published or presented at a professional conference.

The sources and advice offered in this chapter will help you to conceive and conduct your research ethically. The suggestions provided do not cover all the ethical issues you are likely to encounter in your research. Perhaps the fundamental ethical rule is that participants should not be harmed in any way, real or possible, in the name of science. Respect and concern for your own integrity and for your participants' dignity and welfare are the bottom lines of ethical research.

Doing the Right Thing: The Role of Ethics in Action Research

Simply stated, the role of ethics in action research can be considered in terms of how each of us treats the individuals with whom we interact at our school setting: students, parents, volunteers, administrators, and teaching colleagues. As Nolen and Putten contend, "Like the physician and the counselor, the teacher cannot abandon the role of practitioner but must always exercise professional judgment and skill in the best interest of the student" (2007, p. 403). Similarly, Smith (1990) stated, "At a commonsense level, caring, fairness, openness, and truth seem to be the important values undergirding the relationships and the activity of inquiring" (p. 260). However, values such as these invariably take on a different meaning for different people with whom we interact. Nevertheless, the success of your action research project depends on a clear understanding of the intimate nature of the research process and on not harming participants in the name of research.

The vignette of Billabong Elementary School that opened this chapter is a good reminder of why it is important to think about ethical dilemmas before they occur. And although I have seen few instances of where ethical dilemmas have threatened to stall a collaborative action research effort, the very nature of the enterprise provides the potential for conflict and harm. Considering the ethics of action research before commencing the work (and as part of your IRB approval) is one way to ensure that you are prepared to respond in an ethical, caring manner to difficult situations that may arise.

The issue of ethics in qualitative research and action-oriented research has received considerable attention in recent years (cf. Christians, 2000; Creswell, 2002; Eisner, 1991; Flinders, 1992; Gay, Mills, & Airasian, 2009; Nolen & Putten, 2007; Smith, 1990; Soltis, 1990; Wolcott, 1990). Most of this literature describes mistakes made in the research process and how the ethics of the situation were addressed. What makes the subject of ethics particularly challenging for teacher researchers is the intimate and open-ended nature of action research.

Action research is intimate because there is little distance between teacher researchers and their subjects, the students in their classrooms and schools. Qualitatively oriented action research is open ended because the direction of the research often unfolds during the course of the study. This significantly complicates the ability of teacher researchers to obtain students' "fully informed consent" to participate in the research process. Informed consent is central to research ethics. It is the principle that seeks to ensure that all human subjects retain autonomy and the ability to judge for themselves what risks are worth taking for the purpose of furthering scientific knowledge.

In action research the key participants in a study are often the students in our classrooms. How does the concept of informed consent apply to them? Do we need to obtain written permission from parents/guardians before collecting naturally occurring data such as test scores, observations, work samples, and so on? As stated previously, it will depend on whether you need to obtain IRB approval in addition to meeting the local school district protocols. But as you will see in the following discussion, regardless of the kinds of mandatory research approvals it is important that you develop your own criteria for what you consider to be ethical behavior.

Ethical Guidelines

The following commonsense ethical guidelines may help teacher researchers respond appropriately when faced with ethical decisions before, during, and after an action research inquiry.

Informed Consent and Protection from Harm

Informed consent should take the form of a dialogue that mutually shapes the research and the results. Informed consent ensures that research participants enter the research of their free will and with an understanding of the study and any possible dangers that may arise. It is intended to reduce the likelihood that participants will be exploited by a researcher persuading them to participate without fully knowing the study's requirements. Be clear about whether you need to seek permission from participants in the study. For example, if you are using photographs or video recordings as data collection techniques and intend to use these artifacts in a public forum, such as a presentation at a conference, make sure that you have checked whether written permission is necessary. The answer may vary from district to district and university to university depending on how the materials are to be used.

Similarly, consider how to inform students that they are subjects in a study. For example, you may decide to interview a small group to determine how a problem-solving curriculum is being implemented in different classrooms as a follow-up to a survey or an observation. How will you ensure the anonymity of the respondents to protect their privacy? How will you protect the confidentiality of participants? In the case of Billabong Elementary School (from the opening vignette), the action research team wrestled with the issue of informed consent. When they initially presented their project to the faculty at the school, all of the teachers and the principal appeared to want to cooperate with the research team's requests for access to classrooms, curriculum materials and so on. The research team had not collected data without their knowledge. Still, the team wondered if they had done enough. Would the presentation of their data harm the teachers, especially if the teachers had expressed disapproval of the principal? Were the teachers adequately prepared for the risks? After debate, the researchers resolved to share the general findings of the study, rather than singling out any individual teacher's comments. That way, the researchers could protect the confidentiality of participants while at the same time sharing the themes that emerged from the study.

Freedom from harm is focused on not exposing students to risks. It involves issues of confidentiality (to protect students from embarrassment or ridicule) and issues related to personal privacy. Collecting information on participants or observing them without their knowledge or without appropriate permission is not ethical. Furthermore, any information or data that are collected, either from or about a person, should be strictly confidential, especially if it is at all personal. Access to data should be limited to persons directly involved in conducting the research. An individual participant's performance should not be reported or made public using the participant's name, even for an innocuous measure such as an arithmetic test. For example, individuals identified as members of a group that performed poorly on a research instrument might be subjected to ridicule, censure by parents, or lowered teacher expectations.

The use of anonymity or confidentiality to avoid privacy invasion and potential harm is common. **Anonymity** means that the researcher does not know the identities of the participants in the study. On the other hand, confidentiality is when the researcher knows the identities of participants but promises not to release them to anyone else. If the researcher knows participants' identities, there can be confidentiality, but no anonymity. Removing names or coding records is one commonly used way to maintain anonymity. When planning your study you must indicate to participants (students and parents) whether you will provide confidentiality (you'll know but won't tell) or anonymity (you will not know the participants' names) and be sure they know the difference. Clearly, this is a challenge in action research when the focus of the research is on the outcomes of students in the teacher researcher's classroom.

Confidentiality usually involves the use of pseudonyms to conceal identities. However, protecting confidentiality in a qualitatively oriented action research effort is sometimes more problematic than just assigning pseudonyms. For example, a team of teacher researchers who are responsible for driving a schoolwide action research effort will likely be made privy to the intimate details of their colleagues' classrooms. It will be their challenge to make sure that they protect their colleagues from stress, embarrassment, or unwanted publicity that may come from sharing the action research findings. And, of course, all of this must be balanced against their commitment to improve the learning experiences of the students in their school.

Figure 2–2 presents a cover letter written by a principal in support of a doctoral student's proposed study. Note that the student secured not only the principal's permission, but also his strong support and cooperation, by sharing the potential benefits of the study with the principal's students. Figure 2–3 presents the parental consent form that accompanied the cover letter. It addresses many of the ethical and legal concerns discussed in this chapter.

Clearly, human relations are an important factor in conducting research in applied settings. That you should be your usual charming self goes without saying. But you should keep in mind that you are dealing with sincere, concerned educators who may not have your level of research expertise. Therefore, you must make a special effort to discuss your study in plain English (it is possible!) and to never give the impression that you are talking down to them. Also, your task is not over once the study begins. To maintain your participants' initial level of cooperation, monitor their feelings and respond as necessary.

Deception

There is no room for deception in action research (or any other research for that matter). For example, if during an interview a colleague, parent, or student confides in you "off the record," then the substance of the conversation should remain off the record. Regardless of how meaningful the comments, you have a responsibility to act with integrity and to honor your interviewees' requests for confidentiality. Similarly, there is no place for hidden microphones in order to capture interviewees "on tape." If you wish to record a conversation, seek verbal and/or written permission. It is recommended that you not do your action research studies using a topic that requires deception. Your advisor and the Human Subjects Review or IRB Committee at your institution will provide suggestions about ethical ways to carry out your research plan. Note that as the teacher researcher in an action research study it is your responsibility to maintain ethical standards in the research.

SCHOOL OF EDUCATION

BOSTON COLLEGE

January 17, 2005

Mr. Dennis Yacubian
Vice-Principal
Westside High School
Westside, MA 00001

Dear Mr. Yacubian,

The Department of Measurement and Evaluation at Boston College is interested in determining the types of testing, evaluation, research, and statistical needs high school administrators in Massachusetts have. Our intent is to develop a master's level program that provides graduates who can meet the methodological needs of high school administrators. The enclosed questionnaire is designed to obtain information about your needs in the areas of testing, evaluation, research, and statistics. Your responses will be anonymous and seriously considered in developing the planned program. We will also provide you a summary of the results of the survey so that you can examine the responses of other high school administrators. This study has been approved by the university's Human Subjects Review Committee.

We would appreciate your completion of the questionnaire by January 31. We have provided a stamped, addressed envelope for you to use in returning the questionnaire. You do not need to put your name on the questionnaire, but we request that you sign your name on the enclosed postcard and mail it separately from the questionnaire. That way we will know you have replied and will not have to bother you with follow-up letters.

We realize that your schedule is busy and your time is valuable. However, we hope that the 15 minutes it will take you to complete the questionnaire will help lead to a program that will provide a useful service to school administrators.

Thank you in advance for your participation. If you have questions about the study, you can contact me at 555-555-4444.

Yours truly,

James Jones
Department Chair

FIGURE 2–2 *Sample Cover Letter*

Personal Ethical Perspective

Researchers should have an ethical perspective that is very close to their personal ethical position. This may seem like a statement of the obvious except for this caveat: As teacher researchers, we may find ourselves in situations that are foreign to us. For example, in a collaborative action research project focused on the effects of a new math problem-solving curriculum on student achievement and attitude, teachers are asked to administer a student attitude survey. The surveys are then analyzed by a team of teacher researchers representing different grades or benchmark levels in the school. During the analysis, it becomes clear that one group of students

PARENTAL CONSENT FORM

The information provided on this form and the accompanying cover letter is presented to you in order to fulfill legal and ethical requirements for Northwest Eaton College (the institution sponsoring this doctoral dissertation study) and the Department of Health and Human Services (HHS) regulations for the Protection of Human Research Subjects as amended on March 26, 1989. The wording used in this form is utilized for all types of studies and should not be misinterpreted for this particular study.

The dissertation committee at Northern University and the Research Review Committee of Knox County Public Schools have both given approval to conduct this study, "The Relationships Between the Modality Preferences of Elementary Students and Selected Instructional Styles of CAI as They Affect Verbal Learning of Facts." The purpose of this study is to determine the effect on achievement scores when the identified learning styles (visual, audio, tactile/kinesthetic) of elementary students in grades 3 and 5 are matched or mismatched to the instructional methods of specifically selected computer assisted instruction (CAI).

Your child will be involved in this study by way of the following:

1. Pretest on animal facts.
2. Posttest on animal facts.
3. Test on learning styles.
4. Interaction with computer-assisted instruction (CAI-software on the computer)—visual, audio, tactile CAI matching the student's own learning style.

All of these activities should not take more than two hours per student. There are no foreseeable risks to the students involved. In addition, the parent or researcher may remove the student from the study at any time with just cause. Specific information about individual students will be kept *strictly confidential* and will be obtainable from the school principal if desired. The results that are published publicly will not reference any individual students since the study will only analyze relationships among groups of data.

The purpose of this form is to allow your child to participate in the study, and to allow the researcher to use the information already available at the school or information obtained from the actual study to analyze the outcomes of the study. Parental consent for this research study is strictly voluntary without undue influence or penalty. The parent signature below also assumes that the child understands and agrees to participate cooperatively.

If you have additional questions regarding the study, the rights of subjects, or potential problems, please call the principal, Ms. Gwen Gregory, or the researcher, Ms. Joleen Levine (Director of Computer Education, Northern University, 555-5554).

_____

Student's Name

_____   _____

Signature of Parent/Guardian   Date

FIGURE 2–3 *Parental Consent Form for a Proposed Research Study*

is very unhappy with their math instruction and have supported their assertions with negative comments about the teacher. What will you do with the data? Should they be shared in an unedited form with the teacher? Who might be hurt in the process? What potential good can come from sharing the data? Or perhaps the principal hears that there is a problem with one teacher and asks for access to the data so that the teacher can be placed on a "plan of assistance."

How should the research team respond? What assurances of confidentiality were given to the participants prior to collecting the data? How will you respond to the principal when you are stopped in the hallway and asked for your opinion?

This scenario is not meant to scare you away from doing action research. However, these are the kinds of unexpected outcomes that occasionally face teacher researchers who have been made privy to information about their own teaching and that of their colleagues. Smith's (1990) lesson is an important one: You will potentially avoid such awkward situations if you have clarified your own ethical perspectives at the outset. This might take the form of a values clarification activity that can be undertaken individually or collectively (see Task 1 at the end of this chapter). The point is this—be prepared to respond in a manner that is comfortable and natural for you. When you are placed in the "hot seat," there may not be time to give a well-thought out, rational response. This situation will be easier if you can respond in a personal manner.

Social Principles

You should be able to identify broader social principles that are an integral part of who you are as a teacher and a contributing member of the community in which you live. These broader social principles should dictate your ethical stance. For example, democratic processes, social justice, equality, and emancipation may be the principles that guide your ethical behavior in a given situation.

Accuracy

Ensuring the accuracy of your data is a central concern of action research. It is unethical and unscientific to fabricate data in order to substantiate a personal belief or value. For example, your study may have focused on the effectiveness of a newly adopted reading program. Although you personally like the program, the data suggest that it is not effective in improving test scores. You must be able to accept the findings of the study despite your bias toward the reading program. Any attempt to manipulate the data to support a personal position is unethical.

RESEARCH IN ACTION CHECKLIST 2–1

Ethical Guidelines for Action Researchers

_____ Determine whether or not you require Institutional Review Board (IRB) approval and/or school district approval.

_____ If necessary, obtain IRB approval.

_____ Seek your action research participants' informed consent.

_____ Consider confidentiality, anonymity, and avoidance of harm.

_____ Deception is unacceptable.

_____ Develop an ethical research perspective that is close to your personal, ethical position.

_____ Determine the broader social principles that affect your ethical stance.

_____ Ensure that you accurately record data.

The purpose of this discussion on ethics in action research has been to prepare you to think about a whole range of issues that face any researcher. Carefully consider how you will respond when confronted with difficult questions from colleagues, parents, students, and administrators. Taking time to clarify your values and ethical perspectives will help you to respond in a professional, personal, and caring fashion.

As you embark on your action research journey and data collection efforts, remember that you are ultimately condemned to freedom in matters of ethics (Eisner, 1991). There are few absolutes. Working with colleagues through issues related to confidentiality, anonymity, informed consent, and rational judgment in matters of ethics will ensure that you avoid potentially difficult situations that may arise in implementing your action research effort. Gay, Mills, and Airasian (2009) summarize ethical issues as follows:

> Perhaps the fundamental rule of ethics is that participants should not be harmed in any way, real or possible, in the name of science. Respect and concern for your own integrity and for your participants' dignity and welfare are the bottom lines of ethical research. (p. 24)

Remember, you will be undertaking your action research in your own classroom and school—this is the place where you will continue to conduct your professional and personal life long after you have changed your current area of focus. Attention to the fundamental ethical guidelines presented in this chapter will help ensure that, regardless of your area of focus, life in school will not be adversely affected by your quest for excellence. (See Research in Action Checklist 2–1 for ethical guidelines for teacher researchers.)

Summary

The Ethics of Research

1. In research, the ends do not justify the means, and researchers must not put their need to carry out their study above their responsibility to maintain the well-being of the study participants.
2. Many professional organizations have developed codes of ethical conduct for their members. Figure 2–1 presents the general principles of the American Psychological Association for the ethical conduct of researchers.
3. The National Research Act of 1974 requires that, to ensure protection of participants, proposed research activities involving human participants be reviewed and approved by an authorized group prior to the execution of the research.
4. Institutional Review Boards (IRBs) are charged by universities to ensure the ethical conduct of research involving human subjects.
5. The key issue for teacher researchers studying their own practices, and hence, collecting data primarily based on student outcomes, relates to the fact that they are not only acting as the researchers, but also as the change agents who have the power and authority to bring about change in their classrooms.
6. Teachers are active participant observers of their classrooms, continually monitoring and adjusting their teaching based on formal and informal observations of their students.

7. Action researchers should provide IRBs with all the necessary university-based IRB requirements (which vary slightly from university to university).

8. Action researchers should provide IRBs, school district administrators, and parents with data collection plans that clearly minimize data sources that could be construed as providing evidence that could be used in a coercive manner.

9. Action researchers should provide IRBs, school district administrators, and parents with cover letters that explain their studies and include statements about the dual role of teacher and researcher and the sensitivity it takes to conduct research into one's own practice.

10. Action researchers should provide IRBs, school district administrators, and parents with parental consent forms that clearly state how they will guarantee that students will be protected from harm, that is, that students will not be penalized for not participating in a study.

11. Action researchers should include in all data collection instruments a final "yes or no" option such as "Please include my answers in the study," which unobtrusively allows the student to opt out of the study while appearing to participate.

Doing the Right Thing: The Role of Ethics in Action Research

12. The role of ethics in action research can be considered in terms of how each of us treats the individuals with whom we interact at our school setting: students, parents, volunteers, administrators, and teaching colleagues.

13. Action research is intimate because there is little distance between teacher researchers and their subjects, the students in their classrooms and schools. This significantly complicates the ability of teacher researchers to obtain students' informed consent to participate in the research process.

Ethical Guidelines

14. Perhaps the most basic and important ethical issues in research are concerned with participants' informed consent and freedom from harm.

15. Informed consent should take the form of a dialogue that mutually shapes the research and the results.

16. Informed consent ensures that research participants enter the research of their free will and with an understanding of the study and any possible dangers that may arise.

17. The use of confidentiality or anonymity to avoid privacy invasion and potential harm is common.

18. Anonymity means that the researcher does not know the identities of the participants in the study.

19. Confidentiality is when the researcher knows the identities of participants but promises not to release them to anyone else.

20. There is no room for deception in action research.

21. Researchers should have an ethical perspective that is very close to their personal ethical position.

22. You should be able to identify broader social principles that are an integral part of who you are as a teacher and a contributing member of the community in which you live.
23. Ensuring the accuracy of your data is a central concern of action research.
24. Teacher researchers should, to the best of their ability, recognize their own personal biases and develop an ethical perspective that ensures they will do the right thing when confronted with a difficult ethical dilemma.

Task

1. Using the ethical guidelines provided in Checklist 2–1, determine what remains to be done to address all possible ethical dilemmas in your study.

3

Deciding on an Area of Focus

This chapter provides guidelines for clarifying a general idea and an area of focus for action research efforts. Procedures are described for doing reconnaissance and reviewing related literature using online resources such as ERIC, the Internet, university library resources, or articles found in journals published by professional organizations for educators. Finally, this chapter tells how to create an action research plan.

After reading this chapter you should be able to:

1. Select an appropriate area of focus.

2. Do reconnaissance.

3. Review related literature.

4. Write an action plan to guide your work.

Interactive Teen Theater

CATHY MITCHELL

Cathy Mitchell is a substitute teacher who also works with teen theater companies. Her story helps us to see how serendipity can play a role in developing an area of focus. In the beginning of the action research process, Cathy was unsure of her area of focus. However, as the result of an unexpected "intervention" to her teen theater production when an actor did not turn up for a performance, Cathy decided to systematically investigate the effects of improvisation on audience participation.

For the past 10 years I have directed peer education teen theaters. These companies create and perform original plays based on company members' experiences and ideas. The plays are collections of dramatic scenes, comic sketches, and songs; the topics are current issues of concern to young people, including self-esteem, substance abuse, teen pregnancy, love versus lust, violence, family relationships, and sexually transmitted diseases. We tour extensively, performing for high schools and middle schools as well as at juvenile detention facilities.

Although the company is generally very well received, I have felt that there is something stale in the actor/audience relationship. The audience sits attentively, laughs in recognition, and enjoys the variety in their class day, but remains essentially passive. Question sessions after the show, initially planned to generate discussion about important topics, frequently degenerated into boring adulation questions, such as "How long have you been rehearsing this?" or "Do you want to be an actor when you grow up?"

Two years ago, a few actors had to miss a performance. When we arrived at the high school we were scheduled to perform at, we realized the opening scene had two small roles that we could not eliminate but didn't have enough actors to fill. I asked two children from the audience to volunteer, taught them their lines backstage while the rest of the scene was going on, and they walked on stage and finished the scene. The audience was instantly galvanized. Even with this very small change we had broken the division between actor and audience.

This began my experience into interactive theater. For me, this has meant bringing some of the improvisation techniques that we use to develop material during rehearsals onto the stage and inviting the audience to participate in limited ways. I found that involving the audience changed the dynamics from a passive spectator sport to a more participatory dialogue.

Through my research I have arrived at a working description for interactive theater: A short scene is played by workshop actors. The audience is asked to look for opportunities to improve the resolution. The scene is played again, and any time anyone wants to intervene and take any character's place to show a better way of handling the situation, they just shout "Stop!" and take over the role. One scene may be played many times. Often no closure is evident, and the scene ends in unresolved issues and heightened emotions. The actors and audience then discuss the issues generated by the scene.

The purpose of my study was to determine the effects of audience interaction with the actors in teen theater productions on their ability to identify issues and transfer learnings into similar problems in their lives. For example, in the current production of Duct Tape Theater, a company I direct, there is a well-written scene called "Sticks and Stones," which is a collage containing poetry, a song, short monologues, and scenes. It lasts about 20 minutes and confronts issues of prejudice, discrimination, and violence. I decided, as my intervention, to replace this scene with an interactive theater piece developed with the audience. For three performances we included "Sticks and Stones" (my control groups), and for three other performances we included what became known as the "Violence Improv" audience interaction scene. This gave us six audiences: three control groups and three interactive groups.

Some of my methods of data collection for this project—my personal journal and the actors' journals, which are required for actors receiving credit for the class—were already in place. I also asked each teacher to write me a letter commenting on what they observed during the performance. None of these gave me the data I really wanted but which was most difficult to collect— data from the audience. I decided to have my acting company develop this data collection source with me. The actors and I developed a questionnaire to be filled out directly after the performance and a group interview technique that involved three company members meeting with a small group of audience members for about 15 minutes. The goal was to generate as many responses as possible to the scenes about teen violence and harassment. One actor served as the interviewer, one as the scribe, and one kept a running tally of comments and responses.

The data showed four clear themes:

1. The audience clearly judged the performance containing the "Violence Improv" as more relevant to their lives than the control performance of "Sticks and Stones."
2. More individuals participated in discussing the issues of violence and harassment, with more overall comments and more comments that were considered "right on." This data showed that more audience members were able to both iden-

tify issues in the performance and relate these issues to their own lives.
3. The clearest negative response was that the interactive piece made the performance feel "rushed." These data told me that the interactive material threw off the timing of the show. I often wrote in my own journal that I feel exhausted at the end of performances, and teachers wrote to me that we were running into break time and past the end of the period "trying to squeeze everything in."
4. The biggest letdown to me was that there wasn't any significant increase in the number of different issues identified or solutions suggested between the two audiences. Even though the interactive improvisation generated more answers and much more participation, the issues and solutions were pretty much the same.

My action research project confirmed to me that my methods for making teen theater work more meaningful are on the right track. It also became clear, however, that the format I am using is not the best one. I plan to continue working with the teen theater groups, to modify the format I have used in the past, and to monitor the effects of the changes on participants' transfer of learning to their real lives. For me, this is critical work, and the most important result of this project is that I feel renewed energy for my work. Last year at this time I was busily seeking a replacement for myself and announcing to everyone that I wasn't going to direct teens anymore. I didn't even consider that I could examine the problem, address it, and remedy it. It feels really good to expect something to happen in my working life as a result of my own research and reflection.

Not everyone comes to an action research setting with an area of focus in mind. In fact, many teachers initially resist participating in the process. It is not uncommon for teachers and administrators to skeptically claim, "I'm only here because I have to be. No action research—no teaching/administrator license!" In this teen theater example, the "intervention" and "area of focus" emerged quite unexpectedly and led to some important understandings about how to increase audience understanding and participation.

We'll assume, then, that you may not have identified an area of focus. However, you probably do have several interests and concerns: perhaps your content area, a self-contained special education classroom, an at-risk program, an alternative education program, a multi-graded classroom, a single fourth-grade classroom, a reading specialist program, a block-scheduled team teaching program, or even a one-room schoolhouse, to name a few!

Every teacher and administrator who undertakes an action research project starts at the same place: making explicit a question or problem to investigate, or defining an **area of focus**. Finding an area of focus can be hard work if your action research inquiry is going to be engaging and meaningful for you. Taking time in the beginning to ensure that your topic is important—for you—is a critical step in the action research process. No one should tell you what your area of focus is or ought to be. The following guidelines can help you focus your research question.

Clarifying a General Idea and an Area of Focus

In the beginning of the action research process, you need to clarify the general idea that will be the area of focus. The general idea is a statement that links an idea to an action and refers to a situation one wishes to change or improve on (Elliott, 1991). Here are some examples, phrased in the form of a statement based on an observation and followed by a question about how the situation could be improved:

- *Statement/Observation*: Students do not seem to be engaged during teen theater productions.
- *Question*: How can I improve their engagement?
- *Statement/Observation*: Students take a lot of time to learn problem solving in mathematics, but this process doesn't appear to transfer to their acquisition of other mathematics skills and knowledge.
- *Question*: How can I improve the integration and transfer of problem-solving skills in mathematics?
- *Statement/Observation*: Parents are unhappy with regular parent-teacher conferences.
- *Question*: How can I improve the conferencing process using student-led conferences?

Taking time in the beginning of the action research process to identify what you feel passionate about is critical. For some, this will be a relatively short activity—you may have come to an action research setting with a clear sense of a student-centered, teacher-centered, or parent-driven area of focus. For others, gaining a sense of the general idea will be more problematic. Don't rush it. Take time to talk to colleagues, reflect on your daily classroom life, and carefully consider what nags at you when you prepare for work every day.

Criteria for Selecting a General Idea/Area of Focus

There are some important criteria you should keep in mind while identifying your general idea and subsequent area of focus (Creswell, 2008; Elliott, 1991; Sagor, 2000):

- The area of focus should involve teaching and learning and should focus on your own practice.
- The area of focus is something within your locus of control.
- The area of focus is something you feel passionate about.
- The area of focus is something you would like to change or improve.

Applying these criteria early in the process will keep you on track during the early stages of the action research process. They will also remind you of the vital and dynamic dimensions of action research—that it is important work done by teacher researchers for themselves and their students, the results of which will ultimately improve student outcomes. (See Research in Action Checklist 3–1.)

Identifying Your Area of Focus

Is your area of focus an issue that
_____ Involves teaching and learning?
_____ Is within your focus of control?
_____ You feel passionate about?
_____ You would like to change or improve?

Reconnaissance

The next important step in the action research process is **reconnaissance**, or preliminary information gathering. More specifically, reconnaissance is taking time to reflect on your own beliefs and to understand the nature and context of your general idea. Doing reconnaissance takes three forms: self-reflection, description, and explanation.

Gaining Insight into Your Area of Focus Through Self-Reflection

First, try to explore your own understanding of:

- The *theories* that impact your practice.
- The *educational values* you hold.
- How your work in schools fits into the *larger context* of schooling and society.
- The *historical* contexts of your *school* and *schooling* and how things got to be the way they are.
- The *historical* contexts of how you arrived at your *beliefs* about *teaching* and *learning* (Kemmis & McTaggart, 1988, 2000).

If your general idea for your action research inquiry is the question "How can I improve the integration and transfer of problem-solving skills in mathematics?" you might think about the following:

- Based on my experience teaching mathematics and my reading of the subject, I have been influenced by Van de Walle's (2003) *theory* about teaching and learning mathematics developmentally. In particular, the goal of mathematics is *relational understanding*, which is the connection between *conceptual* and *procedural knowledge* in mathematics. This theory of mathematics directly affects the ways in which I think about teaching mathematics to my students.
- I hold the *educational value* that children ought to be able to transfer problem-solving skills to other areas of mathematics as well as to life outside of school. That is, I am committed to relevancy of curriculum.
- I believe that mathematical problem solving, and problem solving in general, fits the *larger context* of schooling and society by providing children with critical lifelong learning skills that can be transferred to all aspects of their life.
- The *historical context* of mathematics teaching suggests a rote method of memorizing facts and algorithms. Although this approach to teaching mathematics worked for me (as a child and young teacher), it no longer suffices as a teaching method today.

- The historical context of how I came to *believe* in the importance of changing how I teach mathematics to children has grown out of my own frustration with knowing what to do to solve a problem, but not knowing *why* I need to use a particular approach or algorithm.
- Given this self-reflection on an area of focus related to the integration and transfer of problem-solving skills in mathematics, I can now better understand the problem before I implement an intervention that addresses my concern for how to best teach a *relevant* problem-solving curriculum.

This is part of the "mind work" or "mental gymnastics" of action research. It is not an activity that will immediately produce new and exciting curricula and/or teaching materials—things that may follow later in the process when you become clearer about an intervention.

Gaining Insight into Your Area of Focus Through Descriptive Activities

Next, try to describe as fully as possible the situation you want to change or improve by focusing on *who, what, when, where,* and *how.* Grappling with these questions will not only clarify the focus area for your action research efforts, but will prevent you from moving ahead with an investigation that was too murky to begin with. For example, in this stage, you might answer these questions:

- What evidence do you have that this issue (the problem-solving skills of math students) is a problem?
- Which students are not able to transfer problem-solving skills to other mathematics tasks?
- How is problem solving presently taught?
- How often is problem solving taught?
- What is the ratio of time spent teaching problem solving to time spent teaching other mathematics skills?

Gaining Insight into Your Area of Focus Through Explanatory Activities

Once you've adequately described the situation you intend to investigate, try to explain it. Focus on the *why.* Can you account for the critical factors that have an impact on the general idea? In essence, this is the step in which you develop a hypothesis stating the expected relationships between variables in your study (Elliott, 1991).

In this case, you might hypothesize that students are struggling with the transfer of problem-solving skills to other mathematics tasks because they are not getting enough practice, they lack fundamental basic math skills, or they have not had sufficient opportunity to use math manipulatives. Given these possible explanations for why children have not been successfully transferring problem-solving skills to other areas of mathematics, you might develop the following hypotheses:

- A relationship exists between a mathematics curriculum that emphasizes the children's ability to know *what* to do and *why* to do it and children's abilities to transfer problem-solving skills.

- A relationship exists between a mathematics curriculum that emphasizes the use of manipulatives (to help children create meaning) and children's abilities to transfer problem-solving skills.

These reconnaissance activities (self-reflection, description, and explanation) help teacher researchers clarify what they already know about the proposed focus of the study; what they believe to be true about the relationships of the factors, variables, and contexts that make up their work environment; and what they believe can improve the situation. Research in Action Checklist 3–2 summarizes the critical activities for reconnaissance that you should perform at this point in the action research process.

Review of Related Literature

At this point you should make an initial foray into the professional literature, the formal record of other people's experiences, to try to better understand the problem on which you are focusing. The literature may suggest other ways of looking at your problem and help you to identify potential *promising practices* that you might use in your classroom to correct the problem. To borrow the words of Kemmis and McTaggart (1988), "Can existing research throw any light on your situation and help you see it more clearly?" (p. 55).

Some authors of action research books debate the importance of reviewing the literature as a strategy in the action research process. Most experts agree, however, that reviewing the literature is a valuable activity for action researchers. For example, Sagor (1992) writes: "I would encourage anyone interested in doing good research to review the literature immediately after engaging in the problem-formulation activities" (p. 76). Although reviewing the literature has long been a well-established component of dissertation and contract research and graduate research classes, its inclusion here signals the importance that teacher researchers have awarded the activity.

Reviewing the literature is a valuable contribution to the action research process that could actually save you time. Often, teacher researchers think that they know what their problem is but become stymied in the process because they weren't really sure what they were asking. Taking time to immerse yourself in the literature allows you to reflect on your own problems

RESEARCH IN ACTION CHECKLIST 3–2

Critical Activities for Doing Reconnaissance

Self-Reflection:
_____ Reflect on your area of focus in light of your values and beliefs; your understandings about the relationships among theory, practice, school, and society; how things got to be the way they are; and what you believe about teaching and learning.

Description:
_____ Describe the situation you wish to change or improve.
_____ Describe the evidence you have that the area of focus is a problem.
_____ Identify the critical factors that affect your area of focus.

Explanation:
_____ Explain the situation you intend to investigate by hypothesizing how and why the critical factors you've identified affect that situation.

through someone else's lens. You can locate yourself within the research literature and find support for what you are doing or be challenged by what other researchers have done and how they have tackled a particular problem.

At the end of the process, you ought to be informed enough about the literature that you could talk to colleagues about the major themes that emerged. Similarly, you should be able to talk about "promising practices" that were discussed.

You might also view this activity as being analogous to the exercise most people undertake before making a major purchase for their family—they immerse themselves in the literature to see what other folks have learned about a particular product. For example, I recently purchased a new automobile. My wife and I discussed the kind of vehicle we wanted in light of our family needs (one child), recreational interests (skiing in the winter and camping in the summer) and, of course, budget (can we really afford a car payment?). In a sense, this activity was akin to selecting an area of focus. In our case, our area of focus was the purchase of a sport utility vehicle (SUV). This led me very naturally to review the related literature about SUVs in such sources as *Consumer Reports, Car and Driver, Edmund's Buying Guide* online, and the *Kelly Blue Book* for reviews and comparative pricing information.

This review of literature was an invaluable exercise for helping me see clearly the issues related to purchasing an SUV. For example: Did we really need all the extras included on a particular vehicle? What size engine did we need to tow our tent trailer? How did the safety and reliability of different vehicles compare? As in action research, immersion into the related literature helped us clarify all the issues that we needed to consider in order to solve a problem.

This activity also helped me identify "promising practices" for purchasing a new vehicle. For example, given the "sticker price," how much should I really pay for the vehicle? Again, the literature identified purchasing strategies that had been used by experienced buyers. These strategies included determining the manufacturer's cost of the vehicle to the dealer; accounting for dealer incentive programs, dealer "holdbacks," and manufacturer-to-buyer "cashback" incentives; and, of course, calculating a "fair" price while still paying the dealer enough to cover advertising costs, commissions, and so on.

After reviewing this literature, I was prepared to implement a "promising practice" (buying strategy) for the SUV we had determined best met our needs and budget. And although the time spent immersing myself in the literature did not guarantee that my intervention would achieve my desired outcomes, I was better prepared to initiate my strategy and informed about how I would know if I achieved my goals—based on what other experts in the field had done in the past.

Sometimes, teacher researchers will claim that they cannot find any published research related to their area of focus. This invariably leads to questions of relevance and importance. After all, if nobody else has researched the problem, perhaps it is not worthy of investigation! Unlike the SUV example above, my illustration here is far more personal and serious. Several years ago my son, who was five years old at the time, inexplicably began to pass blood in his urine—a pretty scary sight for any parent. After many invasive medical tests over a six-month period, we finally opted for a procedure that required general anesthesia in order to determine the cause of the blood. The surgeon emerged from the operating room and pronounced, "I have some good news, and I have some bad news!" The good news was that the surgeon was able to diagnose the cause of the internal bleeding—a rare, benign, and non-life-threatening condition called trigonitis. The bad news was that the surgeon was unable to tell us why our son had developed the condition or how to treat it! I was shocked at this revelation from the surgeon, a pediatric urology specialist. How could my son be bleeding internally and there not be a medical explanation? Simply, the surgeon responded, because the condition was rare, benign, and non-life-threatening it did not warrant research! My point here is not to be melodramatic but rather to make a case for the importance of your own research, regardless of whether it has been researched (and published) by other professionals. Just because your area of focus is unique to you does not make it any less important. It is your problem and you own it. Do not be disheartened if your review of the literature fails to provide you with helpful insights.

Action researchers rely on four main sources of literature to better prepare themselves to undertake research: online searching of the Educational Resources Information Center (ERIC) and similar online resources (for example, Education Index, PyscINFO, Dissertation Abstracts, Readers' Guide to Periodical Literature, and the Annual Review of Psychology), online searching of the Internet and the World Wide Web, membership in professional organizations, and visits to a university library.

Searching Online Resources

Education Resources Information Center (ERIC)

Established in 1966 by the National Library of Education as part of the U.S. Department of Education's Office of Educational Research and Improvement, ERIC is the world's largest database on education. The online database provides information on subjects ranging from early childhood and elementary education to education for gifted children and rural and urban education. ERIC is used by more than 500,000 people each year, providing them with access to more than 1.2 million bibliographic citations and more than 107,000 full-text nonjournal documents. In 2004, the ERIC system was restructured by the Department of Education and now uses the most up-to-date retrieval methods to provide users access to the ERIC databases. As of June 30, 2008, ERIC has added more than 130 education-focused journals to the ERIC collection in addition to the 600 titles it had already indexed.

ERIC also allows users to search the *What Works Clearinghouse* (WWC). The WWC, sponsored by the U.S. Department of Education's Institute of Education Sciences (IES), provides users with a central source of scientific research about what works in education. The WWC claims to promote informed education decision making through easily accessible, high-quality reviews of the research of effective practices intended to improve student outcomes. This is a very valuable resource for action researchers who are focused on identifying specific effective practices that address the needs of an identified area of focus.

With its user-friendly features, ERIC is a quick, easy way to get access to the related literature. In addition, there is no charge associated with conducting an ERIC search online from your home or school computer and accessing full-text ERIC documents. The best starting point for your ERIC explorations is the ERIC home page at www.eric.ed.gov. This home page includes links to all other ERIC sites, most notably, ERIC Search, and the What Works Clearinghouse.

You can conduct a search using ERIC online in several ways. The basic ERIC search prompts you to search using keywords, author only, title only, or ERIC document number. The advanced ERIC search offers the same prompts as the basic search but also allows you to search by ISBN number, journal name, source institution, sponsoring agency, publication types (e.g., book, review, dissertation), ERIC Thesaurus descriptor, publication date, and full-text availability.

The thesaurus search prompts you to search using your own descriptor, which is then matched to one or more ERIC descriptors (remember: garbage in, garbage out!). You must search ERIC using ERIC descriptors. For example, entering the term *achievement tests* results in a suggestion from ERIC to use a narrower search term such as *equivalency tests, mastery tests,* or *national competency tests*. You can browse the thesaurus alphabetically or look for descriptors in the forty-plus categories provided by ERIC. Once you have identified materials that you would like to examine, you need to access these materials. You may notice in your searches that documents are categorized with an ED or EJ designation. An ED designation is generally used for unpublished documents, such as reports, studies, and even lesson plans. ED references are available in university libraries through ERIC's microfiche collection or may be available as full-text online documents. An EJ designation is used for articles that have been published in professional journals. EJ articles are not available in full text from ERIC and must be tracked down in the periodicals collection of a library or purchased from article reprint companies.

Although ERIC is the largest computer database for searches of education literature, it is not the only source available. Other commonly used computer databases in education are described next.

Education Index

The Education Index is an electronic index of educational periodicals with abstracts since 1983. It provides bibliographic information and abstracts of sources (some libraries subscribe to a full-text feature) pertaining to the topic(s) that have been researched. A sample result of an Education Index search is shown in Figure 3–1. In addition to article abstracts, the database includes citations for yearbooks and monograph series, videos, motion picture and computer program reviews, and law cases.

PsycINFO

The PsycINFO database is the online version of Psychological Abstracts, a print source that presents summaries of completed psychological research studies (see www.apa.org/psycinfo). Produced monthly, Psychological Abstracts contains summaries of journal articles, technical reports, book chapters, and books in psychology. It is organized by subject area according to the PsycINFO classification codes for easy browsing. The classification codes also serve as the

---

1. Developing Academic Confidence to Build Literacy; What Teachers Can Do (EJ558072)
AUTHOR(S): Colvin, Carolyn; Schlosser, Linda Kramer
SOURCE: Journal of Adolescent and Adult Literacy, v41 n4 p272-81 Dec-Jan
PUB DATE: 1998-00-00
PUB TYPE(S): Journal Articles; Reports - Research
PEER-REVIEWED: N/A
DESCRIPTORS: Academic Achievement; Intermediate Grades; Junior High Schools; Literacy; Middle School Students; Middle Schools; Self Esteem; Student Attitudes; Teacher Behavior; Teacher Student Relationship
ABSTRACT: Examines how middle school students' literacy behaviors in the classroom relate to their academic achievement, how these behaviors reinforce their developing sense of self, and how teachers can support academic competence in their students. Discusses teachers' influence on efficacious behavior, how students and teachers work together, and students' beliefs about themselves. Offers profiles of students and suggestions for teachers. (SR)

FIGURE 3–1 *Results of an Education Index Search*
Source: Education Resources Information Center (ERIC), U.S. Department of Education. www.eric.ed.gov.

table of contents for Psychological Abstracts, which can be accessed at www.apa.org/psycinfo/training/tips-classcodes.html. These classification codes allow you to retrieve abstracts for studies in a specific category—for example, Developmental Disorders and Autism (3250) or Speech and Language Disorders (3270).

Dissertation Abstracts

Dissertation Abstracts contains bibliographic citations and abstracts from all subject areas for doctoral dissertations and master's theses completed at more than 1,000 accredited colleges and universities worldwide. The database dates back to 1861, with abstracts included from 1980 forward. If after reading an abstract you wish to obtain a copy of the complete dissertation, check to see if it is available in your library. If not, speak to a librarian about how to obtain a copy. The results of a Dissertation Abstracts search are shown in Figure 3–2.

OCLC FirstSearch: Detailed Record
Your requested information from your library BOSTON COL

Dissertation Abstracts Online results for: kw: literacy. Record 2 of 5208

Mark: ☑

Database: Dissertations

Title: **Learning community: An ethnographic study of popular education and homeless women in a shelter-based adult literacy program**

Author(s): Rivera, Lorna

Degree: Ph.D.

Year: 2001

Pages: 00264

Institution: Northeastern University; 0160

Advisor: Adviser Gordana Rabrenovic

Source: DAI, 61, no. 09A (2001): p. 3511

Standard No: ISBN: 0-599-95181-8

Abstract: This dissertation studies the impact of popular education approaches on the lives of fifty homeless and formerly homeless women who participated in the Adult Learners Program at a shelter located in one of Boston's poorest neighborhoods. Data were collected between January 1995 and June 1998. The guiding research questions are: How do poor women interpret the value of education? What poverty-related barriers interfere with their participation in popular education classes? How do the principles and practices of popular education build a sense of community and collective social action?

This ethnographic study utilizes multiple research methods to illustrate how popular education approaches make it possible for poor women to become empowered individually and collectively. Popular education is a methodology of teaching and learning through dialogue that directly links curriculum content to people's lived experience. It's roots are in critical social theory and the work of Paulo Freire. This research shows that poor women place a high value on education. They believe that a high school diploma will provide access to better economic opportunities and they struggle to complete their formal education within the context of homelessness and family violence.

It is argued that popular education's potential to build community is strengthened by the Adult Learners Program's participatory organization and the support services it offers to homeless families. Further, it is argued that popular education had a positive impact on the women's lives, as evidenced by: the women's increased levels of participation in their children's education; the women's participation in efforts to help other poor women in the community; the women's reported increase in self-confidence and group esteem; and, the women becoming stronger advocates for their basic legal rights related to welfare, housing, health, and education.

The research data suggest that the 1995 Massachusetts welfare reform legislation poses a significant barrier to adult literacy for welfare recipients. It is argued that limiting access to education through "work-first" welfare reform policies reproduces social inequalities. This dissertation about homeless women and popular education provides strong evidence in support of the social, political, and economic benefits of popular education programs for the poor.

SUBJECT(S)

Descriptor: EDUCATION, SOCIOLOGY OF
SOCIOLOGY, PUBLIC AND SOCIAL WELFARE
EDUCATION, ADULT AND CONTINUING

Accession No: AAI9988499

FIGURE 3–2 *Results of a Dissertation Abstracts Search*

Source: Screen capture retrieved from OCLC FirstSearch Web site: http://FirstSearch.oclc.org. FirstSearch electronic presentation and platform copyright © 1992–2001 by OCLC. Reprinted by permission. FirstSearch and WorldCat are registered trademarks of OCLC Online Computer Library Center, Inc.

Readers' Guide to Periodical Literature

Readers' Guide to Periodical Literature is an index similar in format to the Education Index. Instead of professional publications, however, it indexes articles in nearly 200 widely read magazines. Articles located through the Readers' Guide will generally be nontechnical, opinion-type references. These can be useful in documenting the significance of your problem. The Readers' Guide lists bibliographic information for each entry. To obtain an article listed in the Readers' Guide, search your library's catalog for the magazine in which the article appears. If your library holds that magazine, it will be located in the periodicals department.

Annual Review of Psychology

The Annual Review of Psychology includes reviews of psychological research that are often relevant to educational research. It provides bibliographic information and abstracts for specific areas such as child development, educational administration, exceptional child education, and language teaching.

Searching the Internet and the World Wide Web

The Internet and the World Wide Web provide information and resources on many educational topics. As we enter the second decade of the twenty-first century, it is increasingly difficult to remember a time when we didn't use the Internet and World Wide Web on an everyday basis. It is a truism to say that the resources you can find on the Web are almost limitless. With just a few clicks, you can access electronic educational journals that provide full-text articles, bibliographic information, and abstracts. You can also obtain up-to-the-minute research reports and information about educational research activities being undertaken at various research centers, and you can access education home pages that provide links to a range of education resources that other researchers have found especially valuable. But be warned—there is little quality control for much that is found on the Internet. At times, the sheer volume of information on the Web can be overwhelming. Be prepared to sift through piles of cyberspace junk to find the diamond in the rough. The best way to become adept at searching the Web efficiently is simply by surfing (browsing) it during your spare time. In this way, you will become familiar with maneuvering from site to site and implementing successful search strategies.

Following are some Web sites that are especially useful to action researchers. Their Internet addresses are in parentheses. In addition, you can access other electronic indexing and abstracting sources by using your computer's search engine (e.g., Lycos, Infoseek, Yahoo!, or Excite) to find some of your own addresses. Addresses containing *ed* or ending in *.edu* are related to educational institutions, and those ending in *.com* are related to commercial enterprises.

- **Uncover Periodical Index** (www.unm.edu/~brosen/uncover.htm). UnCover is a database with brief descriptive information about articles from more than 17,000 multidisciplinary journals. If you register (for a fee) with UnCover REVEAL, an automated alerting service, you will receive monthly tables of contents from your favorite periodicals. The service also allows you to create search strategies for your research topics.
- **NewJour** (http://gort.ucsd.edu/newjour/). This site provides an up-to-date list of journals and newsletters available on the Internet on any subject. Using NewJour's search option, you can do a title search to see if a specific journal is currently on the Web, or do a subject search to find out which journals in a particular subject are available on the Internet. Direct links are provided to available journals.

- **Education Week** (www.edweek.org/). Full-text articles from *Education Week*, a periodical devoted to education reform, schools, and policy, are available at the site. In addition to current and past articles, the site provides background data to enhance current news, resources for teachers, and recommended Web sites to investigate for other information.
- **CSTEEP: The Center for the Study of Testing, Evaluation, and Educational Policy** (www.bc.edu/research/csteep/). The Web site for this educational research organization contains information on testing, evaluation, and public policy studies on school assessment practices and international comparative research.
- **National Center for Education Statistics** (www.nces.ed.gov/). This site contains statistical reports and other information on the condition of U.S. education. It also reports on education activities internationally.
- **Developing Educational Standards** (www.edstandards.org/Standards.html). This site contains a wealth of up-to-date information regarding educational standards and curriculum frameworks from national, state, local, and other sources. Information on standards and frameworks can be linked to by subject area, state, governmental agency, or organization. Entire standards and frameworks are available.
- **Internet Resources for Special Education** (http://specialed.about.com). This site provides links to a variety of topics, including teaching resources for regular and special education teachers; Web sites for students to visit; disability information, resources, and research; disability laws; special education laws; assistive technology; clearinghouses; and information about current topics of interest.
- **U.S. Department of Education** (www.ed.gov/). This site contains links to the U.S. government's education databases (including ERIC). It also makes available full-text reports on current findings on education. In addition, it provides links to research offices and organizations, as well as research publications and products. One Department of Education publication, *A Researcher's Guide to the Department of Education*, helps researchers access the various resources that the department has to offer.

It is is likely that you will need to access information on the World Wide Web that is not available in the Web addresses described above. The easiest and quickest way to find interesting new sites is to use a search engine (such as Google, Yahoo!, Lycos, Excite, or Alta Vista) to look for Web pages containing keywords related to your topic. Once you have entered a keyword or keywords in the appropriate place on the search engine's home page, the search engine examines a selected large portion of the Internet (or a specific domain of the Internet, if you say so) for sites that contain your keyword(s).

To facilitate your search, most search engines offer options for narrowing a search so that only the most relevant sites are identified. An example of using Yahoo! is shown in Figure 3–3. Clicking on the subcategory Education in the Yahoo! Web Directory (Figure 3–3a) will significantly narrow your search to relevant sources in the field of education. After selecting the Education subcategory, a very useful page (shown in Figure 3–3b) appears. Clicking on a subtopic such as Early Childhood Education will then take you to another Web page that provides links to numerous sites pertaining to your topic. Clicking on any of the links shown in Figure 3–3c will access all the information that those particular sites have to offer.

Becoming a Member of Professional Organizations

Another way to access current literature related to your research topic is through membership in professional organizations. The following list gives the names of a few U.S.-based

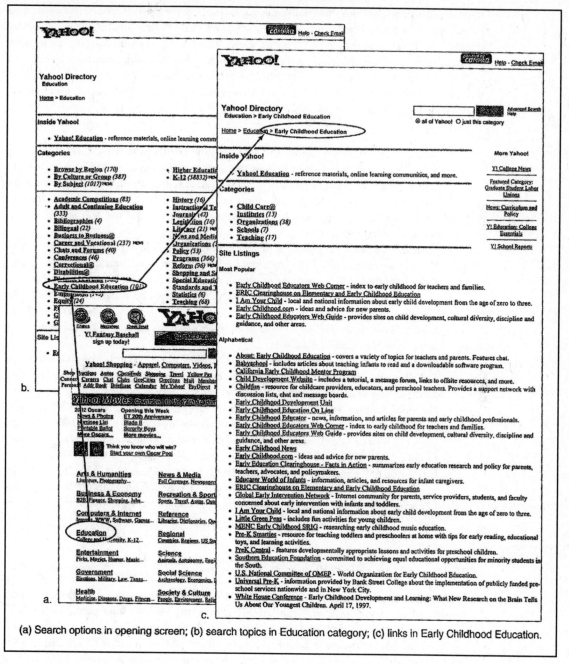

(a) Search options in opening screen; (b) search topics in Education category; (c) links in Early Childhood Education.

FIGURE 3–3: a, b, and c *Sample Search Using Yahoo!*

Source: Reproduced with permission of Yahoo! Inc. © 2009 Yahoo! Inc. YAHOO! and the YAHOO! logo are registered trademarks of Yahoo! Inc.

professional organizations that could be valuable resources for research reports and curriculum materials. Countries other than the United States are likely to have similar organizations that could also be accessed through an Internet search. This list of professional organizations is not intended to be comprehensive, for there are as many professional organizations as there are content areas (reading, writing, mathematics, science, social studies, music, health, and physical education, to name a few) and special interest groups (Montessori education, for example). A search of the Internet will provide a listing of more Web sites than you will have the time or energy to visit!

- **Association for Supervision and Curriculum Development (ASCD)** (www.ascd. org). Boasting 175,000 members in more than 119 countries, ASCD is one of the largest educational organizations in the world. ASCD publishes books, newsletters, audio and video recordings, and some excellent journals that are a valuable resource for teacher researchers, including *Educational Leadership* and the *Journal of Curriculum and Supervision*.
- **National Council of Teachers of Mathematics (NCTM)** (http://nctm.org). With 100,000 members, NCTM is dedicated to the teaching and learning of mathematics and offers vision and leadership for mathematics educators at all age levels. NCTM provides regional and national professional development opportunities and publishes the following journals: *Teaching Children Mathematics*, *Mathematics Teaching in the Middle School*, *Mathematics Teacher*, *Online Journal for School Mathematics*, and the *Journal for Research in Mathematics Education*.
- **National Council for the Social Studies (NCSS)** (www.ncss.org). The NCSS supports and advocates social studies education. Its resources for educators include the following journals: *Social Education* and *Social Studies and the Young Learner*.
- **National Science Teachers Association (NSTA)** (http://nsta.org). The NSTA, with 60,000 members, provides many valuable resources for science teachers. It develops the National Science Education Standards and publishes the following journals: *Science and Children*, *Science Scope*, *The Science Teacher*, and *Journal of College Science Teaching*.
- **International Reading Association (IRA)** (www.reading.org). The IRA provides resources to an international audience of reading teachers through its publication of the following journals: *The Reading Teacher*, *Journal of Adolescent and Adult Literacy*, and the *Reading Research Quarterly*.

Visiting a University Library

With all this talk about user-friendly resources, don't overlook the most valuable, user-friendly resource of all—your university librarian! Most university libraries (and public libraries, for that matter) have a librarian on duty to help with requests. My university has an "education" librarian who has experience in both K–12 and graduate education and is very skilled in helping folks who are intimidated at the thought of navigating around the stacks. However, if a librarian is not available when you make your initial visit, you are likely to find the following important resources that will allow you to start your work:

- *Computers.* Instead of the card catalogues that many of us remember using in the "old days" (it's funny how those old days become an increasingly frequent frame of reference!), you will now find a computer terminal that provides you with access to the library's resources. You may even be able to access other libraries with whom your institution has reciprocal loan agreements if a particular reference is not available at your home library. These electronic databases are extremely user friendly and provide a good place to start your search for literature related to your area of focus.

- *ERIC on CD-ROM.* The same computers that contain the library's electronic database may also provide access to a CD-ROM version of ERIC. You will be able to use the same search strategies outlined in the earlier online discussion.
- *Browsing the stacks.* In all this discussion about electronic databases, we have not considered the old strategy of browsing the stacks. This is similar to the kind of activity you might undertake at a public library when looking for a new fiction book to read. If you can locate the area of the library with books related to your area of focus, it can be productive to browse and pull interesting books off the shelves. You may also find leads to related materials, not necessarily uncovered in your electronic search, by looking at any given book's reference list.

Evaluating Your Sources

When you have a source in hand, you will need to evaluate it. The following questions (summarized in Table 3–1) can serve as a checklist for evaluating your sources. Critically evaluating your sources will save you time and energy reading and abstracting sources that may contribute little to your understanding of a research topic.

- *What was the problem statement of the study?* Obviously, the first thing to do is to determine if it really applies to your research topic. If it does, then it has passed a very important initial screening—it is related to your research topic—and qualifies to be included in a review of related literature. The problem statement is often found in the abstract, which will allow you to determine the relevance of the research to your own research.
- *Who was studied?* That is, what was the sample population? Is it relevant to be included in your own study given your research problem and population under investigation?
- *Where was the source published?* For example, does the information come from a scholarly journal or a popular magazine? Is the information someone's personal opinion or the result of a research study? Clearly, sources of different types merit different weight in your review. For instance, did you find your source in a refereed or a nonrefereed journal? In a **refereed journal**, articles are reviewed by a panel of experts in the field and are thus seen as more scholarly and trustworthy than articles from nonrefereed or popular journals. Research articles in refereed journals are required to comply with strict guidelines regarding not only format but also research procedures. Special care and caution must also be taken when evaluating World Wide Web sources because anyone can post information on the Web. Just because an Internet search identifies a particular source does not mean that the source is accurate or credible. Sources from the World Wide Web must be closely examined for bias,

TABLE 3–1 Questions to Critically Evaluate Literature Sources

What was the problem statement of the study?

Who was studied?

Where was the source published?

When was the research conducted?

How was the study conducted?

subjectivity, intent, and accuracy. These important quality-control questions will help you determine whether or not a source is worthy of inclusion in your review of related literature.

- *When was the research conducted?* An initial appraisal of a source includes looking closely at the date of publication. Look at the copyright date of books that you find and the dates on which articles were published. Appropriate research in topic areas of current interest and continuing development generally require recent, up-to-date references. Finding recent references does not mean that research conducted in the twentieth century should be disregarded; after all, all of us are artifacts of the twentieth century, and we still have something to contribute! Oftentimes, the classics that affected your world view as an educator are still relevant in the twenty-first century. This importance is evident throughout this book, for example, with references to seminal theoretical work conducted in educational psychology by Jean Piaget.

- *How was the study conducted?* It is important to verify that the information presented in a particular source is objective and impartial. Does the author present evidence to support the interpretations? Does the content of the article consist mainly of an individual's opinion, or does it contain appropriately collected and analyzed data? Was an appropriate method used to investigate the problem? Finally, does the source add to the information you have already gathered about your topic? If so, it is useful and worth paying attention to.

Conducting effective library and Internet searches will yield an abundance of useful information about your topic. By using both search methods, you will collect information that is up-to-date and comprehensive. As you become more experienced, you will be able to conduct more efficient searches that are focused appropriately on your topic from the beginning.

Abstracting

After you have identified the primary references related to your topic, you are ready to move on to the next phase of a review of related literature—abstracting the references. Basically, this involves creating abstracts by reviewing, summarizing, and classifying your references. Students sometimes ask why it is necessary to read and abstract original, complete articles (or reports, or whatever) if they already have perfectly good abstracts. There are two basic reasons. First, a provided abstract is not necessarily "perfectly good." It may not be a totally accurate summary of the article's contents. Second, there is a great deal of important information that you can obtain only by reading the complete article. (You'll see.)

To begin the abstracting process, arrange your articles and other sources in reverse chronological order. Beginning with the latest references is a good research strategy because the most recent research is likely to have profited from previous research. Also, recent references may cite preceding studies you may not have identified. For each reference, complete the following steps:

PEARSON
myeducationlab

Go to the Assignments and Activities section of Topic #2, *Defining the Project*, in the MyEducationLab for your course and complete the activity titled "Abstracting an Article." In this activity, you will practice your skills at evaluating and summarizing published research.

1. If the article has an abstract or a summary, which most do, read it to determine the article's relevancy to your problem.
2. Skim the entire article, making mental notes of the main points of the study.
3. On an index card or in a computer database, write a complete bibliographic reference for the work. (The word *reference* can mean either a reference work or a bibliographic reference—a note containing complete bibliographic information on a work.) Include the library call number on the card or in the database if the source work is a book. This

is tedious but important. You will spend much more time trying to find the complete bibliographic information for an article or book you failed to abstract completely than you will abstracting it in the first place. If you know that your final report must follow a particular editorial style, such as that described in the *Publication Manual of the American Psychological Association* (APA), put your bibliographic reference in that form. For example, an APA-style reference for a journal article would look like this:

Snurd, B. J. (1995). The use of white versus yellow chalk in the teaching of advanced calculus. *Journal of Useless Findings, 11,* 1–99.

In this example, 1995 is the date of publication, 11 is the volume number of the journal, and 1–99 are the page numbers. A style manual such as the APA's provides reference formats for all types of sources. Whatever format you use, use it consistently and be certain your bibliographic references are accurate. You never know when you might have to go back and get additional information from an article.

4. Classify and code the article according to some system, and then add the code to the database entry or index card (or a photocopy) in a conspicuous place, such as the upper right corner. The code should be one that can be easily accessed when you want to sort your notes into the categories you devise. Any coding system that makes sense to you will facilitate your task later when you have to sort, organize, analyze, synthesize, and write your review of the literature. Coding and keeping track of articles is key for organization. Useful computer programs that simplify coding and subsequent data retrieval are HyperRESEARCH and EndNote.

5. Abstract, or summarize, the reference (source work) by typing or neatly writing (you're going to have to read your abstracts later) its essential points. If the work is an opinion article, write the main points of the author's position—for example, "Jones believes parent volunteers should be used because [list the reasons]." If it is a study, state the problem, the procedures (including a description of participants and instruments), and the major conclusions. Make special note of any particularly interesting or unique aspect of the study, such as use of a new measuring instrument. Double-check the reference to make sure you have not omitted any pertinent information. If the abstract provided at the beginning of an article contains all the essential information (and that is a big *if*), by all means use it.

6. Indicate any thoughts that come to your mind, such as points on which you disagree (mark them with an *X*, for example) or components that you do not understand (mark with a *?*). For example, if an author stated that he or she had used a double-blind procedure, and you were unfamiliar with that technique, you would put a question mark next to that statement in your database entry, on your index card, or on a photocopy of the page. Later, you could find out what it is.

7. Indicate any statements that are direct quotations or personal reactions: Plagiarism (intentional or not) is an absolute no-no, with the direst of consequences. If you do not put quotation marks around direct quotations on your card or database entry, for example, you might not remember later which statements are, and which are not, direct quotations. You must also record the exact page number of the quotation in case you use it later in your paper. Incidentally, direct quotations should be kept to a minimum in your research plan and report; both should be in *your* words, not those of other researchers. Occasionally, however, a direct quotation may be quite appropriate and useful. Be sure, however, that you record all bibliographic information required in your style manual. (You may choose to photocopy entries from other researchers' reference lists, but the main disadvantage of this is cost.)

Whatever approach you use, guard your notes with your life. Make a copy and put it away in a safe place. When you have completed your reviewing task, those notes will represent many hours of work. Students have been brought to tears because they left their notes on the bus or on a table in the cafeteria or, even worse, lost all their files to a computer virus! Beyond being sympathetic, your instructor can do little more than to tell you to start over. In addition, when the research report is completed, the cards or computer information can be filed (photocopies can be placed in notebooks) and saved for future reference and future studies (nobody can do just one!).

Analyzing, Organizing, and Reporting the Literature

For beginning researchers, the hardest part of writing the literature review for a plan or report is thinking about how hard it is going to be to write the literature review. More time is spent worrying about doing it than actually doing it. This hesitancy stems mostly from a lack of previous experience writing a literature review. A literature review requires a technical form of writing that is unlike most of the writing we do. In technical writing, facts must be documented and opinions substantiated. For example, if you say that Ohio's high school dropout percentage has increased in the last ten years, you must provide a source for this information. Technical writing is precise, requiring clarity of definitions and consistency in the use of terms. If the term *achievement* is important in your review, you must indicate what you mean by it and be consistent in using that meaning throughout the written review. Figure 3–4 summarizes these and other important technical writing guidelines useful in a literature review.

If you have efficiently abstracted the literature related to your problem, and if you approach the task in an equally systematic manner, then analyzing, organizing, and reporting the literature will be relatively painless. To get warmed up, you should read quickly through your notes. This will refresh your memory and help you identify references that no longer seem sufficiently related to your topic. Do not force references into your review that do not

---

- *Document facts and substantiate opinions.* Cite references to support your facts and opinions. Note that facts are usually based on empirical data, while opinions are not. In the hierarchy of persuasiveness, facts are more persuasive than opinions. Differentiate between facts and opinions in the review.
- *Define terms clearly, and be consistent in your use of terms.*
- *Organize content logically.*
- *Direct your writing to a particular audience.* Usually the literature review is aimed at a relatively naive reader, one who has some basic understanding of the topic but requires additional education to understand the topic or issue being studied. Do not assume your audience knows as much as you do about the topic and literature! They don't, so you have to write to educate them.
- *Follow an accepted manual of style.* The manual of style indicates the style in which chapter headings are set up, how tables must be constructed, how footnotes and bibliographies must be prepared, and the like. Commonly used manuals and their current editions are *Publication Manual of the American Psychological Association*, Fifth Edition, and *The Chicago Manual of Style*, Fifteenth Edition.
- *Evade affected verbiage and eschew obfuscation of the obvious.* In other words, limit big words; avoid jargon.
- *Start each major section with a brief overview of the section.* The overview might begin like this: " In this section, three main issues are examined. The first is. . . ."
- *End each major section with a summary of the main ideas.*

FIGURE 3–4 *Guidelines for Technical Writing*

really fit; the review forms the background and rationale for your hypothesis and should contain only references that serve this purpose. The following guidelines—based on experience acquired the hard way—should be helpful to you:

- *Make an outline.* Don't groan; your eighth-grade teacher was right about the virtues of an outline. However you construct it, an outline will save you time and effort in the long run and will increase your probability of having an organized review. The outline does not have to be excessively detailed. Begin by identifying the main topics and the order in which they should be presented. For example, the outline of the review for the problem concerned with salaried paraprofessionals versus parent volunteers might begin with the headings: "Literature on Salaried Paraprofessionals," "Literature on Parent Volunteers," and "Literature Comparing the Two." Note that you can always add or remove topics in the outline as your work progresses. The next step is to differentiate each major heading into logical subheadings. The need for further differentiation will be determined by your topic; the more complex it is, the more subheadings you will require. When you have completed your outline, you will invariably need to rearrange, add, and delete topics. It is much easier, however, to reorganize an outline than it is to reorganize a document written in paragraph form.
- *Analyze each reference in terms of your outline.* In other words, determine the subheading under which each reference fits. Then sort your references into appropriate piles. If you end up with references without a home, there are three logical possibilities: (1) your outline is not correct, (2) the references do not belong in your review and should be discarded, or (3) the references do not belong in your review but do belong somewhere else in your research plan and report introduction. Opinion articles or reports of descriptive research often will be useful in the introduction, whereas formal research studies will be most useful in the review of related literature section.
- *Analyze the references under each subheading for similarities and differences.* If three references say essentially the same thing, you will not need to describe each one; it is much better to make one summary statement and cite the three sources, as in this example:

  > Several studies have found white chalk to be more effective than yellow chalk in the teaching of advanced mathematics (Snurd, 1995; Trivia, 1994; Ziggy, 1984).

- *Give a meaningful overview of past research.* Don't present a series of abstracts or a mere list of findings (Jones found A, Smith found B, and Brown found C). Your task is to organize and summarize the references in a meaningful way. Do not ignore studies that contradict most other studies or your personal bias. Analyze and evaluate contradictory studies and try to determine a possible explanation. For example:

  > Contrary to these studies is the work of Rottenstudee (1998), who found yellow chalk to be more effective than white chalk in the teaching of trigonometry. However, the size of the treatment groups (two students per group) and the duration of the study (one class period) may have seriously affected the results.

- *Discuss the references least related to your problem first and those most related to your problem just prior to the statement of the hypothesis.* Think of a big V. At the bottom of the V is your hypothesis; directly above your hypothesis are the studies most directly related to it, and so forth. The idea is to organize and present your literature in such a way that it leads logically to a tentative, testable conclusion, namely, your hypothesis. Highlight or summarize important aspects of the review to help readers identify them. If your problem has more than one major aspect, you may have either two Vs or one V that logically leads to two tentative, testable conclusions.

- *Conclude the review with a brief summary of the literature and its implications.* The length of this summary depends on the length of the review. It should be detailed enough to clearly show the logic chain you have followed in arriving at your implications and tentative conclusions.

Writing Tools and Suggestions

To assist with writing the literature review I suggest the following tools and strategies:

Literature Matrix

A helpful way to keep track of the literature you are reading is to record it on a matrix (see Figures 3–5 and 3–6). The matrix is a powerful organizer for when you are committing your thoughts to text. Along the Y-axis list the authors' names and year of publication. Along the X-axis list the kinds of variables/themes/issues addressed by the studies. The matrix will provide you with a mental map of what you are reading and what the studies share in common.

Thematic and Chronological Review

Attend to the themes that emerge from the matrix and use these as the subheadings for your written narrative. In this way you can construct a "compare and contrast" of the authors

Author/s	Year	Variables Considered in the Study					

FIGURE 3–5 *Literature Matrix*

Variables Considered in the Study

Author/s	Year	Academic Achievement	Military Personnel	Social Adjustment	Attitude to Change	Discontinuous Education	Caravan Parks	S.E.S.	I.Q.	School Counsellors	Solutions Provided
Cramer, W., & Dorsey, S.	1970	●	●								
Bourke, S. F., & Naylor, D.R.	1971	●	●								
Collins, R. J., & Coulter, F.	1974	●	●	●							
Mackay L. D., & Spicer, B. J.	1975	●	●	●							
Lacey, C., & Blare, D.	1979	●				●					
Parker, L.	1979	●				●	●				
Parker, L.	1981	●		●			●	●			
Bell, D. P.	1962	●					●				
Smith, T. S., Husbands, L. T., & Street, D.	1969	●							●		
Whalen, T.C., & Fried, M. A.	1973	●						●	●		
Black, F. S., & Bargar, R, R.	1975	●									
Goodman, T. L.	1975	●									
Splete, H., & Rasmussen, J.	1977			●						●	●
de Noose, D. A., & Wells, R. M.	1981	●								●	●
Allan, J., & Bardsley, P.	1983									●	●
King, M.	1984	●						●			●
Thomas, B. D.	1978	●				●					●
Rahmani, Z.	1987		●								●
Mills, G. E.	1989	●		●		●					●

FIGURE 3–6 Sample Literature Matrix

Source: From "Transient Children," by G. E. Mills, 1985, Unpublished M. Ed. thesis. Perth, Australia: Western Australian Institute of Technology.

included in your literature review. Similarly, within each category organize the literature chronologically, that is, from the most dated to the most recent. Oftentimes this strategy will reveal the changing trends within the field you are investigating.

A Concluding Statement of the Review

The concluding statement serves a number of purposes that teacher researchers find useful. First, it provides a starting point for your own research in terms of what previous studies have found. Second, it provides support for the importance of your study and the potential your work has to contribute to the existing body of published research. If you are applying for a grant to support your work, linking your area of focus to previous research is an important component. Third, it provides you with an opportunity to share what promising practices have emerged from the research that have the potential to have a positive impact on your own research.

The Action Research Plan

Ideally, your investment of time and energy in the reconnaissance and literature review stages will allow you to synthesize the related literature so that you can see your project more clearly. In addition, it may have helped you to identify promising practices that can become an integral part of your ongoing action research efforts.

At this stage of the action research process, you should create an action plan. An action plan summarizes your action research thoughts in a plan that will guide you through your action research work and includes the following nine steps (adapted from Elliott, 1991; Kemmis & McTaggart, 1988):

PEARSON
myeducationlab

Go to the Assignments and Activities section of Topic #2, *Defining the Project*, in the MyEducationLab for your course and complete the activity titled "Developing an Action Plan." In this activity, you will reflect on planning an intervention.

1. Write an area-of-focus statement.
2. Define the variables.
3. Develop research questions.
4. Describe the intervention or innovations.
5. Describe the membership of the action research group.
6. Describe negotiations that need to be undertaken.
7. Develop a timeline.
8. Develop a statement of resources.
9. Develop data collection ideas.

Write an Area-of-Focus Statement

An area of focus identifies the purpose of your study. To start, write a statement that completes the following sentence: "The purpose of this study is to . . ." For example:

- The purpose of this study is to describe the effects of an integrated problem-solving mathematics curriculum on student transfer of problem-solving skills and the retention of basic math facts and functions.
- The purpose of this study is to describe the impact of bringing audience members into an interactive relationship with teen theater productions on participants' abilities to identify issues and incorporate solutions to similar problems in their own lives.
- The purpose of this study is to describe the effects of student-led conferences on parent and student satisfaction with the conferencing process.

Define the Variables

As part of the area-of-focus statement construction process, write definitions of what you will focus on in the study. These definitions should accurately represent what the factors, contexts, and variables *mean to you*. A **variable** is a characteristic of your study that is subject to change. That is, it might be the way you are going to change how you teach, the curriculum you use, and student outcomes. Definitions may also emerge from the literature, but it is important that you own whatever you are defining and communicate that ownership with others. In the preceding examples, the researchers would define what they mean by transfer of solutions to life's situations, an integrated problem-solving curriculum, transfer of problem-solving skills, the retention of math facts and functions, interactive participation in teen theater, student-led conferences, and parent and student satisfaction with the conferencing processes. If you are clear about what you are examining, it will be easy to determine how you will know it when you see it! That is, your data collection ideas will flow more freely and there will be no confusion when you communicate with your action research collaborators about your purpose.

Develop Research Questions

Develop questions that breathe life into the area-of-focus statement and help provide a focus for your data collection plan. These questions will also help you validate that you have a workable way to proceed with your investigation. For example:

- What is the effect of teen theater audience participation strategies on audience comprehension of issues?
- How does the "Violence Improv" affect the audience's understanding of the issues of violence and harassment?
- What is the effect of incorporating math manipulatives into problem-solving activities on student performance on open-ended problem-solving tests?
- In what ways do students transfer problem-solving skills to other areas of mathematics?
- How do students incorporate problem-solving skills into other curriculum areas?
- How do students transfer problem-solving skills to their life outside of school?

Describe the Intervention or Innovation

Describe what you are going to do to improve the situation you have described. For example, "I will implement a standards-based, integrated problem-solving mathematics curriculum," "I will include audience improvisation as part of the teen theater performances I direct," and "I will incorporate student participation in student-parent-teacher conferences." Remember, this is simply a statement about what you will do in your classroom or school to address the teaching/ learning issue you have identified.

Describe the Membership of the Action Research Group

Describe the membership of your action research group and discuss why its members are important. Will you be working with a site council team? A parent group? If so, what will be the roles and responsibilities of the group's participants? For example:

I will be working with seven other high school math teachers who are all members of the math department. Although we all have different teaching responsibilities within the department, as a group we have decided on problem solving as an area of focus for the department. Each of us will be responsible for implementing curriculum and teaching strategies that reflect the new emphasis on problem solving and for collecting the kinds of data that we decide will help us monitor the effects of our teaching. The department chair will be responsible for keeping the principal informed about our work and securing any necessary resources we need to complete the research. The chair will also write a description of our work to be included in the school newsletter (sent home to all parents), thus informing children and parents of our focus for the year.

Describe Negotiations That Need to Be Undertaken

Describe any negotiations that you will have to undertake with others prior to implementing your plan. Do you need permission from an administrator? Parents? Students? Colleagues? All this assumes that you control the focus of the study and that you undertake the process of negotiation to head off any potential obstacles to implementation of the action plan. It's very frustrating to get immersed in the action research process only to have the project quashed by uncooperative colleagues or administrators.

Develop a Timeline

In developing a timeline, you will need to decide who will be doing *what* and *when*. Although not part of a timeline in the strictest sense, you can also use this stage to anticipate *where* and *how* your inquiry will take place. For example:

- **Phase 1 (August–October).** Identify area of focus, review related literature, develop research questions, reconnaissance.
- **Phase 2 (November–December).** Collect initial data. Analyze video recordings of lessons, do first interviews with children, administer first problem-solving probe.
- **Phase 3 (January–May).** Modify curriculum and instruction as necessary. Continue ongoing data collection. Schedule two team meetings to discuss early analysis of data.
- **Phase 4 (May–June).** Review statewide assessment test data and complete analysis of all data. Develop presentation for faculty. Schedule team meeting to discuss and plan action based on the findings of the study. Assign tasks to be completed prior to year 2 of the study.

Develop a Statement of Resources

Briefly describe what resources you will need to enact your plan. This is akin to listing materials in a lesson plan—there is nothing worse than starting to teach and finding that you don't have all the manipulatives you need to achieve your objectives. For example, to participate in the study of math problem-solving skills, the team determines that it will need teacher release time for planning the project, reviewing related literature, and completing other tasks; funds to purchase classroom sets of manipulatives; and a small budget for copying and printing curriculum materials. After all, there is no sense developing a study that investigates the impact of a new math problem-solving curriculum if you don't have the financial resources to purchase the curriculum.

Develop Data Collection Ideas

Give a preliminary statement of the kinds of data that you think will provide evidence for your reflections on the general idea you are investigating. For example, brainstorm about the kind of intuitive, naturally occurring data that you find in your classroom or school, such as test scores, attendance records, portfolios, and anecdotal records. As we learn more about other types of data that can be collected, this list will grow, but in the early stages think about what you already have easy access to and then be prepared to supplement it with interviews, surveys, questionnaires, video and audio recordings, maps, photos, and observations as the area of focus dictates.

These activities can be undertaken whether you are working individually, in a small group, or as part of a schoolwide action research effort. The resolution of these issues early in the action research process will ensure that you do not waste valuable time backtracking (or even apologizing) once you are well down the action research path. The process of developing an action plan is summarized in the Research in Action Checklist 3–3.

Put the Action Plan into Action

Kemmis and McTaggart (1988) provide the following conclusion to the process of developing a plan:

> Your plan orients you for action, of course; but it is also a reference point for reflection later on, and it is something which you can modify and develop in later plans. Since you have done so much hard thinking to put your plan together, don't skimp when it comes to drafting and redrafting it before you go into action. It represents the fruits of one round of reconnaissance and thinking ahead—it provides you with a benchmark for later reflection and replanning. (p. 77)

With the plan complete, it's time to determine what information (data) you can collect that will increase your understanding about your own practice and its impact on your students. You are now ready to decide how you will monitor the effects of the innovation or intervention you are going to implement and to develop your data collection techniques.

RESEARCH IN ACTION CHECKLIST 3–3

Developing an Action Plan

_____ Write an area-of-focus statement.
_____ Define the variables.
_____ Develop research questions.
_____ Describe the intervention or innovation.
_____ Describe the membership of the action research group.
_____ Describe negotiations that need to be undertaken.
_____ Develop a timeline.
_____ Develop a statement of resources.
_____ Develop data collection ideas.

Summary

Clarifying a General Idea and an Area of Focus

1. In the beginning of the action research process, you need to clarify the general idea that will be the area of focus of your study.
2. The general idea is a statement that links an idea to an action and refers to a situation one wishes to change or improve on.
3. Taking time in the beginning of the action research process to identify what you feel passionate about is critical.
4. The area of focus should involve teaching and learning and should focus on your own practice.
5. The area of focus is something within your locus of control.
6. The area of focus is something you feel passionate about.
7. The area of focus is something you would like to change or improve.

Reconnaissance

8. Reconnaissance is taking time to reflect on your own beliefs and to understand the nature and context of your general idea. Doing reconnaissance takes three forms: self-reflection, description, and explanation.
9. Try to explore your own understanding of:
    a. The theories that impact your practice.
    b. The educational values you hold.
    c. How your work in schools fits into the larger context of schooling and society.
    d. The historical contexts of your school and schooling and how things got to be the way they are.
    e. The historical contexts of how you arrived at your beliefs about teaching and learning.
10. Try to describe as fully as possible the situation you want to change or improve by focusing on the who, what, when, where, and how questions.
11. Try to explain the situation you intend to investigate by hypothesizing how and why the critical factors you've identified affect the situation.

Review of Related Literature

12. The review of related literature involves systematically identifying, locating, and analyzing documents pertaining to the research topic.

13. The major purpose of reviewing the literature is to identify information that already exists about your topic.

14. The literature review can point out research strategies, procedures, and instruments that have and have not been found to be productive in investigating your topic.

15. A smaller, well-organized review is preferred to a review containing many studies that are less related to the problem.

16. Heavily researched areas usually provide enough references directly related to a topic to eliminate the need for reporting less related or secondary studies. Little-researched topics usually require review of any study related in some meaningful way so that the researcher may develop a logical framework and rationale for the study.

17. Most sources have alphabetical subject indexes to help you locate information on your topic. A list of keywords should guide your literature search.

18. A good way to start a review of related literature is with a narrow search of pertinent educational encyclopedias, handbooks, and annual reviews found in libraries. These resources provide broad overviews of issues in various subject areas.

19. An article or report written by the person who conducted the study is a primary source; a brief description of a study written by someone other than the original researcher is a secondary source. Primary sources are preferred in the review.

20. Most libraries use an electronic catalog system that indexes all the sources in the library by author, title, and subject. You should familiarize yourself with your library and its resources.

21. A keyword search uses terms or phrases pertinent to your topic to search for and identify potentially useful sources.

22. Keyword searches can be focused by using the Boolean operators AND, OR, and NOT. Using AND or NOT narrows a search and reduces the number of sources identified; using OR broadens the search and increases the number of sources. It is often best to start with a narrow search.

23. Computer databases can facilitate the identification of relevant primary sources. Among the most used are ERIC, Education Index, PsycINFO (Psychological Abstracts), and Dissertation Abstracts.

24. ERIC is the world's largest database on education and is used by more than 500,000 people each year. ERIC also provides a link to the *What Works Clearinghouse* (WWC) that allows action researchers to search for effective practices that intend to improve student outcomes.

25. The Internet links organizations and individuals all over the world. The World Wide Web is on the Internet.

26. To access the Internet, you need a computer with a modem or Ethernet/cable line and a browser that connects to the Web.

27. The available resources on the World Wide Web are almost limitless, so the best way to become familiar with its use is to "surf" in your spare time.

28. The Web contains a variety of sites relevant to an educational researcher. Each site is reached by using its Internet address. Addresses containing ed or ending in .edu are related to educational institutions, those ending in .com are related to commercial enterprises, those ending in .org refer to organizations (including professional organizations), and those ending in .gov link to government sites..

29. Search engines have established subcategories and also allow keyword searches to review large portions of the World Wide Web quickly.

30. The Web sites for professional organizations maintain links to current research in a particular discipline.

31. Popular professional organizations include Association for Supervision and Curriculum Development, National Council of Teachers of Mathematics, National Council for the Social Studies, National Science Teachers Association, and the International Reading Association.

32. With all of the talk about user-friendly resources, don't overlook the most valuable, user-friendly resource of all—your university librarian.

33. It is important to evaluate all literature sources by asking, "What was the problem statement of the study?" "Who was studied?" "Where was the source published?" "When was the study conducted?" and "How was the study conducted?"

34. Abstracting involves creating summaries by locating, reviewing, summarizing, and classifying your references.

35. The main advantage of beginning with the latest references on your topic is that the most recent studies are likely to have profited from previous research. References in recent studies often contain references to previous studies you have not yet identified.

36. For each source work, list the complete bibliographic record, including author's name, date of publication, title, journal name or book title, volume number, issue number, page numbers, and library call number. Briefly list main ideas. Put quotation marks around quotes taken from the source, and include page numbers. Keep all references in the format required for research reports or dissertations.

37. Make a copy of your references and put it in a safe place.

38. Describing and reporting research call for a specialized style of writing. Technical writing requires documenting facts and substantiating opinions, clarifying definitions and using them consistently, using an accepted style manual, and starting sections with an introduction and ending them with a brief summary.

39. When organizing a review, make an outline; sort references by topic; analyze the similarities and differences between references in a given subheading; give a meaningful overview in which you discuss references least related to the problem first; and conclude with a brief summary of the literature and its implications.

40. A helpful way to keep track of the literature is to use a matrix.

The Action Research Plan

41. Ideally, your investment of time and energy in the reconnaissance and literature review stages will allow you to synthesize the related literature so that you can see your project more clearly. In addition, it may have helped you to identify promising practices that can become an integral part of your ongoing action research efforts.

42. At this stage of the action research process you should create an action research plan summarizes your action research thoughts in a plan that will guide you through your action research work. It should include the following nine steps:
    1. Write an area-of-focus statement.
    2. Define the variables.
    3. Develop research questions.
    4. Describe the intervention or innovations.
    5. Describe the membership of the action research group.
    6. Describe negotiations that need to be undertaken.
    7. Develop a timeline.
    8. Develop a statement of resources.
    9. Develop data collection ideas.

Tasks

1. Complete an action plan that includes an area-of-focus statement, definitions, research questions, a description of the intervention, membership of the action research group, negotiations to be undertaken, a timeline, the necessary resources for the project, and data collection ideas.
2. Identify ten to fifteen good references (sources) that directly relate to your area of focus. The references should include a variety of source types (e.g., books, articles, Internet reports, etc.).
3. Evaluate and abstract those references.
4. Write a review of related literature.

4

Data Collection Techniques

This chapter introduces qualitative and quantitative data collection techniques that can be used to systematically investigate an area of focus. These techniques include using direct observation, interviews, questionnaires, attitude scales, new and existing records, artifacts, teacher-made tests, standardized tests, and school-generated report cards.

After reading this chapter you should be able to:

1 Identify and appropriately utilize qualitative data collection techniques.

2 Identify and appropriately utilize quantitative data collection techniques.

Reflection on Action Research

JAMES ROCKFORD

James Rockford is an elementary teacher in a rural school district in Oregon. James is primarily responsible for teaching music and computer keyboarding skills to young children and initially became involved with action research as part of a statewide action research initiative. As a result of his first attempt at doing action research and his effort to make it a standard part of his teaching, James has also worked as a mentor for other teachers in his region. James's story highlights the importance of collecting data from a variety of sources to fully understand the effects of an intervention on student outcomes.

It seemed to be a perfect match. I had charge of a new computer lab and a mandate to develop a program of instruction to match the curriculum guide, and I needed a "problem" for a collaborative action research class.

The only software that came with the computers was a popular program to teach keyboarding and ClarisWorks. It didn't make any sense to spend several thousand dollars to teach keyboarding, so the problem became, "How does keyboarding instruction enhance students' ability to use word processing, database, spreadsheet, and draw functions?"

Looking at the literature proved to be a formidable problem because there wasn't a good academic library in the area. The local community college had one online computer to access ERIC (Educational Resources Information Center) through the World Wide Web if I gave search terms to the librarian. A little help came, but I preferred to do the search myself. Our school was not yet online, so I resorted to using my son's computer. A quick survey of the literature showed plenty of research on keyboarding, but not much focused on young children. Opinions ranged from "Start them as early as possible" to "Avoid bad habits" to "Don't bother because they can hunt and peck as fast as they can type."

The problem proved to be a little overwhelming in that I had just started an instructional program to teach all the keyboarding skills, and it became obvious that results would be harder to get for database,

spreadsheet, and draw functions. As a result, I decided to look initially only at the effect of teaching keyboarding on word processing for students in grades 4 through 6.

This was supposed to be a collaborative venture, so my first task was to enlist the help of the teachers in grades 4 through 6. We met after school one afternoon so I could explain the purpose of the project. They agreed to help gather data, but only one class actually got into the lab every day. This was disappointing, but it helped make the project more manageable since I would be handling data from only one class instead of three.

What variables might have an effect on students' success in learning to keyboard? I conducted a survey of teacher attitudes and a survey to assess whether students had any prior knowledge, how much time they spent on a computer at home and at school, and whether they had a computer at home. Records were kept for time on computers at school in instructional and free-choice situations.

A well-designed action research project should, as its name declares, lead to some kind of action. The purpose of my action research project was to determine if teaching keyboarding skills to sixth-grade students had enough of an impact on their word processing skills to warrant spending the time and money. It seemed rather obvious that it would, but several students had developed their own unique "hunt-and-peck" system and could already approach the district-mandated target of

Student Self-Evaluation Survey

1. Do you have a computer that you use outside of school?

   (a) Yes   (b) No

2. How many hours a day do you spend at the computer outside of school?

   (a) 0   (b) 1 or less   (c) 1–2   (d) 2–3

3. How much time do you spend at the computer while you're at school?

   (a) 0   (b) 15 minutes   (c) 30 minutes   (d) more than 30 minutes

4. When you type on a keyboard, do you look at the

   (a) monitor (b) keyboard   (c) rough draft   (d) your neighbor

5. I use the computer to (circle all that apply)

   (a) play games   (b) write stories and reports
   (c) draw pictures   (d) collect information and store it
   (e) find information in the library

6. Learning to keyboard in the lab made my life with computers

   (a) easier   (b) more frustrating   (c) no different

7. If I had the chance to do more with computers, I would

   _____

8. The best thing about learning to keyboard is

   _____

9. The hardest thing about learning to keyboard is

   _____

20 words per minute. There are many variables that might affect word processing rates, and that led to the following questions:

1. Do students have a computer at home? How much time do they spend at it per week?
2. What preexisting knowledge do students have about computers?
3. How much time do students spend at the computer when they're at school? How does it affect word processing rates?
4. What is the effect of the keyboarding software used in the lab at school?

The questions were then placed in a data matrix and triangulated as follows (Note: D.S. = data source):

Questions	D.S. 1	D.S. 2	D.S. 3
Preexisting knowledge?	Students' survey	Computer knowledge pretest	
Keyboarding speed?	Pretest	Posttest	Teacher help
Appropriate use (WP)?	Pretest software	Posttest software	Timed typing teacher constructed
Time on computers?	School lab records	Student survey	Parent survey

I collected data using surveys that I developed to measure the following areas:

- Student self-evaluation questionnaire.
- Teacher-constructed vocabulary/facts pretest of general computer knowledge.
- Teacher-constructed timed typing test rates.
- A classroom teacher survey of knowledge/ attitudes about technology.
- A teacher observation record for the computer lab.
- Existing records of students' word processing rates with software.
- Parent survey of student computer use outside of school.

Data were compiled as follows:

- The three variables of time, prior knowledge, and use of keyboarding software were analyzed using a scatter plot graph to determine any correlation to word processing speed.
- Surveys were compiled to show tendencies.
- Keyboarding rates between October and May were compiled in graph form to show progress over time.

In general, the data indicated the following:

- Student time spent on computers out of school had no effect on word processing rate. (They love those computer games!)
- Time spent on computers at school was critical.
- In only 1 month, the class word processing rate mean had increased 300%.

As a result, it was apparent that the keyboarding software was effective, and on that basis I continued its use. Because time on task is critical, teachers were urged to take students to the lab every day and monitor keyboarding habits as well as install keyboarding software on classroom computers so that each student received a minimum of 10 minutes' practice per day. Timed typing tests require greater and different skills than are called for on keyboarding software. In the future, timed typing tests will be given weekly to provide an authentic assessment of student progress, and a tracking system will be used to monitor the acquisition of skill development.

Any research worth its salt appears to generate more questions than it answers. At the completion of this project, I was left wondering if a student's learning style had any impact on the ability to learn word processing skills. Would keyboarding instruction improve students' use of database, spreadsheet, and draw/paint functions? Could other types of authentic assessment be used to determine skill/concept development? These are questions I will continue to investigate.

The project became a springboard to address issues in setting up a computer lab. Instead of being behind the eight ball, I was able to anticipate problems and find solutions. Collaboration was an important part of the process. But perhaps the most powerful part of the action research process was the extent to which I became more reflective about what I was doing in the computer lab. The lab at my school has received a lot of praise from administrators, board members, and teachers, and I believe that going through the action research process has had much to do with the continued success of the lab.

I don't look at classroom problems quite the same way now. For example, I also teach middle school choir and began to notice that the weeks on which I saw eighth graders on Mondays (we're on block scheduling), it was usually a difficult, if not unproductive rehearsal. Keeping some informal data about those days and reflecting about why they were so difficult led me to try some interventions that might help alleviate the problem. It may be a bit corny, but action research has changed my life . . . in the classroom anyway. Student learning is enhanced, I approach problems more systematically, I gather data more carefully and accurately, and my practice is more reflective.

The year following my word processing action research project, I had the good fortune to be a mentor for other teachers learning the action research process. Based on this experience, two observations come to mind. Problem formulation is a difficult process. Extra time spent in this phase of the action research cycle will prevent backtracking, headaches, and frustration down the road. When

Teacher Survey

1. I take my class to the lab

   (a) once a week   (b) twice a week   (c) 3 times a week
   (d) 4 times a week   (e) every day   (f) only when Mr. Rockford
                                                  is there

2. I expect my students to (circle all that apply)

   (a) compose reports/stories   (b) revise reports from written copies
   (c) practice keyboarding   (d) other:_____

3. If I rated my comfort level with computers it would be

   Use it every   Don't want to be in the
   chance I get   same room as one

   5   4   3   2   1

4. I monitor my students' keyboarding technique

   (a) only during lab sessions   (b) any time they're at the computer
   (c) never

5. My students' abilities to use the computer have been enhanced by learning to keyboard

   They're experts!   They're still looking
                                                      for the on switch!

   5   4   3   2   1

6. I would like my students to be able to

   _____

---

teachers do identify something that needs addressing, there appears to be a measurable difference between problems that are student centered and those that arise from a teacher complaint about a teaching situation. It appeared that the problems that are student centered are more likely to result in the improvement of instruction.

Making action research a natural part of the teaching process, in the classroom and the school, is critical to success. Traditionally, teachers are not researchers. The school routine isn't geared to provide teachers with the time and resources that research demands. Teachers are considered to be working only when they're in front of a class. On the other hand, teachers need to develop the attitude that improvement of the teaching/learning process can and should be addressed with data-based decision making formalized through action research.

The decision about what data are collected for an action research area of focus is largely determined by the nature of the problem. There is no one recipe for how to proceed with data collection efforts. Rather, the individual or group must determine what data will contribute to their understanding and resolution of a given problem. Hence, data collection associated with action research is largely an idiosyncratic approach fueled by the desire to understand one's practice and to collect data that is appropriate and accessible.

This chapter will discuss qualitative (experience-based) data collection techniques and quantitative (number-based) techniques. The former includes data sources such as field notes, journals, questionnaires (surveys), maps, and audio and video recordings, whereas the latter focuses on the collection of teacher-made tests (criterion-referenced tests), standardized tests (norm-referenced tests), school-generated report cards, attitude scales, and the results of student achievement reported on statewide assessment tests.

One approach is not *better* than the other. Your area of focus and research questions will determine the best data collection techniques for your research. As discussed earlier, this may involve *qualitative* data sources and *quantitative* sources using a **mixed-methods** design. However, the literature on action research supports the assertion that qualitative methods are more appropriately applied to action research efforts compared with the application of an experimental pretest-posttest control group design in which the teacher researcher randomly assigns children to either a control group or an experimental group in order to receive a "treatment." Qualitative research is not the "easy" way out for teacher researchers who fear statistics (a.k.a. sadistics!). As you will see, the rigor of good qualitatively oriented action research equals the rigor of doing good quantitatively oriented action research. If your area of focus necessitates a more quantitative, experimental approach, then you should consult more quantitatively oriented references such as Gay, Mills, and Airasian (2009, Chapters 6, 7, 8, 9, and 10), or Creswell (2008).

PEARSON
myeducationlab

Go to the Assignments and Activities section of Topic #3, *Data Collection*, in the MyEducationLab for your course and complete the activity titled "Qualitative or Quantitative?" In this activity, you will learn more about the similarities and differences between qualitative and quantitative data.

Qualitative Data Collection Techniques

The receptivity among educators in general, and action researchers in particular, to a qualitative (descriptive) way of examining problems is reflected in the action research literature that emphasizes the following data collection techniques and sources:

- Existing archival sources within a school
- Tools for capturing everyday life
- Tools for questioning
- Conventional sources (surveys, questionnaires, etc.)
- Inventive sources (exhibits, portfolios, etc.)
- Interviews
- Oral history and narrative stories
- Rating scales
- Inventories
- Observation
- Mapping
- Visual recordings

- Photography
- Journals and diaries

(Anderson, Herr, & Nihlen, 1994; Calhoun, 1994; Hendricks, 2006; Sagor, 2000; Stringer, 2004; Wells, 1994)

As you can see from these examples, the kinds of data you collect would include descriptive, narrative, and even nonwritten forms. In many cases, these data occur naturally and are regularly collected by teachers and administrators. In simple terms, we are engaging in an activity that seeks to answer the question: "What is going on here?" It is not a mysterious quest, but is quite simply an effort to collect data that increase our understanding of the phenomenon under investigation. The three primary fieldwork strategies we will discuss in this chapter are *experiencing, enquiring,* and *examining* (Wolcott, 1992, p. 19). Each of these strategies will be discussed in the context of actual teacher researchers' experiences.

Experiencing Through Direct Observation

Teachers who undertake action research have countless opportunities to observe in their own classrooms. They observe as a normal component of their teaching, monitoring and adjusting instruction based on the verbal and nonverbal interactions in their classrooms. Therefore, using direct observation as a data collection strategy is familiar and not overly time consuming. As teachers we are constantly observing our environment and adjusting our teaching based on what we see. Action research gives us a systematic and rigorous way to view this process of observation as a qualitative data collection technique.

Participant Observation

The action research vignettes shared at the beginnings of Chapters 1, 2, 3, and 4 illustrate how teachers "experience" their teaching through observation. James Rockford observed the "hunt-and-peck" keyboarding strategies of his students as a natural part of his teaching. Cathy Mitchell observed audience reactions to the "Violence Improv" and recorded field notes in her daily journal. Deborah South observed the interpersonal interactions of her "study skills" students and recorded her observations in a journal—observations that quickly confirmed the presence of major problems in the classroom. These experiences are all examples of participant observation.

If the researcher is "a genuine participant in the activity being studied," then the researcher is called a **participant observer** (McMillan, 1996, p. 245). According to Spradley (1980), participant observation is undertaken with at least two purposes in mind:

- To observe the activities, people, and physical aspects of a situation; and
- To engage in activities that are appropriate to a given situation that provide useful information.

Participant observation can be done to varying degrees depending on the situation being observed and the opportunities presented: A participant observer can be an *active participant observer*, a *privileged, active observer*, or a *passive observer* (Pelto & Pelto, 1978; Spradley, 1980; Wolcott, 1982, 1997). Depending on the problem, teachers have many opportunities to be active participants in the observation process as they go about their work. However, the tendency with observing is to try to see it all! A good rule of thumb here is to try to do less, but do it better. That is, as you embark on some degree of participant observation, do not be overwhelmed with the task. It is not humanly possible to take in everything that you experience.

Be content with furthering your understanding of your area of focus through *manageable* observations. Avoid trying to do too much and you will be happier with the outcomes.

Active Participant Observer

Teachers, by virtue of teaching, are active participant observers of their teaching practice. When they are actively engaged in teaching, teachers observe the outcomes of their teaching. Each time we teach we monitor the effects of our teaching and adjust our instruction accordingly. As an active participant observer of our own teaching practices, however, we may be so fully immersed in what we are doing that we don't have time to record our observations in a systematic way during the school day. Such recording is a necessary part of being an active participant observer.

In the action research vignettes from Chapters 1, 2, 3, and 4, we saw teachers who were active participant observers of their own teaching. Deborah South observed the "off-task" behavior of her "unmotivated" students during the study skills lessons. Cathy Mitchell observed the nature of the audience participation while she directed the teen theater. James Rockford observed the "hunt-and-peck" strategies used by keyboarding students while he was teaching keyboarding skills. As researchers of our own teaching practices, active participant observation is likely to be the most common "experiencing" data collection technique that we use.

Privileged, Active Observer

Teachers may also have opportunities to observe in a more privileged, active role. That is, they may wish to observe their children during a time when they are not directly responsible for the teaching of a lesson, for example, during a "specialist's" time in music, library, or physical education. These times provide opportunities for teachers to work as a "teacher's aide," while at the same time allowing them to withdraw, stand back, and watch what is happening during a particular teaching episode, moving in and out of the role of teacher, aide, and observer.

Many teachers comment on how valuable these experiences have been in allowing them time to observe the social interactions of students and the impact of a particular instructional strategy on those interactions. By necessity, these privileged, active observer opportunities require teachers to give up valuable time that is often dedicated to duties other than teaching, such as planning, attending team meetings, reading, visiting other classrooms, and relaxing (the all-important "downtime" during a day, if they are fortunate enough to have such a schedule). Taking time to observe one's class is a valuable use of nonteaching time that honors a teacher's effort to improve practice based, in part, on observational data.

Passive Observer

Teachers also have opportunities to be passive observers in classrooms and schools. When teachers take on the role of passive observer, they no longer assume the responsibilities of the teacher—they should focus only on their data collection. A privileged, active observer could be transformed into a passive observer by making explicit to the students and a teaching colleague that the classroom teacher is present only to "see what's going on around here." Students will quickly learn that there are times when their teacher is not going to interact with them as the teacher normally does. The teacher might simply announce that today "I am going to watch and learn from what you are doing!" Taking a step back from the daily rigor of being "on stage" and performing can be refreshing and provide an insightful opportunity for teachers who are unaccustomed to watching their students in a different setting, through a different lens.

Field Notes

The written records of participant observers are often referred to as **field notes**. For teachers undertaking participant observation efforts in their classrooms, these field notes may take the form of anecdotal records compiled as part of a more systematic authentic assessment or portfolio effort. So, what do you write down in these field notes? Well, it depends on what you are looking for! I can offer only limited guidance to help quell your concerns about the "how-to" of writing field notes. But first let me start with an example of how *not* to do field notes!

During my graduate studies at the University of Oregon, I took a class on "Ethnographic Research in Education," and as part of learning how to do ethnography (qualitative research) I was required to conduct a "beginning ethnography" of something that was "culturally different" for me. As an Australian studying in the United States, I had a number of opportunities to study a culturally different phenomenon while at the same time having fun with the project. I chose to study a sorority. As part of this study I participated in one of the regular ceremonies that was part of the sorority members' lives—a formal dinner held each Monday night at which members were required to wear formals and male guests were expected to wear a jacket and tie.

During the course of the dinner, I frequently excused myself to visit the restroom, stopping along the way to take out my notebook so I could try to record quotes and reconstruct events as they were happening, as I tried to capture in great detail all that I was observing. Of course, the irony in this strategy was that I was missing a great deal of the dinner by removing myself from the setting in a futile effort to record everything. The ridiculousness of the situation became evident when one of my dinner hosts asked me if I was feeling well or if the meal was to my satisfaction. After all, why did I keep leaving the dinner table?!

The message here for teacher researchers who wish to use field notes as part of their data collection efforts is clear: You can't physically record everything that is happening during an observational episode, nor should you try to. The following options for observing and recording field notes are useful ways to proceed (adapted from Wolcott, 1994).

Observe and Record Everything You Possibly Can

If you knew exactly what you wanted to observe when you went into an observation, you would find this data collection process inefficient. Engaging in an effort to "record everything" will quickly attune you to what is of most interest to you. During these observational periods, you can start with a broad sweep of the classroom and gradually narrow your focus as you gain a clearer sense of what is most pressing. You can also decide on your strategies for recording observations. You might choose verbatim conversations, maps and illustrations, photographs, video or audio recordings, or even writing furiously in the fashion of a principal or university professor undertaking an evaluation. It is a very idiosyncratic activity, but follow one rule: Don't run off to the restroom every five minutes—you *will* miss something! Do try to maintain a running record of what is happening in a format that will be most helpful for you.

For example, in my study of a school district attempting multiple change efforts (see Mills, 1988), I attended the 37th Annual McKenzie School District Teacher Inservice Day. Part of my field notes from this observation were as follows:

8:30 A.M.   An announcement is made over the public address system requesting that teachers move into the auditorium and take a seat in preparation for the inservice. As the teachers file into the auditorium, the pop song "The Greatest Love of All" is played.

8:41 A.M.	The Assistant Superintendent welcomes the teachers to the inservice with the conviction that it is also the "best district with the best teachers." The brief welcome is then followed by the Pledge of Allegiance and the introduction of the new Assistant Superintendent.
8:45 A.M.	The Assistant Superintendent introduces the Superintendent as "the Superintendent who cares about kids, cares about teachers, and cares about this district."

The next hour of the inservice is focused on introducing new teachers to the district (there were 60 new appointments) and the presentation of information about how a new focus for the district would be at-risk children.

10:00 A.M.	The Superintendent returns to the lyrics of "The Greatest Love of All" and suggests that the message from the song may be suitable as the district's charge: "Everyone is searching for a hero. People need someone to look up to. I never found anyone who fulfilled my needs . . . " The Superintendent compels the teachers to be the heroes for their students and wishes them a successful school year before closing the inservice.

As you can see from this abbreviated example, there is nothing mystical about field notes. They serve as a record of what an observer attended to during the course of an observation and help guide subsequent observations and interviews. This was the beginning of my year-long fieldwork in the McKenzie School District, and this initial observation helped me to frame questions that guided my efforts to understand how central office personnel, principals, and teachers manage and cope with multiple innovations.

Observe and Look for Nothing in Particular

Try to see the routine in new ways. If you can, try to look with "new eyes" and approach the scene as if you were an outsider. Wolcott (1994) offers helpful advice for teachers conducting observations in classrooms that are so familiar that everything seems ordinary and routine:

> Aware of being familiar with classroom routines, an experienced observer might initiate a new set of observations with the strategy that in yet another classroom one simply assumes "business as usual. . . ." The observer sets a sort of radar, scanning constantly for whatever it is that those in the setting are doing to keep the system operating smoothly. (p. 162)

Look for "Bumps" or Paradoxes

In this strategy, you consider the environment you are observing as if it were "flat"; nothing in particular stands out to you. It is an opportunity for observers to look for the "bumps" in the setting. In action research projects these "bumps" might be unexpected student responses to a new curriculum or teaching strategy or an unexpected response to a new classroom management plan, seating arrangement, monitoring strategy, or innovation.

For example, the "bumps" observed by a teacher concerned with gender inequity may become painfully evident when the "locus of control" in a classroom is on one or two boys. That is, by keeping a tally of who commanded most of the teacher's attention by answering and asking questions, it became clear that one or two dominant boys were the focus of the activity during a lesson.

This strategy also suggests that teacher researchers look for contradictions or paradoxes in their classrooms. In a sense, this is not dissimilar to the "looking for bumps" strategy, because a paradox will often stand out in an obvious way to the teacher who has taken the time

Principle Components of Effective Observation

DEGREES OF PARTICIPATION

Participant observer	Engage in activities Observe activities, people, and physical aspects
Privileged observer	A teacher's aide during specialists' time
Passive observer	Present only to observe what's going on

FIELD NOTES

Observe and record everything	Attune to what you actually record through verbatim conversations, maps and illustrations, photos, and video and audio recordings
Observe and look for nothing	Try to see beyond the routine and look with a fresh perspective
Look for paradoxes	What are the unintended consequences of action?

to stand back and look at what is happening in the classroom. (See Key Concept Box 4–1 for a description of the components of effective observation.)

For example, teacher researchers often comment on the unintended consequences of a particular teaching strategy or a curriculum change that has become evident only when they have had an opportunity to stand back and observe the results of their actions. These consequences often present themselves in the form of a paradox—a contradiction in terms. For example, as one teacher researcher commented after attempting to incorporate manipulatives into her math instruction in a primary classroom, "I thought that the use of manipulatives in teaching mathematics would also lead to increased cooperation in group work. Instead, what I saw were my kids fighting over who got to use what and not wanting to share."

Enquiring: When the Researcher Asks

A second major category of data collection techniques can be grouped as data that are collected by the teacher through the asking of questions. Teacher researchers may ask questions of students, parents, and other teachers using **interviewing** and **questionnaire** techniques.

As Agar (1980) suggests, information from interviews can serve as the "methodological core" against which observational data can be used to "feed" ongoing informal interviews. That is, observational data (collected through the "experiencing" techniques described earlier) can suggest questions that can be asked in subsequent interviews with children, parents, teachers—whomever the participants in the study might be. Participants in an interview may omit things. Pairing observation and interviewing provides a valuable way to gather complementary data. For example, Cathy Mitchell's Teen Theater Group (see Chapter 3) developed a group interview technique based on observations of audience reactions to performances. This technique involved three company members meeting with a small group of audience members for about fifteen minutes following a performance so that they could gauge the audience response to the scenes about teen violence and harassment. One actor served as the interviewer, one as the scribe, and one kept a running tally of comments and responses.

Informal Ethnographic Interview

The **informal ethnographic interview** is little more than a casual conversation that allows the teacher, in a conversational style, to inquire into something that has presented itself as an opportunity to learn about their practice. Agar (1980) suggests strategies that allow teacher researchers to have a ready set of questions to ask participants in a study, for example, the "5 Ws and H": *who, what, where, when, why,* and *how.* Using these prompts, teachers will never be at a loss for a question to add to their understanding of what is happening in their classrooms. For example, in considering the example of the teacher researching the impact of manipulatives on math performance, and through observation recognizing the unanticipated consequence of poor sharing of manipulatives, the teacher might ask questions such as these:

- *Who* should be responsible for rotating the materials through the group?
- *What* was the cause of the problem?
- *Where* did the problem originate?
- *When* did the problem of sharing begin?
- *Why* don't you want to share the manipulatives with each other?
- *How* do you think we can solve this problem?

Following the episode, the teacher might briefly jot down in a plan book a summary of what the students had to say and refer back to it later as a valuable data source. Alternatively, the teacher researcher may keep anecdotal records on each student and simply make an entry on the student's file. An example of a student anecdotal record form is presented in Figure 4–1.

Structured Formal Interviews

Teacher researchers may also want to consider formally interviewing children, parents, or colleagues as part of their data collection efforts. Using a structured interview format allows the teacher to ask all the participants the same series of questions. However, a major challenge in constructing any interview is to phrase questions in such a way that they elicit the information you really want. Although this may seem obvious, teacher researchers often feel compelled by tradition and history to ask a lengthy set of questions of which only a part is really their focus. When planning interviews, consider the following options for ensuring the quality of your structured formal interviews:

- **Pilot questions on a similar group of respondents.** That is, if you have developed an interview schedule to use with the students in your classroom, try it out on some similarly aged students (not in your class) to see if it makes sense. Their feedback will quickly confirm, or challenge, the assumptions you have made about appropriate language. Using the feedback from the students, revise the questionnaire before administering it to your class.
- **Use questions that vary from convergent to divergent.** That is, use both "open-ended" and "closed" questions in a structured interview or questionnaire. For example, a closed (convergent) question allows for a brief response such as "Yes/No." Alternatively, an open-ended (divergent) question can conclude with an "Other comments" section,

Student Anecdotal Record Form

Name: _Mary Smith_

Grade: _K_

Date: _10/23_   Comments: _Writing table_
observation. Mary appears unhappy during the time
she spends at the writing table. Her explanation:
"I don't have time to think about my story."

Date: _____   Comments: _____

_____

_____

_____

FIGURE 4–1   *Student Anecdotal Record Form*

or a request for the interviewees to "add anything else" they would like to. In so doing, you will provide students with opportunities to elaborate on questions in ways that you had never anticipated. However, the information gathered through open-ended questions is often more difficult to make sense of. But it does allow the teacher researcher to obtain information that might otherwise be considered "outlying" or "discrepant."

• **Persevere with silence and "wait time" to elicit a response.** Otherwise it becomes too easy to answer your own question!

• **Consider using an audio recorder to capture the interview responses.** One way to ensure that you capture verbatim responses during an interview is to use an audio recorder. After all, you can't write down everything that is said and still maintain rapport with your interviewee. But be warned—this will add to the amount of time that it takes to "write up" your interview. You will need to listen to the recording and transcribe the responses. Furthermore, I seem to suffer from Murphy's Law when it comes to the use of audio recorders!

(That is, if something is going to break or malfunction it will develop a terminal illness on my shift!) I have also interviewed teachers, principals, and superintendents who are very uncomfortable with being recorded. After all, who else will listen to the recording?! Check the body language of whomever you are interviewing to determine if they are okay with the use of the recorder. You may find that your interviewees eventually loosen up!

- **Locate a private place to interview.** Whether you are conducting one-on-one or focus group interviews, be sure to conduct the interview in a private place where you are not likely to be interrupted and where you have the tools for the interview (audio recorder and notepad). You may choose to use your classroom, another teacher's classroom, a study room in the library—anywhere will work as long as you have privacy and your interviewee feels comfortable in the environment. Alternatively, in an informal interview you may choose to talk to students outside during a recess and play a game of some sort. Some of your colleagues may be very comfortable being interviewed in a faculty lounge or lunch room. Take your cues from your interviewees as to where they are most comfortable being interviewed.

- **Carefully choose who you will interview.** Teacher researchers have considerable flexibility about how they will choose who they interview. The decision to interview will largely depend on the questions you are trying to answer and whether the interviewee is "information rich" (Patton, 1990, p. 169). This is perhaps a statement of the obvious—it doesn't make a lot of sense to interview folks who don't know anything about your area of focus! But at some point you will make a conscious decision about who you will interview. Will you interview all the children in your class/school? All the teachers? The answer is probably "No." Therefore, you will choose who to talk to based on a number of factors: knowledge and experience of the area of focus, verbal skills, and willingness to be interviewed. For most teacher researchers the choice will be fairly limited—the students in their classes will be the primary targets for interviews. Depending on the number of students in your classes, you may choose to conduct a combination of focus group and individual interviews in order to develop a comprehensive understanding of your area of focus.

- **Take notes during the interview.** Regardless of whether you use an audio recorder during an interview, be sure to take notes to capture the essence of the conversation. This is also an antidote for Murphy's Law! No matter how quickly you can write, you will not be able to capture everything that transpires during the interview. The notes taken during the interview will serve as a roadmap for you so that you can fill in the blanks as soon as possible after the actual interview. Your interviewees will also appreciate the rapport that you establish with them and not be distracted by your fervent scratching on a notepad! Note taking is largely an idiosyncratic activity. What works for one person may not work for another. I tend to use a combination of verbatim quotes (taken in longhand), abbreviations, and sketches (uses of arrows to link comments that are repeated, smiley faces to capture the interviewee's body language, etc.) to enable me to reconstruct an interview. Given my increasing number of "senior moments," it also speaks to the importance of taking time *as soon as possible after the interview* to write up the field notes for the interview! (The components of interviewing are listed in Key Concepts Box 4–2.)

Focus Groups

Another valuable interview technique is the use of focus groups with several individuals who can contribute to your understanding of your area of focus. One way to think of focus groups is as a group interview where you are trying to "collect shared understanding from several

KEY CONCEPTS BOX 4–2

Components of Interviewing

INFORMAL INTERVIEWS	5 Ws AND H: *WHO, WHAT, WHERE, WHEN, WHY, AND HOW?*
Structured formal interviews	Pilot the interview. Use a variety of question formats. Use divergent and convergent questions. Allow ample "wait time" to elicit a response. Consider using an audio recorder to capture the interview responses. Locate a private place to conduct the interview. Carefully choose who you will interview. Take notes during the interview.

individuals as well as to get views from specific people" (Creswell, 2008, p. 226). Focus groups are a particularly useful technique when the interaction among individuals will lead to a shared understanding of the questions being posed by the teacher researcher. For example, James Rockford may have conducted a focus group with the parents of students in his word processing classes to determine a collective view of computer use in the home.

When conducting focus groups it is important to ensure that all participants have their say and to nurture a group agreement to take turns; that is, participants should understand that the focus group is a sharing activity and that one or two participants should not dominate it. Using a structured or semistructured interview schedule, the teacher researcher can pose questions to the group and encourage all participants to respond. To use sporting metaphors, use a basketball versus a ping-pong questioning style. That is, ask the question, elicit a response, and pass it off to another participant (basketball) versus ask the question, accept the response, and ask another question. Get as much information out of each question as you possibly can and, in the process, ensure that all group participants have an opportunity to respond.

Ideally, the teacher researcher will use an interview to capture the responses from the focus group and then later transcribe the discussion. This is a time-consuming process—perhaps even more so than individual interviews, so be prepared to allocate time to ferreting out the nuances of the focus group interview and the shared understandings that emerge.

E-Mail Interviews

Another relatively new approach to interviewing that can be used effectively by teacher researchers is the use of e-mail interviews. With schools becoming increasingly networked, it is easy to use e-mail to interview colleagues and students. For busy teachers, it may be a far more effective use of time to engage in an ongoing conversation using e-mail. Busy professionals can respond to an e-mail either synchronously (during a "live" conversation) or asynchronously (at some other time when you are not sitting at your computer).

There are some pros and cons associated with the use of e-mail interviews. For example, one advantage of the e-mail interview is that the transcription of the interview has already been done for you by the respondent! That is, you don't have to transcribe a recorded interview with a colleague or student. However, there are ethical issues associated with assuring your respondent that their text response will be confidential and anonymous. I am not an expert when it comes to technology, but I do not trust that once I have sent an e-mail to someone that it is not sitting on a server somewhere that is accessible to other curious folks! This paranoia is further enhanced by the amount of "spam" (junk e-mail) I receive that has been forwarded from someone else's computer.

In spite of these technical and ethical challenges associated with the use of e-mail interviews, such interviews may be a useful tool to use at your school. If your colleagues are like mine, it is difficult to find time during a day when we can sit down face-to-face to talk. Using e-mail will allow your colleagues and students to respond on their own timeline—perhaps from the comfort of their home or the quiet of their classroom or library after school.

Questionnaires

Perhaps the major difference between a structured interview schedule and a questionnaire is that the student or parent will write out the responses on the form provided. Clearly there are positives and negatives with each approach: Questionnaires allow the teacher researcher to collect large amounts of data in a relatively short amount of time (compared with interviewing the same number of students or parents), whereas interviews allow an opportunity for the teacher to intimately know how each student (and parent) feels about a particular issue, but in a time-consuming fashion that few teacher researchers feel is justified. A compromise is to use a questionnaire (when appropriate) and to conduct follow-up interviews with students who have provided written feedback that warrants further investigation. For example, in a conversational way, teachers as part of their regular teaching may ask, "Mary, in the questionnaire you returned you commented that . . . Can you tell me a little more about that?" Similarly, as part of a parent-teacher conference the teacher may follow up with parents who have returned questionnaires.

PEARSON
myeducationlab

Go to the Building Research Skills section of Topic #3, *Data Collection*, in the MyEducationLab for your course and complete the activity titled "Data Collection Techniques." As you work through the learning unit, you will have an opportunity to explore various types of data and methods for collecting data.

Clearly, one major assumption associated with the use of a questionnaire is that the student can read and write. Many teacher researchers exclude the use of a questionnaire on this basis alone, but also compromise the time it takes to interview all their students by interviewing only a "representative sample" in their class.

A solid data collection instrument will help to ensure useful responses. Consider the following guidelines for developing and presenting questionnaires:

1. **Carefully proofread questionnaires** (or better still have a "critical" friend read your questionnaire) before sending them out. Nothing will turn parents off more quickly than receiving a message from their child's teacher that is filled with errors. Alternatively, students may be thrilled by the chance to point out that there is an error in their teacher's written work.
2. **Avoid a sloppy presentation.** Make the survey attractive and consider using BIG print if necessary.
3. **Avoid a lengthy questionnaire.** Piloting the instrument will give you a realistic sense of how long it will take for your students (or parents) to complete the task. Remember, no matter how much they want to help you, if the questionnaire is too long, it will find its way into the "circular file" instead of back into your hands.
4. **Do not ask unnecessary questions.** This is akin to teachers developing tests that don't match what was taught—a common complaint directed toward the administration of standardized tests. Often, we feel compelled to ask a great deal of trivial information on a questionnaire that is tangential to our stated purpose.

5. **Use structured items with a variety of possible responses.** (See the discussion of Likert scales in this chapter.) Indicate what you mean by "often" and "frequently" and how they differ from each other. Otherwise, your respondents will interpret the meaning of the terms in quite different ways.

6. **Whenever possible, allow for an "Other Comments" section.** This provides respondents with an opportunity to respond openly to your questions. These comments also provide you with an excellent source of "discrepant" data ("I hadn't expected someone to say that!") and an opportunity to follow up with an informal interview to elicit more information from the respondent as your time, energy, and inquisitiveness allow. For example, "In your response to question 3 you stated that . . . Can you tell me a little more about what you meant?"

7. **Decide whether you want respondents to put their names on the questionnaires or whether you will use a number to keep track of who has responded.** You should assure respondents (students, parents, colleagues) that their confidentiality will be protected throughout the process. However, you can protect respondents while also keeping track of who has responded and deciding whether they have made comments that you feel warrant a follow-up conversation. The key issue here is to assure the students, parents, and colleagues that they will not suffer any negative consequences for anything they might share with you. If we want respondents to be honest and forthright in their answers, we must assure them that they will not be persecuted if they tell us something we don't want to read or hear. (For further discussion of this matter, see the discussion of ethics in Chapter 2.) See Research in Action Checklist 4–1 for guidelines for devising a questionnaire.

Online/Web-Based Survey Tools

The Internet offers a veritable smorgasbord of Web-based survey tools to support the design and analysis of survey (questionnaire) research instruments, and many commercial survey research providers have popular online products that cater to action researchers' needs for survey instruments. Often, universities will provide students with free access to survey tool software hosted on the university server. However, do not be lured into a false sense of security by these user-friendly online providers. Remember the guiding principle of "garbage in—garbage out"! Action researchers must still follow the steps in the research process to ensure that a

RESEARCH IN ACTION CHECKLIST 4–1

Guidelines for Devising Questionnaires
_____ Proofread the questionnaire carefully.
_____ Avoid a sloppy presentation.
_____ Avoid a lengthy questionnaire.
_____ Do not ask unnecessary questions.
_____ Use structured items with a variety of possible responses.
_____ Include an "Other Comments" section.
_____ Decide whether to use respondents' names.
_____ Pilot the questionnaire.
_____ Use a variety of question formats.

survey tool based on an existing (commercially available) instrument collects the information necessary to answer the research questions. What follows is a brief description of two selected online survey sites.

SurveyMonkey.com

SurveyMonkey.com provides templates for the development of questionnaires using a variety of response strategies (e.g., multiple choice, rating scales, and drop-down menus), as well as the ability to administer the survey using e-mail invitations, with a record of respondents and nonrespondents and the ability to analyze results as soon as data arrive. Data are easily downloaded into statistical and spreadsheet programs such as SPSS and Excel but can also be viewed through SurveyMonkey.com in graphic or table form. For detailed information including pricing and guided tutorials for the development of a survey instrument, visit the SurveyMonkey.com homepage. SurveyMonkey.com also provides links to other online providers, so potential users can conduct a comparison of the services provided.

Zoomerang

Zoomerang provides survey researchers with a free trial to create an online survey, including the ability to pilot the tool on a small sample and to analyze the results of the trial. Like other commercial online survey providers, Zoomerang provides users with survey templates and the ability to conduct sophisticated statistical analyses of the results. Zoomerang charges users for its regular services but provides a discount for educational institutions. For detailed information including pricing and a free trial, visit the Zoomerang.com homepage.

Examining: Using and Making Records

This third category for data collection techniques suggests a catch-all term to describe everything else that a teacher researcher may collect. Again, many of these data sources are naturally occurring and require only that teachers locate them within their school setting.

Archival Documents

Like classrooms, schools are repositories for all sorts of records—student records, minutes of meetings (faculty, PTA, school board), newspaper clippings about significant events in the community, and so on. With permission, the teacher researcher can use these sources of data to gain valuable historical insights, identify potential trends, and explain how things got to be the way they are. Clearly, there are many archival data sources that can be accessed by teacher researchers if indicated by their focus areas. Often, clerical assistants, school aides, and student teachers are happy to help with uncovering archival data and organizing them in a way that is most useful to the classroom teacher if they believe that it is contributing to the collective understanding of a pressing educational issue. Don't be bashful about asking for assistance with this task.

Calhoun (1994) lists several archival data sources that exist in schools:

- Attendance rates
- Retention rates
- Discipline referrals
- Dropout rates
- Suspension rates

- Attendance rates at parent-teacher conferences
- Disaggregated data by grade level for student performance on statewide assessments in math, reading, writing, etc.
- Standardized test scores
- Student participation rates in extracurricular activities

Journals

Daily journals kept by both students and teachers are also a valuable data source. As Anderson, Herr, and Nihlen (1994) point out:

> The journal acts as a narrative technique and records events, thoughts, and feelings that have importance for the writer. As a record kept by a student, it can inform the teacher researcher about changing thoughts and new ideas and the progression of learning. (p. 153)

Students' journals can provide teachers with a valuable window into the students' world (in much the same way that homework assignments provide parents with insights into their children's daily experiences). Teachers can also use daily journals to keep a narrative account of their perspectives of what is happening in their classrooms.

Cochran-Smith and Lytle (1993) have incorporated teachers' journals as a central part of their work with teacher researchers and offer a somewhat expanded definition of what journals might incorporate:

- Journals are records of classroom life in which teachers write observations and reflect on their teaching over time.
- Journals are a collection of descriptions, analyses, and interpretations.
- Journals capture the essence of what is happening with students in classrooms and what this means for future teaching episodes.
- Journals provide teachers with a way to revisit, analyze, and evaluate their experiences over time.
- Journals provide windows on what goes on in school through teachers' eyes (pp. 26–27).

Journals, conceptualized in this way, are more than a single data source—they are an ongoing attempt by teachers to systematically reflect on their practice by constructing a narrative that honors the unique and powerful voice of the teachers' language. Regardless of your specific area of focus, journaling is recommended as a way to keep track of not only observations but feelings associated with the action research process.

Making Maps, Video Recordings, Audio Recordings, Photographs, Film, and Artifacts

These nonwritten sources of data can also be extremely helpful for teacher researchers trying to monitor movements in a classroom—data that are not always easily recorded in a narrative form.

Construction of Maps

Teacher researchers find class maps and school maps useful for a number of reasons. They provide contextual insights for people who have not visited the school, and they provide the teacher researcher with a reflective tool—a way of rethinking the way things are in their classrooms. For example, why are the computers in the classroom placed in a "bank" along one wall, and what are the effects of individual student computer time on other seat-work activities? A map can also record traffic flow in a classroom as well as teacher movement during instruction.

The school map may also prove useful for teams of teachers who are concerned about the movement and interactions of different grade levels of students and any problems that emerge from the traffic flow. Quite simply, maps are easy, useful tools that help teacher researchers and the people with whom they are sharing their research locate particular teaching episodes in the space of the teacher's classroom or school. For qualitatively oriented classroom researchers, context is everything! Figure 4–2 shows an example of a classroom map.

Video Recording, Audio Recording, Photographs, and Film

Video and audio recordings provide teacher researchers with another data source when the teacher is fully engaged in teaching but still wants to capture classroom events and interactions. Of course, there are drawbacks to these techniques. For example, their presence may elicit the usual "funny faces" and bizarre comments that we normally associate with the presence of such technology in a classroom for the first time. One way of moving ahead with these efforts is to introduce them into a classroom early in an action research project and provide the illusion that the "camera is running" when, in fact, there is no film in the camera. Alternatively, be prepared to make a lot of recordings! However, with the move to outcome-based performance assessment and "capstone" experiences, children are often required to demonstrate knowledge and skills through presentations to peers or panels of teachers and parents. Video recording is an excellent

FIGURE 4–2 *Classroom Map Example*

way to capture these events and to provide an opportunity for teachers and students alike to reflect on content, skills, and attitudes demonstrated by the students. Similarly, I have seen teacher researchers effectively use still photographs (of the traditional 35mm kind and digital photos) to capture events in their classrooms that are central to their given area of focus. For example, James Rockford might have considered the use of photographs to capture the kinds of activities engaged in by students learning word processing.

Assuming there are no technical problems (and that is a pretty big assumption!), using audio and video recordings also raises the serious issue of time—the time it takes to watch, listen, and record observations from these sources. Although finding enough time is probably the number one challenge for teachers doing action research, it is important for us to weigh the potential benefits and drawbacks of these data sources. These techniques have the potential to be more time consuming and, thus, potentially threatening to the goodwill of any action research endeavor. However, many teacher researchers use these methods to great advantage—which only confirms the idiosyncratic nature of data collection efforts!

Artifacts

Classrooms are rich sources of what we might call **artifacts**—written or visual sources of data that contribute to our understanding of what is happening in our classrooms and schools. The category of artifact can include almost everything else that we haven't already discussed. For example, there has been a trend in schools to move toward "authentic assessment" techniques, including the use of student portfolios—a presentation of work that captures individual student's work samples over time and the relative growth of that work. Portfolios, although difficult to quantify, provide the teacher with valuable outcome data that get at the heart of the qualitatively different samples of work. Such artifacts are a valuable data source that teachers may use as a starting point for conversation with their students. For example, a teacher may ask students to explain the differences they see between the work they included in their portfolios earlier and later in the school year. Key Concepts Box 4–3 shows the components of using and making records.

Hence, we have gone full circle in looking at how teacher researchers could use the contents of student portfolios as the basis for an informal interview with their students as they search for greater understanding of the students' perspectives of their learning. For example, a teacher may ask a student to elaborate on the thinking behind a piece of creative writing,

KEY CONCEPTS BOX 4–3

Components of Using and Making Records	
Archival sources	Minutes of meetings Attendance rates, retention rates, dropout rates, suspension rates Discipline referrals Statewide assessment scores Newspaper clippings
Journals	Daily observations and analysis Reflections Record keeping
Artifacts	Maps and seating charts Photographs, audio recordings, and video recordings Portfolios or less formal examples of student work

Qualitative Data Collection Techniques

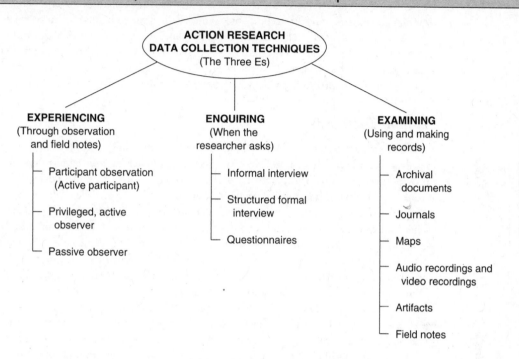

artwork, or explanation of an open-ended mathematics problem-solving solution. Utilize Agar's "5Ws and H" to informally engage students in conversation about their work—you'll be pleased with the outcome and the return for your investment of time. Key Concepts Box 4–4 shows the taxonomy of action research qualitative data collection techniques.

Quantitative Data Collection Techniques

Many data collection techniques can be used by action researchers that represent common "evaluation" practices in schools and provide the teachers with data that can be reduced to numbers. Action researchers must not confuse the quantitative collection of data with the application of a quantitative research design. Experimental quantitative research requires students to be randomly assigned to a control group or an experimental group, and involves manipulation of the independent variables in order to control group assignments. In classrooms, it is usually not feasible for classroom teachers to structure their classroom instruction in this way. However, even if action researchers can't control all of the variables in their classrooms, they can still make use of quantitative data collection techniques to gather useful information about their students that can be analyzed and interpreted using the descriptive statistical techniques.

Teacher-Made Tests

Perhaps one of the most common quantitative data collection techniques used by teachers to aid them in their ability to monitor and adjust instruction is the use of teacher-made tests.

That is, teachers will not rely solely on the unit tests provided by textbook companies to determine whether their students have achieved mastery of specific goals and objectives. Oftentimes, teachers *adapt* rather than *adopt* commercial curriculum materials and therefore cannot rely on the unit test accompanying the curriculum to be a valid measure of student performance. Similarly, teachers are expert at developing innovative curricula to address a particular area of focus and must make their own tests from scratch. Gathering data from teacher-made tests provide classroom teachers with accessible information about how well their students are responding to a particular teaching or curriculum innovation.

Standardized Tests

Teachers are all too familiar with the kind of standardized tests that have swept the nation as a result of No Child Left Behind (NCLB) legislation. These standardized tests are intended to provide teachers, principals, parents, and state and federal education officials with individual student achievement data. These data are often reported as percentile ranks or stanines (see Appendix B) and provide teachers with data about the relative performance of their students. That is, these data provide teachers with a snapshot of how their students are performing on a given subject test relative to all other students taking the test. These data are also aggregated to provide policy makers (for example, principals and superintendents) with information about whether groups of students and schools are meeting Adequate Yearly Progress (AYP). In the United States, AYP is a critical component of the federal NCLB act. Under this legislation, all states must establish student achievement targets that gradually increase over time so that by the 2013–14 school year all students in the state are proficient on state assessments. Schools that do not attain AYP for two or more years in a row receive state and federal sanctions (usually related to funding). Needless to say, teachers are increasingly finding these quantitative data sources to be a critical component of any action research data collection plan.

Teacher researchers are often pressured or required to use standardized tests. It is not possible to list here all of the standardized tests that exist. We should acknowledge, however, that standardized test scores are another data source that contributes to our understanding of how teaching practices affect our students. A good source for teachers who are investigating standardized tests is the *Mental Measurements Yearbook* (MMY). The MMYs are published by the Buros Institute of Mental Measurements and are a major source of test information for educational researchers. The yearbooks, which can be found in most large libraries, provide information and reviews of published tests in various school subject areas (such as English, mathematics, and reading), as well as personality, intelligence, aptitude, speech and hearing, and vocational tests. The Web addresses for the Buros Institute and its catalogs are www.unl. edu/buros/ and www.unl.edu/buros/bimm/html/catalog.html.

School-Generated Report Cards

As the parent of a high-school-aged child, I have intimate knowledge of the kind of report cards provided to children and parents to map student progress. My son, Jonathan, is proud to display his report card on the front of our refrigerator along with all the other important family artifacts that are commonly found on the family fridge (e.g., pictures of family and friends, special vacation places, and of course the family dog, Jesse). Along with the teachers' comments (e.g., "Jonathan is an awesome writer." A chip off the old block I would say!) there are the all important credits earned and the even more important GRADE! At Jonathan's school, grades are reported as letters (A–F) that are ultimately translated into numbers (0–4) in order to calculate a grade point average (GPA). Students who earn a 3.5 GPA or higher, with a minimum of four credits, qualify for Honor Roll and their names appear in the local newspaper. Hence, school-generated report cards are a valuable data source for teachers (who can quantify student achievement) and for students and parents (who can interpret the data and set goals accordingly).

Attitude Scales

Many teacher researchers are curious about the impact of their work on students' attitudes. Scales that are often used to measure attitudes, such as Likert scales and semantic differentials, are useful tools for the action researcher. The use of attitude scales allows teacher researchers to determine "what an individual believes, perceives, or feels" (Gay, Mills, & Airasian, 2009, p. 150). Nearly all of the action research vignettes in this book include examples of how teacher researchers wanted to know how children "felt" about something (a keyboarding software program, the violence and harassment scenes presented by the Teen Theater group, the absenteeism policy at the school, and the de-emphasis of grades). In some cases, these teacher researchers used an attitude scale, whereas others used open-ended questions, such as "How do you feel about the school's absenteeism policy?"

Likert Scales

A **Likert scale** asks students to respond to a series of statements indicating whether they strongly agree (SA), agree (A), are undecided (U), disagree (D), or strongly disagree (SD) with each statement. Each response corresponds with a point value and a score is determined by adding the point values for each statement. For example, the following point values might be assigned for positive responses: SA = 5, A = 4, U = 3, D = 2, SD = 1. As Gay and colleagues (2009) point out, "A high point value on a positively stated item would indicate a positive attitude and a high total score on the test would be indicative of a positive attitude" (p. 130).

Although these instruments provide teacher researchers with quantitative (numerical) data, these data can still be considered descriptive. The responses to such a survey can be reduced to numbers (for example, the average response was 4.2), but the data are still largely descriptive and analyzed using descriptive statistics, such as mean and standard deviation (see Appendix B) and an accompanying narrative. (For example, "the average response was 4.2 and was supported by the following comments . . .")

To illustrate, students experiencing a new math curriculum that emphasizes problem-solving strategies may be asked to respond to the following item on a questionnaire:

Please respond to the following items by drawing a circle around the response that most closely reflects your opinion: strongly agree (SA), agree (A), undecided (U), disagree (D), or strongly disagree (SD).

1. I believe that the problem-solving skills I learn in class help me make good problem-solving decisions outside of school.

   SA   A   U   D   SD

By assigning the following point values, SA = 5, A = 4, U = 3, D = 2, SD = 1, the teacher researcher would be able to infer whether the students felt positively or negatively about the effect of math problem-solving skills outside of the classroom.

Semantic Differential

A **semantic differential** asks a student (or parent) to give a quantitative rating to the subject of the rating scale on a number of bipolar adjectives. For example, following the implementation of a new math curriculum, students might be asked to rate the curriculum in terms of whether it was exciting or boring, relevant or irrelevant, or enjoyable or unenjoyable.

Each location on the continuum between the bipolar words has an associated score:

Boring	__ __ __ __ __ __ __	Exciting
	-3 -2 -1 0 1 2 3	
Irrelevant	__ __ __ __ __ __ __	Relevant
	-3 -2 -1 0 1 2 3	
Unenjoyable	__ __ __ __ __ __ __	Enjoyable
	-3 -2 -1 0 1 2 3	

By totaling scores for all items on the semantic differential, the teacher researcher can determine whether a child's attitude is positive or negative. Semantic differential scales usually have five to seven intervals, with a neutral attitude being assigned a value of zero.

A child who checked the first interval on each of these items would be expressing a positive attitude toward mathematics (for further discussion of semantic differentials, see Gay, Mills, & Airasian, 2009; Pelto & Pelto, 1978). Key Concepts Box 4–5 lists quantitative data collection techniques.

Triangulation

In research terms the desire to use multiple sources of data is referred to as **triangulation**. It is generally accepted in action research circles that researchers should not rely on any single source of data, interview, observation, or instrument. Sagor (2000) has suggested that action researchers complete a "triangulation matrix—a simple grid that shows the various data sources that will be used to answer each research question" (pp. 19–20). In the vignette that opened this chapter you can see how Rockford has laid out his triangulation matrix to address issues related to bias in the data collection. (See Figure 4–3 for an example of a triangulation matrix.) We will adopt a less prescriptive approach here, but we support the triangulation principle. That is, the strength of educational research lies in its triangulation, collecting information in many ways, rather than relying solely on one (Wolcott, 1988). Pelto and Pelto (1978) have described this as a "multi-instrument" approach (p. 122). For our purposes in doing action research, this suggests that the teacher is the research instrument who, in collecting data, utilizes a variety of techniques over an extended period of time, "ferreting out varying perspectives on complex issues and events" (Wolcott, 1988, p. 192).

KEY CONCEPTS BOX 4–5

Quantitative Data Collection Techniques

- Teacher-made tests
- Standardized tests
- School-generated report cards
- Attitude scales
- Likert scales
- Semantic differential

Research Questions	Data Source		
	1	2	3
1. Preexisting Knowledge?	Student Survey	Computer Knowledge Pretest	
2. Keyboarding Speed?	Pretest	Posttest	Teacher Help
3. Appropriate Use (WP)?	Pretest Software	Posttest Software	Timed Typing Teacher Constructed
4. Time on Computers?	School Lab Records	Student Survey	Parent Survey

FIGURE 4–3   *Triangulation Matrix Example*

It should be noted that this "ferreting out" may involve the combination of qualitative and quantitative approaches by including both qualitative and quantitative data in a single study. For example, a teacher may be shocked to see the steady decline of student performance on statewide reading assessments. In order to better understand the reasons behind the decline, the teacher develops and administers a survey to students that is focused on out of school reading behaviors. Analysis of the survey may reveal that students do not like the choice of reading materials provided by the school and as a result have stopped reading after school. The teacher uses this data as the basis for interviews with some of the students (and parent perhaps) in order to better understand the kinds of reading materials students would find interesting to read out of school. Therefore, our triangulation of data may involve collecting qualitative and quantitative data, allowing us to build on the synergy and strength that exists between qualitative and quantitative research methods. This approach will enable us to understand a phenomenon more fully than is possible using either qualitative or quantitative methods alone. As we begin to focus our data collection efforts, we must keep in mind the principle of triangulation and apply it to our regular data collection efforts.

Realign Your Area of Focus and Action Research Plan When Necessary

By this point in the action research process, teacher researchers have already articulated their area of focus in a problem statement and reviewed the literature based on that idea. However, once they start their data collection, many teacher researchers find themselves drawn into other directions that appear more interesting, relevant, or problematic. That is the very nature of action research; it is intimate, open-ended, and often serendipitous. Being clear about a problem is critical in the beginning, but once teacher researchers begin to systematically collect their data, the area of focus will become even clearer.

Be prepared to modify and adjust your action research plan if necessary. For example, a group of teachers started their action research project with an area of focus on the impact of early literacy development on problem-solving skills in mathematics. As their study evolved, it became clear to the participants that their real focus was not on the transfer of literacy to problem solving but rather on the effects of a phonemic skills curriculum on early literacy development. When this focus became clear after some initial data collection, the group decided to change their research questions to more accurately reflect the real nature of their work.

There is nothing wrong with realigning your inquiry midway through it. Remember, action research is done to benefit you and the students in your classroom. The process is a spiral. If you discover a question or a method that seems more fruitful than the one you are currently using, adjust your action research plan and continue on!

Summary

1. The decision about what data are collected for an action research area of focus is largely determined by the nature of the problem.
2. Qualitative data collection techniques include data sources such as field notes, journals, interviews, maps, and audio and video recordings.
3. Quantitative data collection techniques include data sources such as questionnaires (surveys), attitude scales, teacher-made tests (criterion-referenced tests), standardized tests (norm-referenced tests), school-generated reports cards, and the results of student achievement reported on statewide assessment tests.
4. One approach is not better than the other. Your area of focus and research questions will determine the best data collection techniques for your research.
5. A research project might use both qualitative and quantitative sources of data using a mixed-methods design. Mixed-methods research designs combine qualitative and quantitative approaches by including both qualitative and quantitative data in a single study.

Qualitative Data Collection Techniques

6. Qualitative data collection techniques may include the following: existing archival tools within a school, tools for capturing everyday life, tools for questioning, conventional sources (e.g., surveys and questionnaires), inventive sources (e.g., exhibits and portfolios), interviews, oral history and narrative stories, rating scales, inventories, observation, mapping, visual recordings, photography, journals and diaries.
7. Three qualitative fieldwork strategies include experiencing, enquiring, and examining.
8. In action research the teacher researcher is the primary data collection instrument.

Experiencing Through Direct Observation

9. When qualitative researchers obtain data by watching the participants, they are observing.
10. A researcher who becomes a part of and a participant in the situation under observation is called a participant observer.
11. A researcher can be an active participant observer; a privileged, active observer; or a passive observer.
12. A passive observer watches but does not participate in the situation while observing it.

13. Field notes are the records of what the observer has seen or heard. Field notes contain literal descriptions as well as personal reactions and comments on what the observer has experienced and thought about during an observation session. Field notes may be guided by a protocol developed prior to the observation session.

Enquiring: When the Researcher Asks

14. The unstructured interview is like a casual conversation and allows the qualitative researcher to inquire into and learn about something that is going on at the research setting.
15. In a structured interview, the researcher has a specified set of questions designed to elicit the same kind of information from all respondents.
16. For interviews, researchers should include convergent and divergent questions and pilot test them with a group of respondents similar to the target sample.
17. Interviewers should take notes during the interview, write notes after the interview, or (preferably) audio or video record the interview and later transcribe it.
18. A focus group is a group interview. Researchers conducting focus groups should ensure that all participants have a chance to state their points of view.
19. An e-mail interview can be used to elicit responses from busy professionals, who can respond to an e-mail either synchronously or asynchronously.
20. A questionnaire is a written collection of self-report questions to be answered by a selected group of research participants.
21. Developing and presenting questionnaires takes care; questions should be relevant and the presentation should be attractive. Be sure to protect participants' confidential information.
22. The Internet offers a veritable smorgasbord of Web-based survey tools to support the design and analysis of survey (questionnaire) research instruments, and many commercial survey research providers have popular online products that cater to action researchers' needs for survey instruments.
23. SurveyMonkey.com provides templates for the development of questionnaires using a variety of response strategies (e.g., multiple choice, rating scales, and drop-down menus), as well as the ability to administer the survey using e-mail invitations, with a record of respondents and nonrespondents and the ability to analyze results as soon as data arrive.
24. Zoomerang provides survey researchers with a free trial to create an online survey, including the ability to pilot the tool on a small sample and to analyze the results of the trial. Like other commercial online survey providers, Zoomerang provides users with survey templates and the ability to conduct sophisticated statistical analyses of the results.

Examining: Using and Making Records

25. Useful educational records include archival documents, journals, maps, video and audio recordings, and artifacts.
26. There are many archival data sources that teacher researchers can access: student records, minutes of meetings (faculty, PTA, school board), newspaper clippings about significant events in the community, and so on.
27. Students' journals can provide teachers with a valuable window into the students' world (in much the same way that homework assignments provide parents with insights into their children's daily experiences). Teachers can also use a daily journal to keep a narrative account of their perspectives of what is happening in their classrooms.

28. Maps can also be extremely helpful for teacher researchers trying to monitor movements in a classroom—data that are not always easily recorded in a narrative form.

29. Video and audio recordings provide teacher researchers with another data source when the teacher is fully engaged in teaching but still wants to capture classroom events and interactions.

30. Classrooms are rich sources of what we might call artifacts—written or visual sources of data that contribute to our understanding of what is happening in our classrooms and schools.

Quantitative Data Collection Techniques

31. Many data collection techniques can be used by action researchers that represent common "evaluation" practices in schools and provide the teachers with data that can be reduced to numbers. Action researchers must not confuse the quantitative collection of data with the application of a quantitative research design.

32. Quantitative data collection techniques include teacher-made tests, standardized tests, school-generated report cards, attitude scales, Likert scales, and semantic differentials.

33. Teacher-made tests. Perhaps one of the most common quantitative data collection techniques used by teachers to aid them in their ability to monitor and adjust instruction is the teacher-made test. That is, teachers will not rely solely on the unit tests provided by textbook companies to determine whether their students have achieved mastery of specific goals and objectives.

34. Standardized tests are intended to provide teachers, principals, parents, and state and federal education officials with individual student achievement data. These data are often reported as percentile ranks or stanines (see Appendix B) and provide teachers with data about the relative performance of their students.

35. A good source for teachers who are investigating standardized tests is the *Mental Measurements Yearbook* (MMY). The MMYs are published by the Buros Institute of Mental Measurements and are a major source of test information for educational researchers.

36. School-generated report cards are a readily available data source for teachers. Different schools will use different approaches to how student success data is reported but will usually include a letter grade and narrative teacher comment.

37. Attitude scales allow teacher researchers to determine what an individual believes, perceives, or feels; they often use a Likert scale or semantic differential.

38. A Likert scale asks students to respond to a series of statements indicating whether they strongly agree (SA), agree (A), are undecided (U), disagree (D), or strongly disagree (SD) with each statement. Each response corresponds with a point value and a score is determined by adding the point values for each statement.

39. A semantic differential asks a student (or parent) to give a quantitative rating to the subject of the rating scale on a number of bipolar adjectives.

Triangulation

40. In research terms the desire to use multiple sources of data is referred to as triangulation. It is generally accepted in action research circles that researchers should not rely on any single source of data, interview, observation, or instrument.

Research Questions	Data Source		
	1	2	3
1.			
2.			
3.			
4.			
5.			

FIGURE 4–4 *Triangulation Matrix Exercise*

Realign Your Area of Focus and Action Research Plan When Necessary

41. Be prepared to modify and adjust your action research plan if necessary.
42. There is nothing wrong with realigning your inquiry midway through it. Remember, action research is done to benefit you and the students in your classroom. The process is a spiral. If you discover a question or a method that seems more fruitful than the one you are currently using, adjust your action research plan and continue on.

Tasks

1. Identify data collection techniques you can use to answer each of your research questions.
2. Identify data collection instruments you need to locate or develop.
3. Complete a triangulation matrix (Figure 4–4) for your proposed study. (Reminder: Don't force the issue of three data sources for each question. In some cases you may have more than three data sources that you wish to use, and in other cases, for example, standardized test scores, it may not be possible to include more than one data source.)

Data Collection Considerations: Validity, Reliability, and Generalizability

This chapter addresses the importance of validity, reliability, and generalizability as ways to ensure the quality of qualitatively oriented action research.

After reading this chapter you should be able to:

1. Understand the concept of validity as it applies to quantitative research.
2. Understand the concept of validity as it applies to qualitative research.
3. Understand the concepts of reliability and generalizability as they apply to action research.

Improving Student Understanding and Motivation of Multiplication Facts

ALYSON MARLAND

Alyson Marland, a student teacher in a fourth-grade classroom, was a participant in an action research class. Like many elementary teachers, Alyson was challenged about how best to teach elementary students basic number facts, while at the same time keeping the children motivated to learn. Alyson's story illustrates the importance of using multiple data sources (qualitative and quantitative) to address issues of validity and reliability that ensured the quality, and robustness, of her action research findings.

This action research project focuses on promoting student understanding and motivation while teaching the basic multiplication facts (0–9). The study examined the effectiveness of teaching methods with an emphasis on rote memorization, compared to those focusing on problem solving. Research advocates the use of problem solving when introducing and teaching basic facts, and holding off on drill and practice methods until after they've developed an understanding. The participants in the study consist of thirty-five fourth-grade students. The students participated in lessons on arrays and multiplication games, and they discussed efficient versus inefficient counting strategies. Data were collected from their old timed tests, state math scores, interviews, and worksheets. The results of the study suggest a positive relationship between balancing conceptual understanding and procedural skills, and student success with basic facts. The results also show a positive relationship between playing games and student motivation for studying the basic facts.

Introduction

Research suggests that for every time you do something wrong, you have to do it right seventeen times before your brain gets used to doing it correctly. These findings are startling when you consider the vast amount of drill and practice methods used in the classroom to teach students their basic math facts. The purpose of my action research project was to seek out and examine effective and efficient methods for teaching the basic facts. My second objective for this project was to develop effective strategies for increasing student motivation in terms of studying their multiplication facts. Students are often frustrated and bored studying things they don't understand, or when using tedious study methods.

Background

According to the 2004–2005 Oregon State Standards, by the end of fourth grade students are expected to have developed efficient strategies for solving multiplication problems. They should be fluent with these strategies and able to solve all basic fact problems mentally within three seconds. Unfortunately, researchers have found that an alarming number of eighth-grade students still resort to finger counting and other inefficient strategies when solving simple problems (Isaacs, Carroll, & Bell, 2001). These strategies are inefficient because they take too much time and are not done mentally.

One promising practice is to reduce the use of drill and practice methods (Jones, 1995). These methods include timed tests, flash cards, and worksheets with rows of basic facts. One reason researchers advise educators to stay away from drill and practice methods is because they don't aid in students' conceptual understanding of multiplication. These methods provide students with procedural skills that they are taught to mimic. Teaching in this way makes it hard for students to apply multiplication concepts to word problems or real-life situations.

Effective strategies for teaching basic facts include balancing procedural skills and conceptual knowledge. Teaching with balance includes the use of word problems, arrays, and open-ended problem-solving assignments. Isaacs et al. (2001) recommend practicing multiplication in a variety of contexts and situations to increase the students' ability to transfer the skill/concept.

Other promising practices suggest three components to use when teaching basic facts. The first component is developing a strong understanding of the operations of number relationships. The second focuses on trading inefficient strategies for efficient ones, and the third component is providing students with drill and practice assignments. Van de Walle (2003) stresses the importance of not moving to step three until after the students have developed efficient strategies. If you introduce drill before the students have mastered one or more efficient strategies, the practice will only reinforce the inefficient strategies. Inefficient strategies include counting on fingers, adding the numbers instead of multiplying them, using manipulatives, drawing pictures, etc. Inefficient methods are inefficient because they take a long time and cannot be done mentally. Efficient methods include skip counting, simplifying the problem, and ultimately, memorization.

Intervention

My planned intervention to address students' understanding of, and motivation to learn, basic number facts included the following:

- Lessons focused on building students' conceptual understanding of the multiplication process.
- Teaching students efficient strategies for solving basic facts.
- Introducing students to fun games they could play while studying their basic number facts.

Data Collection

The data collection tools I used were:

1. Students' scores on state math tests
2. Results of timed tests
3. Informal interviews
4. Students' written work

Data Analysis

The data I collected from the students' state math test was surprising. I was shocked to find that eleven students (about thirty-five percent of the class) did not meet the state standards in math. The students who did not meet state standards were consistent with the students who were not passing their timed tests. I decided I would need to spend some extra time working with these eleven students.

The data I collected from students' timed tests were by far the most helpful in planning my intervention and understanding where students were having the most trouble. The data I collected from the timed tests focused on the types of errors students were making. Edelman, Abdit, and Valentin (1995) describe four types of errors humans make when multiplying; they include operand, table, operation, and non-table errors. Operand errors occur when the incorrect answer given is correct for another problem that shares an operand (e.g., $4 \times 2 = 16$, when 16 is the correct answer for 4×4). Table errors occur when the incorrect answer given does not share an operand with the correct answer, but the answer given does reside in the multiplication table (e.g., $6 \times 9 = 56$). Humans make operation errors when they perform a different operation, such as adding or subtracting, when solving a multiplication problem (e.g., $9 \times 0 = 9$). The final error is a non-table error, and it occurs when the incorrect answer is not an answer to any problem in the multiplication table (e.g., $5 \times 6 = 31$). Operand errors were by far the most common error made by the students. They accounted for fifty-five percent of the error total. This data told me that students were associating the incorrect answer with one of the operands, and the early emphasis on drill and practice has reinforced these wrong answers. Non-table errors accounted for twenty-three percent of the errors. I believe students are making a high amount of non-table errors because they are miscounting on their fingers. Solving 6×7 on your fingers is both hard and confusing, so I assumed students who rely on their fingers make the majority of the table errors. Operation errors occur mostly in problems containing an operand of zero or one. The students often switch to addition and solve the problem by adding zero or one to the other number. This error occurs mostly when the zero or one is on the bottom. I didn't feel the error occurred consistently enough to be considered a problem, so I decided not to focus on it during my intervention.

I also used the students' timed tests to identify which multiplication facts they were having the most trouble with. The problems I found gave students the most trouble were 6×7, 7×6, 7×4, 7×7, 8×8, 8×7, 6×6, 8×6, and 6×8. In general, though, any problem including an operand of six, seven, eight, and/or nine was answered incorrectly by the majority of students. This data was especially helpful in adjusting my interventions, because it allowed me to focus on the problems with which students were having the most trouble.

The informal interviews provided me with insight into what the students thought about timed tests, what strategies they used to solve basic fact problems, and how well they could transfer their skills to real-world situations. I was surprised to find that every student answered "yes" to the question about whether or not they felt timed tests were helpful. The majority of students supported their answer stating that timed tests gave them a chance to practice their multiplication facts. The interviews also allowed me to discover which strategy each student relied on when solving multiplication facts.

Discussion

The purpose of my action research project was to seek out and examine effective and efficient methods for teaching basic math facts. Upon completion of my action research project, I feel confident that I will be able to effectively and efficiently teach basic facts to any grade, first through sixth. I am now aware of the common misconceptions regarding rote memorization and the premature use of timed tests.

My results tell me that timed tests can be beneficial when used as a form of practice. Students should be able to correct their own tests, allowing for immediate feedback on which problems they got wrong and what the correct answer should have been. Teachers should also consider not grading the tests so students can focus on improving their skills and not on a grade.

From my research, experience, and results I was also able to infer that effective teaching strategies center around balancing conceptual understanding and procedural skills. To provide this balance, educators should emphasize problem-solving strategies at an early age. Problem-solving methods provide students with flexibility in their learning, making it easier for them to transfer their knowledge to various math problems and real-life situations. Also, teachers should teach one concept at a time, and teach it to master before moving on.

To motivate their students, educators must first develop their understanding of the multiplication procedure and concept. This understanding will boost the students' self-esteem, giving them confidence and motivating them intrinsically. The second step in motivating students is introducing fun ways for them to learn, study, and memorize the basic facts. In my experience, students preferred competitive games, especially when playing against the teacher. The participants in my study were really excited about having a "multiplication bowl," where the two fourth-grade classes would face off in a multiplication competition. I am excited to continue to test these teaching strategies in the next cycle of my action research journey.

References

Edelman, B., Abdit, H., & Valentin, D. (1995). Multiplication number facts: Modeling human performance with connectionist networks. *Psychologica Belgica*, 36: 31–63.

Isaacs, A., Carroll, W., & Bell, M. (2001). UCSMP Everyday Mathematics Curriculum. *Journal of Mathematical Behavior*, 19: 49–62.

Jones, S. C. (1995). Review of cognitive research. *Educational Memory Aids*, 2: 57–60.

Van de Walle, J. A. (2003). Elementary and middle school mathematics: Teaching developmentally. Upper Saddle River, NJ: Pearson, 156–176.

Attention to the three important concepts of validity, reliability, and generalizability will help teacher researchers ensure the quality of their work. These concepts are also important for teacher researchers who are reviewing published and unpublished research. That is, to both do action research and measure the quality of the action research you're reading about, you need a basic understanding of the concepts of validity, reliability, and generalizability.

Qualitative researchers, action researchers, and quantitative researchers disagree about the value of applying these concepts of validity, reliability, and generalizability to qualitatively oriented action research. In part, this debate takes place because such concepts have their roots in traditional quantitative research—research that uses mostly numerical data and that has different purposes from action research (see Chapter 1).

However, teacher researchers must understand the meanings of these terms to be knowledgeable consumers of research as well as producers of research that we hope will be trustworthy and persuasive in their own eyes and in the eyes of their audience.

Validity

The word *validity* is common in our everyday professional language. For example, teachers will ask, "Are the results of the California Achievement Test really valid?" Or, my preservice teachers will often comment, "My students did poorly on the history test I gave them, but I'm not sure it's an accurate representation of what they really know." Recently, I have also heard teachers discuss whether open-ended assessment strategies really measure their students' ability. All these examples are questions about **validity**, or how we know that the data we collect (test scores, for example) accurately gauge what we are trying to measure (in this case, what it is that our children "know" about history). To put it technically, "validity refers to the degree to which scientific observations actually measure or record what they purport to measure" (Pelto & Pelto, 1978, p. 33).

Validity in Quantitative Research

Historically, validity was linked to numerically based research conducted in the positivistic tradition. For example, Cronbach and Meehl (1955) developed criteria for four different types of validity. These types of validity served to convince the researcher and the researchee that the "results" of the research were "right," "accurate," and could withstand scrutiny from other researchers. In quantitative research, validity is linked to the kind of research being conducted: survey, correlational, causal-comparative, experimental, and single-subject designs. Each of these types of quantitative research addresses the concept of validity in a slightly different way. For our purposes, we will briefly consider validity in quantitative research in terms of internal validity and external validity. **Internal validity** is the degree to which observed differences on the dependent variable are a direct result of manipulation of the independent variable, not some other variable. In other words, an examination of internal validity focuses on threats or rival explanations that influence the outcomes of a quantitative study but are not due to the independent variable. For example, Alyson Marland's mixed-methods vignette at the start of this chapter attempted to determine if the planned intervention (independent variable) of using students' conceptual understanding of the multiplication process along with efficient basic facts strategies impacted students' scores on state math tests (dependent variable). The degree to which Marland's research results are attributable to the independent variable and not to another rival explanation is the degree to which the study is internally valid. In her study, Marland discovered that in fact 35 percent of her students were not meeting state standards in math, in spite of her planned intervention. However, this discovery led her to a deeper understanding of the impact of her teaching strategies on student achievement on the statewide assessment test.

In quantitative research we must also consider the external validity of the research. **External validity** is the degree to which study results are generalizable, or applicable, to groups and environments outside of the research setting. In other words, an examination of external validity focuses on threats or rival explanations that disallow the results of a study to be generalized to other settings or groups. Marland made no claims to external validity in her study of 35 fourth-grade students in her class. In order to make claims to findings that would have external validity, Marland would need to satisfy the tenets of experimental research, including the random assignment of her students to a control group and experimental group. This was clearly not the goal of her research, which focused on promoting student understanding and motivation while learning basic number facts. It is beyond the scope of this book to address all of the issues related to validity across different styles of quantitative research. For a comprehensive discussion of these issues I recommend Gay, Mills, and Airasian (2009), *Educational Research: Competencies for Analysis and Applications*.

Validity in Qualitative Research

As many types of qualitative research became more popular in classroom settings in the late 1970s and early 1980s, it became common for qualitative researchers to begin to justify and defend the validity of their studies according to the criteria that had previously been applied to quantitative studies. For example, as a graduate student completing a research-based master's thesis on the effects of high geographic mobility on the children of low-income families, I was required by my advisors to dedicate considerable time and effort to justifying and defending the accuracy of my account. They confronted me with the question, "How will your readers know that your case studies accurately portray the lives of these children?" (Mills, 1985).

PEARSON
myeducationlab

Go to the Assignments and Activities section of Topic #3, *Data Collection*, in the MyEducationLab for your course and complete the activity titled "Evaluating the Validity of Qualitative Measures." In this activity, you will learn more about how trustworthiness and understanding are key to determining the validity of action research data.

In the early days of my career this seemed like an overwhelming task, because there was a paucity of literature that specifically dealt with the issue. Since then, individuals have been experimenting with a new vocabulary that captures the essence of the term *validity* in a way that applies specifically to the methods of qualitative research. Kincheloe (1991) asks, "Is *trustworthiness* a more appropriate word to use?" (p. 135), whereas Wolcott (1994) suggests, "*understanding* seems to encapsulate the idea as well as any other everyday term" (p. 367). Greenwood and Levin (2000) argue that because action researchers do not make claims to context-free knowledge (that is, by its very nature action research is based in the context of our own classrooms and schools), issues of credibility, validity, and reliability in action research are measured by the willingness of teacher researchers (and the stakeholders in our studies) "to act on the results of the action research, thereby risking their welfare on the 'validity' of their ideas and the degree to which the outcomes meet their expectations" (p. 98). In short, the validity of our action research depends on whether the actual solution to a problem (our planned intervention) actually solves our problem!

Let's look at two systems for measuring the quality of qualitative research based on these two terms: trustworthiness and understanding.

Guba's Criteria for Validity of Qualitative Research

Guba's article "Criteria for Assessing the Trustworthiness of Naturalistic Inquiries" (1981) speaks directly to qualitative researchers. Guba argued that the **trustworthiness** of qualitative inquiry could be established by addressing the following characteristics of a study: *credibility, transferability, dependability,* and *confirmability.*

Credibility

The **credibility** of the study refers to the researcher's ability to take into account the complexities that present themselves in a study and to deal with patterns that are not easily explained. To do this, Guba (1981) suggested that the following methods be used:

- *Do prolonged participation at the study site* to overcome distortions produced by the presence of researchers and to provide researchers with the opportunity to test biases and perceptions. By virtue of studying your own school, classroom, and students, you will be immersed in the setting and spend a prolonged amount of time at the site—probably close to 180 days per year!
- *Do persistent observation* to identify pervasive qualities as well as atypical characteristics.
- *Do peer debriefing* to provide researchers with the opportunity to test their growing insights through interactions with other professionals. For example, most of us will be able to identify a "critical friend," a colleague, or a "significant other"—somebody who is willing and able to help us reflect on our own situations by listening, prompting, and recording our insights throughout the process.
- *Practice triangulation* (discussed in Chapter 4) to compare a variety of data sources and different methods with one another in order to cross-check data.
- *Collect documents, films, video recordings, audio recordings, artifacts, and other "raw" or "slice-of-life" data items.*
- *Do member checks* to test the overall report with the study's participants before sharing it in final form (pp. 84–86).
- *Establish structural corroboration or coherence* to ensure that there are no internal conflicts or contradictions.
- *Establish referential adequacy*; that is, test analyses and interpretations against documents, recordings, films, and the like that were collected as part of the study.

Transferability

Guba's (1981) second criteria of **transferability** refers to qualitative researchers' beliefs that everything they study is context bound and that the goal of their work is not to develop "truth" statements that can be generalized to larger groups of people. To facilitate the development of descriptive, context-relevant statements, Guba proposed that the researcher should:

- *Collect detailed descriptive data* that will permit comparison of a given context (classroom/school) to other possible contexts to which transfer might be contemplated.
- *Develop detailed descriptions of the context* to make judgments about fittingness with other contexts possible.

The transferability of an action research account depends largely on whether the consumer of the research can identify with the setting. Include as much detail as possible to allow the recipients of your work to "see" the setting for themselves.

Dependability

According to Guba (1981), **dependability** refers to the stability of the data. To address issues related to the dependability of the data we collect, Guba recommended the following steps:

- *Overlap methods* (similar to a triangulation process). Use two or more methods in such a way that the weakness of one is compensated by the strength of another. For example, interviews with students may be used to contribute to your understanding of what you observed happening during a lesson.

- *Establish an audit trail.* This process makes it possible for an external "auditor" (maybe a critical friend, principal, or graduate student) to examine the processes of data collection, analysis, and interpretation. This audit trail may take the form of a written description of each process and perhaps even access to original field notes, artifacts, video recordings, pictures, archival data, and so on.

Confirmability

The final characteristic that Guba (1981) addresses is the **confirmability** of the data, or the neutrality or objectivity of the data that has been collected. Guba argues that the following two steps can be taken to address this issue:

- *Practice triangulation* (discussed in Chapter 4), whereby a variety of data sources and different methods are compared with one another to cross-check data.
- *Practice reflexivity*; that is, to intentionally reveal underlying assumptions or biases that cause the researcher to formulate a set of questions in a particular way and to present findings in a particular way. One technique for doing this is to keep a journal in which reflections/musings are recorded on a regular basis. Key Concepts Box 5–1 lists Guba's criteria for validity of qualitative research.

KEY CONCEPTS BOX 5–1

Guba's Criteria for Validity of Qualitative Research

CRITERIA	DEFINITION	STRATEGIES
Credibility	The researcher's ability to take into account the complexities that present themselves in a study and to deal with patterns that are not easily explained.	Do prolonged participation at study site. Do persistent observation. Do peer debriefing. Practice triangulation. Collect "slice-of-life" data items. Do member checks. Establish structural corroboration or coherence. Establish referential adequacy.
Transferability	The researcher's belief that everything is context-bound.	Collect detailed descriptive data. Develop detailed descriptions of the context.
Dependability	The stability of the data.	Overlap methods. Establish an audit trail.
Confirmability	The neutrality or objectivity of the data collected.	Practice triangulation. Practice reflexivity.

Source: Adapted from "Criteria for assessing the trustworthiness of naturalistic inquiries," by E. G. Guba, 1981, *Educational Communication and Technology, 2*(1), pp. 75–91.

Maxwell's Criteria for Validity of Qualitative Research

More recently, Maxwell (1992) has adopted a stance more consistent with that of Wolcott (1990), that is, "that **understanding** is a more fundamental concept for qualitative research than validity" (p. 281; emphasis added). Maxwell's typology based on understanding includes *descriptive validity, interpretive validity, theoretical validity, generalizability,* and *evaluative validity.*

Descriptive Validity

Maxwell (1992) proposes that **descriptive validity**, or factual accuracy, is fundamental to any qualitative, descriptive account:

> The first concern of most qualitative researchers is with the factual accuracy of their account—that is, that they are not making up or distorting things they saw and heard. If you report that an informant made a particular statement in an interview, is this correct? (pp. 285–286)

According to this criterion, any matters related to descriptive validity could be validated by checking with the informant (or the audio or video recorded account of the interview) that the quote that has been reproduced in the account is correct.

For example, in a study I was working on related to documenting the implementation of the National Council of Teachers of Mathematics (NCTM) Standards, I conducted interviews with teachers, principals, students, and district superintendents throughout the United States and Canada. At one of these sites, the superintendent responded to a question about how best to change the way high school teachers teach math in the following way: "I think that the only way to change the way high school math teachers teach math is to line them up and shoot them!" In a case study I wrote about the site, I used the quote to illustrate the frustration the superintendent felt toward the implementation of the NCTM Standards in high schools in the district. When the account was shared with the participants in the study to check the accuracy of the story, the superintendent had a violent reaction to the quote. He responded to me that he never said such a thing and that the account bordered on "tabloid journalism."

To check the descriptive validity of the account, I returned to the taped interview, the transcript of the interview, and to my field notes and the field notes of my co-researcher who was present at the interview. Sure enough, the quote was accurate, and I felt justified in incorporating it into the account. The project director, however, was more concerned about the "potential harm" of the quote, and in a subsequent draft of the case study the account was "paraphrased." Nevertheless, I had established the descriptive validity of a questionable section of the account by returning to data sources to double-check the accuracy of what was said by whom.

Interpretive Validity

Maxwell (1992) describes **interpretive validity** as the concern researchers have with the meaning attributed to behaviors by the people who have been studied; that is, it is concerned with what is commonly called the "participants' perspective":

> Interpretive accounts are grounded in the language of the people studied and rely as much as possible on their own words and concepts. The issue, again, is not the appropriateness of these concepts for the account, but their accuracy as applied to the perspective of the individuals included in the account. (p. 289)

To return to the story of the superintendent who was upset with my use of the "shoot the math teachers" quote, the issue was also related to interpretive validity. How might someone at the site reading the account interpret the language of "line them up and shoot them"? For example, a high school math teacher in the district might interpret the remark as an indication that all high school math teachers in the district will be fired—literally! Indeed, this was not the superintendent's intent, and that alone was a good enough reason to change the account and forgo the use of the quote.

Theoretical Validity

Theoretical validity refers to the ability of the research report to explain the phenomenon that has been studied and described:

> Theoretical validity thus refers to an account's validity as a theory of some phenomenon. Any theory has two components: the concepts or categories that the theory employs, and the relationships that are thought to exist among the concepts. (Maxwell, 1992, p. 291)

For example, to return to my superintendent's story, the language used by the superintendent to describe the difficult nature of changing high school math teaching might be labeled as an act that perpetuates the traditional power relationships that exist in school districts and the resistance to educational reform efforts in general. For this interpretation to be theoretically valid, the reader of the account would need to apply a theoretical construct to the description and, based on that theory, extrapolate to other aspects of the school community.

Generalizability

According to Maxwell, there are two aspects of **generalizability**: generalizability within the community that has been studied (internal generalizability) and generalizability to settings that were not studied by the researcher (external generalizability). Internal generalizability is more important than external generalizability because qualitative researchers (and action researchers) rarely make claims about the external generalizability of their research (Maxwell, 1992).

For example, my reliance on the data I had collected through an interview with the superintendent may have had descriptive and interpretive validity, but I may have missed other aspects of the superintendent's perspective that were not evident during the interview. In this case, the internal generalizability of the account was threatened by the interpretation of the interview. However, by inviting the superintendent to respond to the account, I was able to add to the superintendent's perspective in his own words and to increase the internal generalizability of the account.

The relevance of generalizability will be discussed in greater detail later in this chapter.

Evaluative Validity

Evaluative validity has to do with whether the researcher was objective enough to report the data in as unbiased a way as possible, rather than making judgments and evaluations of the data. No account is immune to questions of whether the teacher researcher was focusing on being evaluative instead of being concerned with describing and understanding the phenomenon that was studied. Clearly, the superintendent thought that I had fabricated the "shoot them" quote to make an evaluative statement about the superintendent and the district. I, on the other hand, maintained that my purpose in doing the research was to increase our understanding of the phenomenon under investigation—not to evaluate the mathematics programs

CRITERIA	DEFINITION
Maxwell's Criteria for Validity of Qualitative Research	
Descriptive validity	Factual accuracy.
Interpretive validity	Concern for the participants' perspective.
Theoretical validity	The ability of the research report to explain the phenomenon that has been studied and described.
Generalizability	*Internal generalizability:* Generalizability within the community that has been studied.
	External generalizability: Generalizability to settings that were not studied by the researcher.
Evaluative validity	Whether the researcher was able to present the data without being evaluative or judgmental.

Source: Adapted from "Understanding and validity in qualitative research," by J. A. Maxwell, 1992, *Harvard Educational Review*, 62(3), pp. 279–300.

in the district. Key Concepts Box 5–2 shows Maxwell's criteria for validity of qualitative research.

Anderson, Herr, and Nihlen's Criteria for Validity in Action Research

For most qualitative researchers, it is helpful to apply words such as *trustworthiness* and *understanding* to indicate the validity of our research. Using these criteria provides us with an opportunity (and challenge) to ensure that our research satisfies professional standards. However, Anderson, Herr, and Nihlen (1994) argued that action researchers need a system for judging the quality of their inquiries that is specifically tailored to their classroom-based research projects:

> If practitioner researchers are to be accepted in a larger dialogue about education, they must develop some inquiry criteria for their research. This is not to say that they need to justify themselves by the same inquiry criteria as academic research, but rather that they must make the case for a different conception of validity. This conception of validity should respond to the purposes and conditions of practitioner research and the uniqueness of its contribution to the dialogue. (p. 29)

To this end, Anderson and colleagues (1994) offered the following criteria for the validity of action research: *democratic validity, outcome validity, process validity, catalytic validity,* and *dialogic validity.*

Democratic Validity

Democratic validity requires that the multiple perspectives of all the participants in the study (teachers, principals, parents, and students) have been accurately represented. The question for teacher researchers will be how to ensure that participants' multiple perspectives are captured.

One way to ensure that there is democratic validity to an action research study will be to involve teachers and administrators in a collaborative effort with participants representing the group being studied. Make sure "the problems emerge from a particular context and solutions are appropriate to that context" (Cunningham, 1983, p. 30).

Outcome Validity

Outcome validity requires that the action emerging from a particular study leads to the successful resolution of the problem that was being studied; that is, your study can be considered valid if you learn something that can be applied to the subsequent research cycle. For example, Jack Reston's study of Eastview's absenteeism policy (see Chapter 7) led to a number of "findings" that affected the development of a new policy. These findings included a need to address:

- The "respectfulness of students."
- Issues related to "feeling safe" in a school.
- The reteaching of conflict management skills.
- The feeling of children in the upper grades that school rules were unfair.
- Student perception that absenteeism added to the image of being "bad."
- The fact that 75 percent of the general school population and students with excessive absenteeism had attended the school for more than two years.

All of these outcomes led to action that has helped to address the school's absenteeism problems.

Process Validity

Process validity requires that a study has been conducted in a "dependable" and "competent" manner. It is possible in any study to find support for any feasible perspective. However, we ought to engage in research processes that help us combat the tendency to present our studies as only glowing validations of existing exemplary practices! One way to address this issue is to be vigilant in reflecting on the suitability of your data collection techniques and to modify your strategies if the data you are collecting are not answering your questions.

Catalytic Validity

The criteria of **catalytic validity** require that the participants in a study are moved to take action on the basis of their heightened understanding of the subject of the study. The results of your study should serve as a "catalyst" for action! According to this schema, your action research effort is valid if it moves you and others involved to action (see Chapter 7, "Action Planning for Educational Change").

Dialogic Validity

Dialogic comes from the word *dialogue*, to have a conversation. Thus, **dialogic validity** involves having a critical conversation with others about your research findings and practices. Dialogic validity requires that the "goodness" of the research is established by application of a peer review process (similar to what already exists in traditional publication circles). For example, the teacher researchers with whom I work use an electronic bulletin board as a venue to share their research with the wider (cyberspace) professional community.

See Key Concepts Box 5–3 for Anderson's criteria for validity of action research.

KEY CONCEPTS BOX 5–3

Anderson's Criteria for Validity of Action Research

CRITERIA	TEST QUESTION
Democratic validity	Have the multiple perspectives of all of the individuals in the study been accurately represented?
Outcome validity	Did the action emerging from the study lead to the successful resolution of the problem?
Process validity	Was the study conducted in a dependable and competent manner?
Catalytic validity	Were the results of the study a catalyst for action?
Dialogic validity	Was the study reviewed by peers?

Wolcott's Strategies for Ensuring the Validity of Action Research

Taken in concert with the previous discussion about validity criteria, the following strategies provide teacher researchers with practical options for making sure their research is the best it can be (adapted from Wolcott, 1994).

Talk Little; Listen a Lot

This strategy suggests that teacher researchers who are conducting interviews, asking questions, or engaging children, parents, and colleagues in discussions about the problem being studied ought to carefully monitor the ratio of listening to talking. For example, interviewing children can be difficult work—our best thought-out questions elicit painfully brief replies, and we are left wondering what to do next. As teachers we are in the business of talking for a living, so it comes quite naturally to us to jump in with our own answer for the child. The trustworthiness of our inquiries will be enhanced if we can bite our tongue, think of some other probing questions, and wait patiently (one thousand . . . two thousand . . . three thousand . . .). As a teacher I have never been very comfortable with silence in my classroom, particularly when I thought that I had asked an engaging question. My advice is to be patient and allow the respondents time to respond. Avoid being your own best informant.

Record Observations Accurately

When conducting classroom research, recording observations while you are teaching is nearly impossible. However, you should record observations as soon as possible following a teaching episode to accurately capture the essence of what transpired. Although audio and video recordings can assist with our efforts to record accurately, there will still be many occasions when, as participant observers, we have to rely on our field notes, our journals, or our memories. And for me, relying on my memory is becoming an increasingly scary thing!

Begin Writing Early

In a work day that is already crunched by the pressures of time, finding time to write in journals is often difficult. However, if we rely solely on our memories of what has been happening in our classrooms over an extended period of time, we are likely to fall victim to writing romanticized versions of classroom and school life. Make time to write down your reflections. The act of writing down your recollections of a teaching episode or observation will make evident to you what blanks need to be filled in, for example, what questions need to be asked the next day or what should be the focus of your observations.

Let Readers "See" for Themselves

Include primary data in any account to let the readers of your action research accounts (colleagues, principals, university professors) see the data for themselves. As Wolcott (1994) suggests, "In striking the delicate balance between providing too much detail and too little, I would rather err on the side of too much; conversely, between overanalyzing and underanalyzing data, I would rather say too little" (p. 350). This is particularly true in a schoolwide action research effort in which you are seeking support for possible change based on data that you must present to colleagues who may not have had a central role in the conduct of the study. When sharing your research reports with colleagues, let them see the data. This may mean using charts, graphs, photographs, film—whatever you have collected. In doing so, you will bring the recipient of your work along in the process and perhaps earn their buy-in to the next action research cycle. Showing can be more persuasive than telling.

Report Fully

In our quest to find neat answers and solutions to our problems, it is often easy to avoid keeping track of discrepant events and data. Just when we think we know the answer, some data come along to shatter the illusion of having neatly resolved the problem! We do not need to be fearful of discrepant data. After all, it is all grist for the research mill, and although we do not need to report everything, it is helpful to keep track of the discrepant data and to seek further explanation to understand what is happening in our classrooms/schools.

Be Candid

Teacher researchers should be candid about their work, and if writing a narrative that they hope to publish or share with a broader audience, they should make explicit any biases that they may have about the inquiry they have undertaken. Teacher researchers should also make explicit the things about which they have made judgments, because it is easy to slip into a narrative that seeks to validate one's position. Being candid may also provide an opportunity to be explicit about events that occurred during the study and that may have affected the outcomes. For example, high student turnover rates may provide an explanation for fluctuating test scores.

Seek Feedback

It is always a good idea to seek feedback from colleagues (and perhaps even students, parents, volunteers, and administrators) on your written study. Other readers will help raise questions about what you as the writer will have taken for granted. They will raise questions about the accuracy of the account and help you to go back to your classroom in your quest to get the story right (or at least, not all wrong).

Write Accurately

Once you have written a description of your action research, it is a good idea to read the account aloud or to ask a close colleague to read the account carefully to look for contradictions in the text. Often we are too close to the investigation to really see the contradictions that may be blatantly obvious to an outsider. Although we are assuming in this discussion that

Wolcott's Strategies for Ensuring the Validity of Action Research

_____ Talk little; listen a lot.
_____ Record accurately.
_____ Begin writing early.
_____ Let readers "see" for themselves.
_____ Report fully.
_____ Be candid.
_____ Seek feedback.
_____ Write accurately.

Source: Adapted from Wolcott, H. F. (1994). *Transforming Qualitative Data*, pp. 348–370.

teacher researchers will generate a written account of their action research efforts, we will see in Chapter 8 some alternative formats that can be used for sharing the outcomes of an action research effort. Nevertheless, the accuracy of the account (whether written or "performed") is critical to the validity of the study. (For further discussion of these points and a discussion of "When It Really Matters, Does Validity Really Matter?" see Wolcott, 1994, pp. 348–370.) See Research in Action Checklist 5–1 for Wolcott's strategies for ensuring the validity of qualitative action research.

Reliability

In everyday English, reliability means dependability or trustworthiness. The term means essentially the same thing with respect to measurement. Basically, **reliability** is the degree to which a test consistently measures whatever it measures. The more reliable a test is, the more confidence we can have that the scores obtained from the administration of the test are essentially the same scores that would be obtained if the test were readministered. An unreliable test is essentially useless; if a test is unreliable, then scores for a given sample would be expected to be different every time the test was administered. If an intelligence test was unreliable, for example, then a student scoring an IQ of 120 today might score an IQ of 140 tomorrow, and a 95 the day after tomorrow. If the test was reliable, and if the student's IQ was 110, then we would not expect his or her score to fluctuate too greatly from testing to testing; a score of 105 would not be unusual, but a score of 145 would be very unlikely. If you have ever administered standardized tests to students, you will be familiar with the reliability coefficients that are presented in the administration manuals. The numbers are meant to convey to the test user the peace of mind that, if the test were administered on a future occasion, individual students would score roughly the same.

Reliability is expressed numerically, usually as a coefficient; a high coefficient indicates high reliability. If a test were perfectly reliable, the coefficient would be 1.00; this would mean that a student's score perfectly reflected her or his true status with respect to the variable being measured. However, no test is perfectly reliable. Scores are invariably affected by errors of measurement resulting from a variety of causes. High reliability indicates

PEARSON myeducationlab

Go to the Assignments and Activities section of Topic #3, *Data Collection*, in the MyEducationLab for your course and complete the activity titled "Evaluating Reliability." In this activity, you will learn more about how to measure the reliability of qualitative data.

minimum error variance; if a test has high reliability, then the effect of errors of measurement has been reduced. Errors of measurement affect scores in a random fashion; some scores may be increased while others are decreased. Errors of measurement can be caused by characteristics of the test itself (ambiguous test items, for example, that some students just happen to interpret correctly), by conditions of administration (directions not properly followed, for example), by the current status of the persons taking the test (some may be tired, others unmotivated), or by a combination of any of the above. High reliability indicates that these sources of error have been eliminated as much as possible.

Errors of measurement that affect reliability are random errors; systematic or constant errors affect validity. If an achievement test was too difficult for a given group of students, all scores would be systematically lowered; the test would have low validity for that group (remember, "valid for whom?"). The test might, however, yield consistent scores (i.e., might be reliable); in other words, the scores might be systematically lowered in the same way every time. A given student whose "true" achievement score was 80 and who scored 60 on the test (invalidity) might score 60 every time he took the test (reliability). This illustrates an interesting relationship between validity and reliability: a valid test is always reliable but a reliable test is not necessarily valid. In other words, if a test is measuring what it is supposed to be measuring, it will be reliable and do so every time, but a reliable test can consistently measure the wrong thing and be invalid!

For qualitatively oriented action researchers the message is simple: As you think about the results of your inquiry, consider whether you think that your data would be consistently collected if the same techniques were utilized over time. Or if you are working as a member of a team that is collecting data, work out how to resolve any differences among observers so you can agree on the descriptive accuracy of an account.

The Difference Between Reliability and Validity

To review, reliability "is the degree to which a test consistently measures whatever it is measuring" (Gay et al., 2009, p. 378). And validity is "the degree to which a test measures what it is supposed to measure" (Gay et al., 2009, p. 375). Reliability, however, is not the same thing as validity. Remember, a valid test that measures what it purports to measure will do so consistently over time. A reliable test may consistently measure the wrong thing.

Generalizability

Historically, research in education concerned itself with **generalizability**, a term that refers to the applicability of findings to settings and contexts different from the one in which they were obtained; that is, based on the behavior of a small group of individuals, researchers try to explain the behavior of a wider group of people. This view of generalizability, however, is not directly applicable to teacher action research—even though there is still a mindset among some teachers, administrators, and policy makers that the findings of action research studies should be transferable. Many of these people believe that we should be able to generalize from the outcomes of a study in one classroom, one school, and one district to all similar classrooms in the state or country. This is not the nature of the research in which we are engaged.

The goal of action research is to understand what is happening in your school or classroom and to determine what might improve things in that context (Sagor, 1992). Therefore, action researchers don't need to worry about the generalizability of data because they are not seeking to define ultimate truths. However, one of the reviewers for this book had the following reaction to this dismissal of generalizability:

> I fear, however, that this approach lends credence to many of my colleagues' beliefs that action research is unscientific, biased, and not generalizable. Some go so far as to call it "garbage research." The question that they often pose is what good is research that is not generalizable? (Anonymous reviewer)

Indeed, action research has faced a self-esteem problem among many "academics" who question the worthiness of the activity as "scientific" inquiry. Confronted with a similar argument, Stringer (1996) offered the following response:

> Whether or not action research is accepted as "scientific" depends on the way in which science is defined. Certainly it is, in one sense, rigorously empirical, insofar as it requires people to define clearly and observe the phenomenon under investigation. What is also evident, however, is that action research does not follow the carefully prescribed procedures that have become inscribed as scientific method. (p. 145)

Stringer goes on to argue that in spite of the success of the scientific method in advancing our knowledge in the "hard sciences," the applicability of this method to inquiries of human behavior has met with little success in increasing the predictability of human behavior. Other textbooks on educational research agree that action research is a different type of inquiry entirely and as such should not be focused on generalizability. For example, Vockell and Asher (1996) state:

> Action research refers to the practical application of the scientific method or other forms of disciplined inquiry to the process of dealing with everyday problems. It is particularly focused on teachers and other educators doing action research in order to make their particular educational activities more productive. It is more concerned with specific classes and programs and less concerned with generalized conclusions about other classes and programs. (p. 10)

Action research is not "garbage research" at the classroom/school level. As teacher researchers we are challenging the experimental researcher's view that the only credible research is that which can be generalized to a larger population. Many examples of teacher research are generalizable to other classroom settings, but the power of action research is not in its generalizability. It is in the relevance of the findings to the researcher or the audience of the research.

Personal Bias in the Conduct of Action Research

Related to the issue of generalizability of research is the issue of personal bias. If we conduct our research in a systematic, disciplined manner, we will go a long way toward minimizing personal bias in our findings. However, in an intimate activity such as action research, it is a challenge to remain "objective" and open, to look into the mirror of our findings and reflect on what we see. It is relatively easy in any research, should we so choose, to collect data that simply validates our existing practices, to maintain the status quo, to pat ourselves on our collective backs, and to ignore discrepant data or discredit research results. The same can be said for reviewing related literature—we may choose to review only the literature that supports a particular thesis that we wish to promote. None of these are acceptable approaches for reconciling the biased collection of data.

Propositions

One way for teacher researchers to get in touch with their biases about the subject they are investigating is to develop a list of propositions about what they think they will find during the course of their investigations. These propositions provide a window into the belief system and personal biases that can, and often do, creep into the investigation. These statements also provide a good starting point for examining teacher researchers' theories about teaching and learning and for understanding where those theories came from.

For example, a teacher who wishes to investigate the effects of manipulatives on student achievement in mathematics may generate propositions such as:

1. The use of manipulatives when teaching mathematics will increase students' conceptual knowledge of mathematics.
2. The use of manipulatives will help overcome math anxiety because the children will have more fun doing math.
3. The use of manipulatives will improve students' basic number facts skills.

Teacher researchers will find it useful to examine their propositions closely so that they can explore what they believe they will find before they start their investigations and what they might do to ensure that they remain vigilant in the fidelity with which they collect their data (thus addressing the concerns of researcher bias). Similarly, this activity helps to clarify teacher researchers' conceptual frameworks for their investigations by making explicit the theories that affect what they do before, during, and after the research.

Summary

1. Attention to the three important concepts of validity, reliability, and generalizability will help teacher researchers ensure the quality of their work. These concepts are also important for teacher researchers who are reviewing published and unpublished research.
2. Qualitative researchers, action researchers, and quantitative researchers disagree about the value of applying these concepts of validity, reliability, and generalizability to qualitatively oriented action research.
3. Teacher researchers must understand the meanings of validity, reliability, and generalizability to be knowledgeable consumers of research, as well as producers of research that we hope will be trustworthy and persuasive in their own eyes and in the eyes of their audience.

Validity

4. Validity is "the degree to which scientific observations actually measure or record what they purport to measure" (Pelto & Pelto, 1978, p. 33).

5. Validity in quantitative research can be thought of in terms of internal validity and external validity.

6. Internal validity is the degree to which observed differences on the dependent variable are a direct result of manipulation of the independent variable, not some other variable.

7. External validity is the degree to which study results are generalizable, or applicable, to groups and environments outside of the research setting.

8. Action researchers do not make claims to context-free knowledge (that is, by its very nature action research is based in the context of our own classrooms and schools); issues of credibility, validity, and reliability in action research are measured by the willingness of teacher researchers (and the stakeholders in our studies) "to act on the results of the action research" (Greenwood & Levin, 2000, p. 98).

9. The validity of our action research depends on whether the actual solution to a problem (our planned intervention) actually solves our problem.

10. Guba (1981) argued that the trustworthiness of qualitative inquiry could be established by addressing the following characteristics of a study: credibility, transferability, dependability, and confirmability.

11. The credibility of a study refers to the researcher's ability to take into account the complexities that present themselves in a study and to deal with patterns that are not easily explained.

12. Transferability refers to qualitative researchers' beliefs that everything they study is context bound and that the goal of their work is not to develop "truth" statements that can be generalized to larger groups of people.

13. Dependability refers to the stability of the data.

14. Confirmability of the data refers to the neutrality or objectivity of the data that have been collected.

15. Maxwell (1992) has adopted a stance that understanding is a more fundamental concept for qualitative research than validity and has proposed the following typology: descriptive validity, interpretive validity, theoretical validity, generalizability, and evaluative validity.

16. Descriptive validity, or factual accuracy, is fundamental to any qualitative, descriptive account. According to this criterion, any matters related to descriptive validity could be validated by checking with the informant, or the audio or video recorded account of the interview that the quote that has been reproduced in the account is correct.

17. Interpretive validity refers to the concern researchers have with the meaning attributed to behaviors by the people who have been studied; that is, it is concerned with what is commonly called the "participants' perspective."

18. Theoretical validity refers to the ability of the research report to explain the phenomenon that has been studied and described. "Theoretical validity thus refers to an account's validity as a theory of some phenomenon" (Maxwell, 1992, p. 291).

19. Generalizability. According to Maxwell, there are two aspects of generalizability: generalizability within the community that has been studied (internal generalizability) and generalizability to settings that were not studied by the researcher (external generalizability).

20. Evaluative validity has to do with whether the researcher was objective enough to report the data in as unbiased a way as possible, rather than making judgments and evaluations of the data. No account is immune to questions of whether the teacher researcher was focusing on being evaluative instead of being concerned with describing and understanding the phenomenon that was studied.

21. Anderson, Herr, and Nihlen (1994) have proposed that action researchers need a system for judging the quality of their inquiries that is specifically tailored to their classroom-based research projects and includes the criteria of democratic validity, outcome validity, process validity, catalytic validity, and dialogic validity.

22. Democratic validity requires that the multiple perspectives of all the participants in the study (teachers, principals, parents, and students) have been accurately represented. One way to ensure that there is democratic validity to an action research study is to involve teachers and administrators in a collaborative effort with participants representing the group being studied.

23. Outcome validity requires that the action emerging from a particular study leads to the successful resolution of the problem that was being studied; that is, your study can be considered valid if you learn something that can be applied to the subsequent research cycle.

24. Process validity requires that a study has been conducted in a "dependable" and "competent" manner. One way to address this criterion is to be vigilant in reflecting on the suitability of your data collection techniques and to modify your strategies if the data you are collecting are not answering your questions.

25. Catalytic validity requires that the participants in a study are moved to take action on the basis of their heightened understanding of the subject of the study. That is, the results of your study should serve as a catalyst for action.

26. Dialogic validity involves having a critical conversation with others about your research findings and practices. Dialogic validity requires that the "goodness" of the research is established by application of a peer review process.

27. Given this book's focus on qualitatively oriented action research, teacher researchers should pay close attention to the following strategies based on Wolcott's (1994) strategies for ensuring validity of action research: talk little, listen a lot; record observations accurately; begin writing early; let readers "see" for themselves; report fully; be candid; seek feedback; and write accurately.

28. Talk Little; Listen a Lot. This strategy suggests that teacher researchers who are conducting interviews ought to carefully monitor the ratio of listening to talking. The trustworthiness of our inquiries will be enhanced if we can bite our tongue, think of some other probing questions, and wait patiently. Avoid being your own best informant.

29. Record Observations Accurately. When conducting research in your own classroom, recording observations while you are teaching is nearly impossible. However, you should record observations as soon as possible following a teaching episode to accurately capture the essence of what transpired.

30. Begin Writing Early. The act of writing down your recollections of a teaching episode or observation will make evident to you what blanks need to be filled in, for example, what questions need to be asked the next day or what should be the focus of your observations.

31. Let Readers "See" for Themselves. Include primary data in any account to let the readers of your action research accounts "see" the data for themselves. This may mean using charts, graphs, and photographs—whatever you have collected—to provide the reader with a window into your research. Showing can be more persuasive than telling.

32. Report Fully. In our quest to find neat answers and solutions to our problems, it is often easy to avoid keeping track of discrepant events and data. We do not need to be fearful

of discrepant data that may help us to seek further explanation to understand what is happening in our classrooms and schools.

33. Be Candid. Teacher researchers should be candid about their work, and if writing a narrative that they hope to publish or share with a broader audience, they should make explicit any biases that they may have about the inquiry they have undertaken.

34. Seek Feedback. It is always a good idea to seek feedback from colleagues on your written study. Other readers will raise questions about what you as the writer will have taken for granted and about the accuracy of the account.

35. Write Accurately. Once you have written a description of your action research, it is a good idea to read the account aloud or to ask a close colleague to read the account carefully to look for contradictions in the text.

Reliability

36. Reliability is the degree to which a test consistently measures whatever it measures. The more reliable a test is, the more confidence we can have that the scores obtained from the administration of the test are essentially the same scores that would be obtained if the test were readministered.

37. Remember, a valid test is always reliable but a reliable test is not necessarily valid. In other words, if a test is measuring what it is supposed to be measuring, it will be reliable and do so every time, but a reliable test can consistently measure the wrong thing and be invalid!

38. For qualitatively oriented action researchers the message is simple: As you think about the results of your inquiry, consider whether you think that your data would be consistently collected if the same techniques were utilized over time.

Generalizability

39. Historically, research in education concerned itself with generalizability, a term that refers to the applicability of findings to settings and contexts different from the one in which they were obtained; that is, based on the behavior of a small group of individuals, researchers try to explain the behavior of a wider group of people. This view of generalizability, however, is not directly applicable to teacher action research.

40. The goal of action research is to understand what is happening in your school or classroom and to determine what might improve things in that context (Sagor, 1992). Therefore, action researchers don't need to worry about the generalizability of findings because they are not seeking to define ultimate truths.

Personal Bias in the Conduct of Action Research

41. Related to the issue of generalizability of research is the issue of personal bias. If we conduct our research in a systematic, disciplined manner, we will go a long way toward minimizing personal bias in our findings.

42. Propositions. One way for teacher researchers to get in touch with their biases about the subject they are investigating is to develop a list of propositions about what they think they will find during the course of their investigations. These propositions provide a window into the belief system and personal biases that can, and often do, creep into the investigation. These statements also provide a good starting point for examining teacher researchers' theories about teaching and learning and for understanding where those theories came from.

Tasks

1. Describe how you have addressed the issues of validity, reliability, and generalizability in your action research inquiry. Specifically, how will you know that your planned intervention actually solves your problem?

2. Develop a list of propositions about the subject you are investigating (see the section on "Personal Bias in the Conduct of Action Research"). What do each of these propositions tell you about your belief system and biases?

6

Data Analysis and Interpretation

After collecting your data, the next steps in the action research process are to review what you have learned and to draw conclusions about what you think your data mean. This chapter provides guidelines and techniques for data analysis (the attempt to fully and accurately summarize and represent the data that has been collected) and data interpretation (the attempt to find meaning in that data, to answer the question "So what?").

After reading this chapter you should be able to:

1 Define data analysis and data interpretation.

2 Identify appropriate qualitative data analysis techniques for your action research project.

3 Identify appropriate quantitative data analysis and interpretation techniques for your action research project.

4 Identify appropriate qualitative data interpretation techniques for your action research project.

Emphasizing Learning by Deemphasizing Grades

LAUREN FAGEL, PAUL SWANSON,
JOHN GORLESKI, AND JOE SENESE
HIGHLAND PARK HIGH SCHOOL

Lauren Fagel, Paul Swanson, John Gorleski, and Joe Senese are all members of the Action Research Laboratory (ARL) at Highland Park High School (HPHS) near Chicago, Illinois. This project provides a good example of a team approach to collaborative action research and the kinds of analysis and interpretations that can flow from various data sources.

The scene is a common one for teachers: Papers are returned to students who immediately search for the grade, sigh, take out calculators, tabulate quarter grades, and then compare grades with their neighbors! The rich comments and constructive feedback on the papers usually go unheeded—the all-important grade is the prime focus of the students' gazes!

This study was conducted at Highland Park High School, one of two large public high schools in Township District 113. Our student population consists of 1509 students with an ethnic makeup of 3% Asian American, 2% African American, 13% Hispanic American, and 82% White. Ninety-two percent of the student body is college-bound, and the parent community strongly encourages high student achievement. Many students enroll in Advanced Placement (AP) classes, strive to become members of the Highland Park Honor Society, and compete to become senior class valedictorian or salutatorian. This ARL group, which included an English teacher, a health teacher, and a history teacher, was concerned about the immense amount of pressure placed on students to receive good grades. We questioned the number system teachers use to assign grades, and we wondered whether grades actually represent what students have learned. We discussed the role of the teacher as assessor, questioning whether we act as true evaluators of student work or simply as "sorters" of students. We lamented the all-encompassing role grades play in the HPHS academic environment. We decided to conduct research in this area, investigating how a deemphasis of grades could, in turn, emphasize learning in the classroom. The research questions were as follows:

1. How does an elimination of number and letter grades throughout the year (with the exception of quarter and semester grades) affect student attitudes toward learning?
2. How does an elimination of number and letter grades throughout the year (with the exception of quarter and semester grades) affect our teaching styles, use of assessments, and choice of curriculum materials?
3. How does an extensive use of student self-assessment affect student growth, improvement, and achievement over the course of a school year?
4. How does deemphasizing grades allow us to enrich our teaching?

We began the year by informing students of our involvement in the ARL and presenting a rationale for deemphasizing grades and emphasizing learning. Teachers were still required to assign a grade at the end of each quarter, and students were curious about how their final grade would be determined. We explained how the system would work and followed up by asking students to write down what they thought they would like about the system, what they thought they would not like, and what they did not understand. A letter was also sent home to parents explaining the system and encouraging them to contact us with any questions, concerns, or comments.

Approximately once a month, we met as a team for an entire day of reflection, discussion, brainstorming, and future planning. We quickly found out that certain aspects of our system were working, while others needed refining, and still others needed to be eliminated or replaced.

With the exception of one major project during third quarter, we returned all student work without a number or letter grade. Instead, we used several different types of markings to indicate to students how well they performed on a particular assessment. On homework assignments, including journal entries, we wrote comments and then assigned a u, u1, or u2. On long-term projects, we either assessed different aspects of the final product on a scale of 1 to 5 and wrote one or two sentences to the student, or we did not use any scale and instead wrote extensive comments. On tests and quizzes we marked objective items wrong when appropriate, assigned a u, u1, or u2 to short-answer and other types of subjective questions, and wrote general comments throughout the test or quiz. Most students were able to tell how well they performed on a particular assessment, and only a very few students persisted by asking us how our comments would translate into a letter grade. In these cases, we found that students were less argumentative than our students had been in the previous year (prior to deemphasizing grades). This year we found ourselves more open to criticism about the way test questions were written and exams were formatted because students seemed to be more genuine in their questioning. They were not arguing for points because there were no points! This created a more community-like setting in the classroom, with all of us aiming for the same goal—learning.

Self-Assessment Worksheet

After some modification during the first semester, we adopted a self-assessment worksheet that encouraged students to reflect on their progress periodically throughout the year. The worksheet included the following headings: Content Mastery, Skill Mastery, Completion of Work, and In-Class Activity. This worksheet evolved into an end of quarter self-evaluation that asked students to select a grade they felt they deserved and then to provide evidence by referring to specific assignments, tests, quizzes, and projects. Finally, by the end of the school year, we were using an end-of-quarter evaluation sheet that listed the student's mid-quarter grade range, the marks they received on specific homework assignments completed since the previous student-teacher-parent conference,

and a general comment for each major test, quiz, and project they had completed since mid-quarter. Students' grades were then assigned without holding an end-of-quarter conference.

Another important part of this project was that students accepted responsibility for their grades and participated in developing criteria that would be used to assess the quality of work. The following criteria are an example of what evolved from involving students in the decision-making process:

"A" Criteria

Participates actively in class
Shows a great deal of effort
Does all homework
Does well on tests
Is on time for class
Shows respect and works well with others
Is always prepared

"B" Criteria

Shows good participation
Misses no more than 1 to 2 assignments
Has 1 to 2 tardies
Shows good knowledge of material
Has no unauthorized absences
Shows some effort
Demonstrates respect for others

"C" Criteria

Demonstrates some knowledge of material and
    passes all tests
Work is frequently late or not turned in
Rarely participates in class
Shows little effort
Has several tardies
Has unauthorized absences
Is frequently not prepared

"D" Criteria

Doesn't show knowledge of material and performs
    poorly on tests
Has large number of assignments not turned in
Shows no effort or participation
Shows little respect for others
Has several unauthorized absences

Is disruptive in class
Is often tardy

By using this rubric, students had guidelines they could use as a reference to accurately assess their performance. The onus on defending a grade now became the students' responsibility and not the teachers'. If students could justify their self-evaluation grade, based on the criteria we had agreed to, that was the grade they received. As a result of this ownership, students had few complaints regarding their grades.

Student-Teacher Conferences

Students appeared to have a difficult time assigning and defending their grades during student-teacher conferences. For many years, students had been conditioned to accept the grades given to them by a teacher without question. They had rarely been asked to participate actively in assigning their own grade. The most valuable part of these conferences was the opportunity to speak with all students and to get a sense of how they were feeling about the class in general. Often the discussion of grade came at the end of the conference and was the shortest part of the conversation. Students were asked to suggest a grade (before the teacher), but there was a sense that a guessing game was in progress as we tried to balance the teacher's expectations with those of individual students.

The data collected from surveys, observations, and interviews with children suggest that the majority of students were either happy with the grading system or neutral about it. A majority of students indicated that the alternative grading system did affect their academic preparation and performance in class (in a positive way), and that they had a more positive attitude toward the class.

Grades

As we reflected on grade distributions, comparing this year to the previous year, there appeared to be a significant increase in the number of students whose grades fell in the A/A minus range (55% this year compared with 27% last year). There is no way of knowing exactly what accounted for the increase of As and A minuses; however, we believe that students' involvement in deciding their own grade, as well as the less objective nature of the way grades were assigned (that is, not

entirely based on the percentages scored on tests), had something to do with the outcomes. We believe that the increased focus on personal learning, growth, and improvement that evolved from deemphasizing grades made it less likely for students to fail and more likely for students to accept responsibility for their learning and to provide the evidence that they had learned.

The end-of-year survey revealed that 71% of students agreed with the following statement: "I feel that the grading practices used in this course helped me to focus more on my learning than on my grade." Seventy-four percent agreed that "they would recommend that this teacher continue using these grading practices because they help students learn better." We believe that these kinds of statements indicate student support for our deemphasized grading practices and that learning can occur in an environment where the pressure to earn grades is reduced. Students made supporting comments such as these:

"I felt I could concentrate on education."
"It helped me concentrate on improving myself."
"It helps you focus more on information and less on what the teacher wants."
"It relieved a lot of stress and I was able to work at my ability without the competition of grades."
"In comparison to the traditional grading system, this system is the most effective way of assessing my level of performance."
"This method helps me perform best because it's personal to my needs."

It was very reassuring to us to see the pride that students showed and the importance they placed on giving accurate self-evaluation grades. The following two comments illustrate the integrity with which the majority of students approached this responsibility:

"I knew I had to be honest with myself."
"Integrity defines you, and if you die tomorrow, people won't remember your grades or your statistics; they remember how true and real you were with yourself."

We learned a tremendous amount through this research, but like any research we were left with more questions than we answered. For example:

- Is the total elimination of letter and number grades (with the exception of quarter and semester grades) the best way to deemphasize grades?

- Is there a way to deemphasize grades that requires less paperwork on the teacher's part? (After all, one of the things we learned through the implementation of this intervention is that grades are expedient and convenient for a harried teacher!)
- What is an appropriate role for students to play in determining their own grades?
- How can we deemphasize grades and still maintain very specific criteria/outcomes for students?

By far the most rewarding part of working on an action research team was the opportunity to learn and grow with a small group of teacher colleagues. This experience of mutual commitment provided a wonderful staff development experience; by working with these colleagues consistently throughout the year, we were able to explore new ideas and take risks in the classroom with a type of "safety net" in place. For that reason alone, as well as our desire to explore the new questions and challenges raised by our research, we will continue to conduct action research into the effectiveness of our teaching and grading practices.

Giving up grading practices and beliefs that we have held for years can be a very scary proposition. It is not always easy to turn over some of our control to others. Perhaps our first action research steps need to be "baby steps." This action research project freed us from the grading merry-go-round and provided a new way to address assessment issues. By taking these steps, we were able to devote less time to pencil pushing and calculator crunching and to spend more time with our most important job: helping our students reach their full potential as we strive to reach our full potential as teachers.

Perhaps the most difficult part of action research is the process of trying to make sense of the mountains of data collected over the course of the study. This task is often daunting for action researchers who, while engaged in the regular, ongoing collection of data, must change their focus and adopt a more analytical and interpretive lens. They must move beyond the description of the phenomenon they have studied and make sense of what they have learned.

The Highland Park High School example richly illustrates how a team of teachers worked together to increase their understanding of how deemphasizing grades could help reemphasize student learning. In so doing, the teachers were able to encapsulate the "findings" of their research into "sound bites" that could be shared with other teachers and participants.

Considering how to best proceed with data analysis and data interpretation is critical before, during, and after the action research process and will be impacted by the type of research you have conducted: qualitative, quantitative, or mixed-methods. It is important to think about "How am I going to make sense of this data?" prior to conducting the study to avoid collecting data that is not important or data that comes in a form that cannot be understood. Similarly, during the study, teacher researchers should reflect on what they are finding and how it can inform their ongoing data collection efforts. Finally, as the systematic collection of data concludes, teacher researchers should determine what they want to "celebrate" and share in their findings.

Ongoing Analysis and Reflection

Action research studies provide teacher researchers with data that can be used formatively and summatively; that is, much of the data collected during the study can be used to positively affect teaching throughout the study. For example, teachers have always reflected on their teaching before, during, and after a particular teaching episode—it's part of our professional disposition. Action research is no different. We can and should take time to analyze our data during the study to decide if what we are learning is what we had hoped to learn. For example, the HPHS team discovered early in their research that some aspects of their deemphasized grading system were working, whereas others needed to be refined or eliminated. Pausing to analyze and reflect during the action research process is essential.

Anderson, Herr, and Nihlen (1994) maintained that "it is very important to recognize that at various intervals you must stop gathering data and reflect on what you have thus far" (p. 155). For example, these authors suggested that teacher researchers answer two questions to guide their work and reflections:

1. Is your research question still answerable and worth answering?
2. Are your data collection techniques catching the kind of data you wanted and filtering out the data that you don't? (p. 155)

Similarly, Hendricks (2006) discusses the importance of *interim analysis*, a step in the action research process that allows the researcher to make changes to data collection strategies during the research based on the kinds of questions and issues that arise during the ongoing data analysis process. Consciously "pausing" during the investigation will allow you to reflect on what you are attending to and what you are leaving out. Such a reflective stance will continue to guide your efforts (in process) as well as to allow for early "hunches" about what you are seeing so far. As Anderson and colleagues (1994) suggested:

> Stopping periodically in the data collection process also allows you to see if you have any gaps in the data, holes where you need data to answer the questions. Seeing this early on in the research allows you to develop the correct techniques for a complete study. (p. 156)

Another way to think of this is in terms of Lewin's (1952) original action research model and the attention given to rethinking, reflecting, discussing, replanning, understanding, and learning during the action research process.

Avoid Premature Action

Although ongoing analysis and reflection is a natural part of the action research process, you should avoid premature actions based on early analysis and interpretation of data. Action researchers—especially those who are inexperienced—often make rash or impulsive decisions based on limited or no data. Neophyte teacher researchers engaged in the first systematic study of their own teaching tend to zealously collect, analyze, and interpret data in a rapid-fire fashion. Their efforts go awry as they become their own best informants and jump to hasty conclusions and impulsive actions.

The action research process takes time. Teacher researchers must be wary of the lure of quick-fix strategies and patient enough to avoid the pitfalls of basing actions on premature analysis. Rarely will a few days of observation provide enough insight to enact a quick-fix strategy! Although it is much easier to start a study with a preconceived notion about what you will find, it's a far greater test of patience, endurance, and integrity to let the action research inquiry slowly unfold over the course of a semester or two.

The Role of Analysis and Interpretation

You will reach a point in the research process where you will want to summarize what you have learned and what you think it means for your students. You will want to share your findings without having to share all of your data and use these findings to identify what will happen next in the action research process. This critical component of the action research process is called data analysis and interpretation, and it needs to be carefully thought out.

Data analysis is an attempt by the teacher researcher to summarize collected data in a dependable and accurate manner. The type of data you collect will determine the data analysis techniques you will use. For example, if you collect narrative, descriptive, and nonnumerical data, such as field notes from observations or interviews, questionnaires, or pictures, qualitative data analysis will be best suited for your needs. It is not possible to "number crunch" and reduce this type of data to a manageable form, as is the case in quantitative data analysis. However, at times quantitative data analysis will be the most appropriate way to summarize your findings, such as when you need to summarize test scores. In this chapter we will discuss how to analyze both qualitative and quantitative data sources.

After analyzing your data, you will be faced with the task of trying to understand it. **Data interpretation** is an attempt by the researcher to find meaning in the data, to answer the "So what?" question in terms of the implications of the study's findings. Put simply, analysis involves summarizing what's in the data, whereas interpretation involves making sense of—finding meaning in—that data.

Data analysis and interpretation are critical stages in the action research process that require the teacher researcher to both know and understand the data. When analyzing and interpreting data, challenge yourself to explore every possible angle and try to find patterns and seek out new understandings among the data. Remember Deborah South from the Chapter 1 vignette on "How to motivate unmotivated students"? At first, she was convinced that the only feasible interpretation of her data was that her class and her teaching were the causes of the dramatic drop in students' scores. After all, it was the only experience these 18 students had in common during the term! However, as Deborah revisited her data and as her fellow action researchers pushed her to examine other possibilities, it became clear that the homogeneous grouping of "low-achieving" and "unmotivated" students contributed to a "critical mass of negativity" in the classroom. As a result of her commitment to quality data analysis and interpretation, Deborah was able to use her action research findings to make a persuasive argument for the school principal to investigate other "interventions" that might more effectively address the problems of the "unmotivated" student.

PEARSON
myeducationlab

Go to the Assignments and Activities section of Topic #4, *Data Analysis and Interpretation*, in the MyEducationLab for your course and complete the activity titled "Organizing Data for Analysis." In this activity, you will have an opportunity to practice working with qualitative data.

Qualitative Data Organization

If data are to be thoroughly analyzed, they must be organized. Ideally, the teacher researcher will have carefully managed notes, records, and artifacts as they were collected; however, as a former classroom teacher, I know sometimes that chaos reigns! So, it is with this sensitivity to the realties of classroom life that I offer some additional organizational tips to "tidy up" your data, ensure their completeness, and make them easier to study. After the data are organized, the analysis can begin in earnest (see Figure 6–1, Data Organization Activities).

One way to proceed with analysis is to follow three iterative, or repeating, steps: reading/memoing, describing what is going on in the setting, and classifying research data. The process focuses on (1) becoming familiar with the data and identifying potential themes (i.e., reading/memoing); (2) examining the data in depth to provide detailed descriptions of the setting, participants, and activity (i.e., describing); and (3) categorizing and coding pieces of data and grouping them into themes (i.e., classifying).

- Write dates (month, day, year) on all notes.

- Sequence all notes with labels (e.g., 6th set of notes).

- Label notes according to type (such as observer's notes, memo to self, transcript from interview).

- Make two photocopies of all notes (field notes, transcripts etc.) and retain original copies.

- Organize computer files into folders according to data type and stages of analysis.

- Make backup copies of all files.

- Read through data and make sure all information is complete and legible before proceeding to analysis and interpretation.

- Begin to note themes and patterns that emerge.

FIGURE 6–1 *Data Organization Activities*

The interrelations among these steps are not necessarily linear. At the start of data analysis, the logical sequence of activities is from reading/memoing to description, to classifying, and finally to interpretation. However, as a researcher begins to internalize and reflect on the data, the initial ordered sequence may lose its structure and become more flexible. If you've ever been driving home pondering some issue or problem and out of the blue had a sudden flash of understanding that provides a solution, you have a sense of how qualitative data analysis takes place. Once you are *into* the data, it is not the three steps that lead to understanding; it is your ability to think, imagine, create, intuit, and analyze that guides the data analysis. Knowing the steps is not enough; the thinker, imaginer, and hypothesizer—that is, the teacher researcher—is the data analyzer, and the quality of the research analysis depends heavily on the intellectual qualities of the teacher researcher. Let me be very clear about this process: It is a process of digesting the contents of your qualitative data and finding related threads in it. You will not meaningfully accomplish these tasks with one or two or more readings of your data. To make the kinds of connections needed to analyze and interpret qualitative data, you must know your data—really know it, in your head, not just on paper. The process can be tedious, time-consuming, and repetitious; however, the steps can help you understand, describe, and classify qualitative data.

Reading/Memoing

The first step in analysis is to read and write memos about all field notes, transcripts, and observer comments to get an initial sense of the data. To begin, find a quiet place and plan to spend a few hours at a time reading through the data. Krathwohl wisely pointed out that "the first time you sit down to read your data is the only time you come to that particular set fresh" (1998, p. 309). It is important that you write notes in the margins or underline sections or issues that seem important to you so that you will have a record of your initial thoughts and sense of the data. Later, when you are deeper into the analysis, you may find that many of these early impressions are not useful; however, you may also find that some initial impressions hold up throughout. At this stage of analysis you should also begin the search for recurring themes or common threads.

Describing

The next step, describing, involves developing thorough and comprehensive descriptions of the participants, the setting, and the phenomenon studied in order to convey the rich complexity of the research. The descriptions are based on your collected observations, interview data, field notes, and artifacts. The aim of this step is to provide a narrative picture of the setting and events that take place in it so you will have an understanding of the context in which the study is taking place. Attention to the research context is a common and important theme in qualitative research because the context influences participants' actions and understandings. Because meaning is influenced by context, analysis (and therefore, interpretation) is hampered without a thorough description of the context, actions, and interactions of participants.

An important concern of teacher researchers is portraying the views of the research participants accurately. The descriptions of the research context, meanings, and social relations can be presented in a number of forms. For example, you can describe events in chronological order, create a composite of a typical day in the life of a participant in the setting, focus on key contextual episodes, or illuminate different perspectives of the participants. Regardless of the form, it is crucial that you describe thoroughly how participants define situations and explain their actions. Also, your descriptions should make note of how interactions and social relations among the participants may have changed during the course of the study.

Classifying

Qualitative data analysis is a process of breaking down data into smaller units, determining their import, and putting the pertinent units together in a more general, analytical form. Qualitative data are typically broken down through the process of classifying or *coding*; the pieces of data are then categorized. A *category* is a classification of ideas or concepts; categorization, then, is grouping the data into themes. When concepts in the data are examined and compared to one another and connections are made, categories are formed.

As an example, consider a teacher researcher who is conducting a qualitative study on characteristics of fifth-grade students' study methods. Suppose the researcher had collected twenty sets of field notes (i.e., based on observations) or twenty transcripts of interviews. The researcher's task is to read through all the notes or transcripts and categorize the meanings or understandings that emerge from the data. The categories provide the basis for structuring the analysis and interpretation—without data that are classified and grouped, a researcher has no reasonable way to analyze qualitative studies. However, the categories identified by one researcher would not necessarily be the same as those identified by another researcher, even if they analyzed the same data. There is no single "correct" way to organize and analyze the data. Different researchers produce different categories from the same data for many reasons, including researcher biases, personal interests, style, and interpretive focus.

Qualitative Data Analysis Techniques

Picture this: After weeks (months, years) of data collection using a variety of qualitative data collection techniques (observations, interviews, surveys, audio recordings, and the like), you sit in your living room (classroom, faculty lounge) with colleagues (or by yourself perhaps being observed by a curious significant other!) surrounded by files (boxes) of stuff (data in all shapes and forms)! This less-than-romantic image of the teacher researcher is a common one. Having immersed themselves in the systematic study of a significant problem, teachers (individually and collectively) are confronted with the somewhat daunting task of data analysis, engaging in analysis that will represent the mountains of descriptive data in a "correct," "accurate," "reliable," and "right" way. There is no easy way to do this work: It is difficult, time consuming, and challenging. And yet, it is potentially the most important step in the action research process as we try to understand what we have learned through our investigations.

The strategies outlined in the following sections will serve as guideposts and prompts to move you through your analysis as efficiently as possible. There is no substitute for taking time to fully immerse yourself in your data. Literally bury yourself in what you have. Read and reread, listen and relisten, watch and rewatch. Get to know intimately what you have collected. Struggle with the nuances and caveats, the subtleties, the persuasive, the incomplete. Avoid premature judgment and action and try to remain aware of what will ultimately improve the lives of the children in your care. These are lofty goals, but they are at the heart of what we are trying to achieve with data analysis.

Identifying Themes

One place to start your analysis is to work inductively as you begin to analyze the data: Consider the big picture and start to list "themes" that you have seen emerge in your literature review and in the data collection. Are there patterns that emerge, such as events that keep repeating themselves, key phrases that participants use to describe their feelings, or survey responses that seem to "match" one another? Consider the Highland Park High School action research team in the opening vignette of this chapter. As they gathered their data, they realized that they were dealing with many recurrent themes in their efforts to deemphasize grades—the stress on students created by grades, the satisfaction gained from the renewed focus on learning, the amount of time it took for teachers to assess student work not using traditional grades, and the issues of honesty and integrity, for example.

Coding Surveys, Interviews, and Questionnaires

One of the most frequent data analysis activities undertaken by action researchers is coding, the process of trying to find patterns and meaning in data collected through the use of surveys, interviews, and questionnaires. Working with these types of data is common because surveys, interviews, and questionnaires are generally accepted as part of the school culture, and they provide a great deal of information in a relatively short amount of time.

As you analyze your data, you may need to reduce that data to a manageable form. One way to proceed when working with field notes, transcripts of taped interviews, pictures, maps, charts, and so on is to try to record data on 3" × 5" index cards so your data will be manageable and allow for sorting. Visual data such as pictures, maps, charts, and video recordings may be reduced to a summary statement that captures the themes identified in the data. As you read and reread your data (possibly now reduced to fit on your cards), organize it into categories or themes. Although there is nothing magical about this process, it does take time and a willingness to check that the mountains of descriptive data have been analyzed in a "correct," "accurate," "reliable," and "right" way.

If you can imagine playing a game of cards and not knowing what the symbols on the cards mean, the following analogy might work: You have a deck of cards, each of which contains data. The order of the cards is random. As you initially scan the cards, you have an intuitive sense that the data on some of the cards look similar to that on other cards. You finish carefully looking at all of the cards and reshuffle the deck. Again you look through the deck, but this time you group together the cards (data) that look alike. You end up with thirteen collections of four cards that have some kind of trait in common (the number or face value of the card). Again, you reshuffle the cards. This time as you start to sort through the cards, you notice a different theme (the suit of the card) and end up with four piles of thirteen cards. This is puzzling. Not to be thwarted in your efforts, you again reshuffle the deck and attempt to settle on an organizing theme. You group together cards (data) that have sufficient common characteristics that you feel confident that your analysis of the data is undeniably accurate. But there is just one problem: What do you do with the Joker that found its way into the pack?! And what about that wildcard?! Where did they come from and where do they fit?! Just when you thought you had it all worked out, in crept something that challenges the themes you have used to organize and represent the data you have collected. The process of shuffling and sorting continues.

A few commonsense guidelines may make this somewhat overwhelming activity of coding mountains of data more manageable:

1. Read through all the data and attach working labels to blocks of text. These labels ought to have meaning for you—a kind of shorthand that will serve as a reference point when you return to the text later in the process.
2. Literally cut and paste the blocks of text onto 3" × 5" cards (similar to the card-playing analogy earlier) so that your data are in a manageable form. Use some kind of numbering system so that you can track the block of text back to the original context in which it appeared. For example, noting date and time (1/26/02, 10:15) will help you to locate the reference in your journal or field notes. Remember: Context is important and you will want to check that you have correctly labeled the text you are trying to funnel into a category with similar text. Trying to shuffle reams of paper can be a difficult task, so cards are beneficial.
3. Start to group together cards that contain the same or similar labels.
4. Revisit each pile of cards and see if, in fact, the label still fits or whether similar labels actually warrant their own category. This process is not dissimilar to brainstorming and seeking categories that will encapsulate similar thoughts and ideas.

For example, in my study of school district change (Mills, 1988), I found myself with a large pile of 3" × 5" cards that included some of the following notations:

Card 1. Assistant superintendent urges principals not to reinvent the wheel but to share ideas with each other as they attempt to deal with an identified problem. (In this case the problem was low test scores on the California Achievement Test [CAT].) The assistant superintendent states to the principals, "I don't want any of you to think that you are alone out there."

Card 2. One of the principals at the meeting comments, "Clearly, the CAT does not test what we teach in our schools. The test was designed for California, not Oregon."

Card 3. The next meeting of principals following the release of the CAT scores and the directive from the superintendent that "all schools will develop action plans to address areas of weakness identified by the test scores" does not include any discussion of action plan development.

Card 4. A principal sums up his feelings about standardized testing as follows, "The district makes us go through a whole lot of garbage for little outcome or benefit to the teachers and the students."

Card 5. Principals' meeting 3 months following the release of test scores and action plan mandate. Action plans were due to the Curriculum Director 7 weeks ago. Principals are instructed that they can have another 2 weeks to complete the plans.

Card 6. The assistant superintendent announces that he will be meeting with principals on an individual basis to discuss how action plans for school improvement will be implemented. It is 4 weeks before the end of the school year, and 16 weeks since the initial directive to develop school improvement action plans.

Card 7. One principal commented on the development of the action plan/school improvement plan, "Do I write plans of improvement just to let the central office know that it has been done so that they are satisfied and can get on with doing whatever it is that they do with all the paper work? I admit that I have written plans and never followed up on them because I'm too busy getting on with the real business of school."

By following the four commonsense guidelines presented earlier, the first step of "attaching working labels" to blocks of text that are then "cut and pasted" onto cards resulted in the following grouping of cards: Cards 1, 3, and 5 were labeled "Statement of school district approach to school change." Cards 2 and 4 were labeled "Principals' challenges to school district approach." And cards 6 and 7 were labeled "Inaction of school district approach."

These cards are indicative of the comments that were captured during interviews with individual principals and observations of principals' meetings; collectively, the comments provided the context and understanding for the analysis that resulted in a statement of a theme titled "inaction." In writing about school change as it related to the McKenzie School District, I included in my data analysis a "Taxonomy of Managing and Coping Strategies for Educational Change," which incorporated such themes as "inaction" to describe the change process; that is, one of the ways that the McKenzie School District personnel managed and coped with educational change was to do nothing! Although the story of the change process was fascinating, I have included this example to demonstrate how a theme emerges from the data you collect. I chose the term "inaction" as a theme because it was descriptive (to me) of what was occurring in the district. The same will be true for your own analysis—as you code your data and reduce them to a manageable form, a label will emerge that describes a pattern of behavior. You will be well on your way to making sense of your data!

Analyzing an Interview

Another common form of qualitative data that action researchers analyze is interview data, most commonly in the form of a transcript from the audio recording of the interview. What follows is an annotated interview between a researcher and a bilingual education teacher as an example of the researcher's analysis of the themes that emerged from the interview.

As this example illustrates, the process of analyzing an interview transcript involves a careful reading of the transcript to identify broad themes that emerge from the data that will help answer your research questions. This in-depth, intimate knowledge and examination of the data allows teacher researchers to categorize themes and ideas that will contribute to their understanding of the phenomenon under investigation. In this bilingual education teacher example, fear of change is a pervasive, recurring theme that contributes to the researcher's understanding of the phenomenon and possibly provides an answer to a research question.

Asking Key Questions

Another approach to data analysis involves the use of key questions. According to Stringer (1996), working through a series of questions can enable action researchers to "extend their understanding of the problems and contexts" (p. 87) they have investigated. These key questions may be the very questions with which you began your action research inquiry, the questions mentioned in Chapter 3 that involve the who, what, where, when, why, and how of the educational process. For example: Who is centrally involved? Who has resources? Which ones? What major activities, events, or issues are relevant to the problem? How do acts, activities, and events happen? When does this problem occur? and so on. Although not all these questions will be applicable to any single situation, they may provide a starting point for teacher researchers who are engaged individually or collectively in analysis.

To illustrate, the Highland Park High School team raised questions such as: What is an appropriate role for students to play in determining their own grades? How can grades be deemphasized while teachers maintain specific criteria/outcomes for students? Answers to these and other questions will help extend the team's understanding of the problems associated with deemphasizing grades while emphasizing the importance of learning.

Coding from a Sample Interview Transcript

Codes		Themes (and Other Ideas)
	Q: Why do you think that English-only teachers fear bilingual education?	
Culture	A: I think the <u>fear factor</u> is on a real gut-level and personal level. Teachers feel it's kind of a one-way system in that the teachers who are in the all-English program are <u>fearful</u> at a real basic visceral level that their jobs and their livelihood are at risk. Not to mention their culture, their society, and their known world is at risk by this other language coming into the schools and being acknowledged in the schools. And the teacher might say, "Oh well, because I don't have Spanish that means I am going to be out of a job. Am I going to be replaced by a bilingual teacher? If you have this program in my school that means you're going to need bilingual teachers. I am not bilingual so my job is at risk."	Fear Fear of change Job stability Fear of new job
	Q: Do you think that there is resistance towards expecting all children to learn English?	
Nativistic movements Patriotic	A: I think that's an interpretation that comes out of a model like a 90/10. When the child needs to come into the first year and has 90% in Spanish and 10% in English, it's easily perceived that we are <u>withholding English</u> from the child. That is a perception. A 50/50 model is a little more amenable to that because it's obvious that 50% of the time the child isn't getting English.	
	Q: There is the old adage that teachers who oppose bilingual education say "My ancestors never received bilingual education services in public schools and they did just fine." How do you respond to that kind of attitude toward bilingual education?	
	A: I say that's old thinking. I think that what your parents or your grandparents had to do when they came here from Italy or Norway, or wherever they came from, to learn another language, the language demand was less than it is today. Employment was easier to obtain, let's say a hundred years ago on a manual labor kind of thing. So a person could come here and speak 80% Scottish and 20% English and still be able to get a job because he could manage to do the labor that was required with that little bit of English. It wasn't an academic level of English that he needed, or that my grandfather needed, coming here speaking Norwegian.	
	Q: What about the attitude, "Well they are in the United States and we speak English here so they can learn English. That's all there is to it." How would you respond to this attitude?	
	A: That's a big one. That's huge. I think that's a whole cultural, you know, it's <u>based again in fear</u>. Based again in the fact that the United States is a very	Fear

isolated island in that we are closed in by two oceans and we have never had the habit of stretching out beyond our borders much, or valuing much of what is beyond our borders. We are <u>xenophobic</u> in that sense. So we haven't traditionally learned other languages, or been interested in other languages. "Why bother, we're America, the biggest, the toughest, so why would we value anybody else's culture or language?" And I think that's an old thinking as well. It's an old habit.

Q: Do you think that this attitude is changing?

A: Well, I'm not sure. With September 11th and Homeland Security and all that, I think we have had a big reversal. I think we were going to be able to look at a global perspective and we were on the track of maybe reaching out and saying, "Oh, yeah, this is interesting. Wow, this is great. Look at what we are getting from South America. Look at what we are learning from the Greeks. Look at what we are learning from folks traveling in Africa or traveling in Asia. We are gaining so much. We are taking in so much, it's been great." And then September 11th kind of closed that down and kind of put us back in our cave again and made us a little more <u>fearful</u>. I think the other phenomenon is, and I can speak from the point of view of my father, a good old Idaho boy, you know. Like, "If those folks are coming into our culture and they don't learn English. And they don't learn about Thanksgiving and the 4th of July and how we celebrate Valentine's Day and do it the same way we do, then they are going to change our culture. My culture. And if they change my culture then I won't know how to act. And it's my culture in the first place so if they want to be here they need to accept that."

Q: I hear in my class all the time, "If I go to Mexico they aren't going to speak English. They are going to expect me to speak Spanish and adhere to their culture." Why are we different? Why should we be more open?

A: Why should we be? Well, there is a big difference between a tourist going to Mexico and somebody coming here for two weeks, or somebody coming here to spend a lifetime and raise their children. That's a really big different set of elements that we are dealing with. So, one of the things about the United States is that we have always said we are a pluralistic culture. You can come here, settle, raise your family, bring your poor, humble, weak, and we will be collectively a nation. So it starts with the idea, the salad bowl idea, that we can all be individuals but we are going to make a collective nation. And the contradiction of that is that we want to all be on the same page because we need to be united. <u>I think the fear</u> that we are not united is seen in the commonly held belief that the word "multicultural" is a nasty word. It's an eight letter word or whatever it is, because it means that we are separating out into our little ghettos, into our little cultures, and we've got Latinos over here and Russians over here, and we've got the Afghanis over here and we've got the Vietnamese here in San Francisco, and they are going to be separated and not be pulling together in one United States. So that goes for elections and social security and achieving resources and services that are federally provided. Schools for example. The thinking would be "Why would we want all those really diverse thinkers? Like maybe we've got a whole bunch of people who are adhering to Islam and they want to come into the public schools and we should educate them? But Islam is apparently against the Anglo-Protestant way of the United States? Why would we let them access our services?" So that is from my father's point of view. Not from mine. But that is from that conservative, older generation in this country.

Fear

Nativistic
movement
Patriotic

Fear

Fear

Fear

Doing an Organizational Review

Another approach Stringer (1996) suggested is undertaking an organizational review that focuses on the following features of the organization (in this case, a school): vision and mission, goals and objectives, structure of the organization, operation, and problems, issues, and concerns (p. 90). Stringer noted: "As participants work through these issues, they will extend their understanding of the organization and aspects of its operation that are relevant to their problems, issues, and concerns" (pp. 90–91). A review of the school, with these features in mind, may provide insight into the data you have collected.

For example, in the Highland Park High School example that opened this chapter, an organizational review of the school's grading policies and communication policies with students and parents would include seeking answers to questions such as:

What is the school's mission and vision?

What is the school's policy on grading?

How is the school organized to provide effective communication with students and parents?

What issues arise when a change in grading policy is put in to effect?

Answers to these questions would provide the teacher researchers at Highland Park High School with additional insights into the data they collected. However, the questions asked by teacher researchers as part of an organizational review will depend on the organization and the area of focus.

Developing a Concept Map

Stringer (1996) suggested that concept maps are another useful strategy that helps action research participants to visualize the major influences that have affected the study. For example, what were the perspectives of the students? Parents? Teachers? Administrators? A concept map gives participants an opportunity to display their analysis of the problem and to determine consistencies and inconsistencies that may exist between the disparate groups. The steps for developing a concept map include the following:

1. List the major influences that have affected the study of your area of focus.
2. Develop a visual representation of the major influences (factors) connecting the influences with relationships you know exist (using solid lines) and influences you have a "hunch" about (using dotted lines).
3. Review the concept map to determine any consistencies or inconsistencies that exist among the influences. This forces you back to your data to see "what's missing."

For example, Jack Reston at Eastview Elementary School (see Chapter 7) concluded that the following factors were major influences on the success of the school's absenteeism policy: respectfulness, safety, conflict management, discipline, school rules, behavior, getting along, self-esteem, and academics. Further, Jack believed that some relationships (real and perceived) existed among these factors (see Figure 6–2).

Analyzing Antecedents and Consequences

Stringer (1996) also suggested a process of mapping antecedents (causes) and consequences (effects) to help action researchers identify the major elements of their analysis. Using this

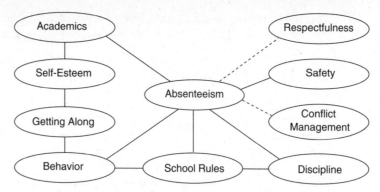

FIGURE 6–2   *Eastview's Concept Map of the Factors Affecting Absenteeism*

framework provides a visual representation of the causal relationships that you, the teacher researcher, now believe exist. It is also helpful to revisit the causal relationships uncovered in your review of the literature to determine challenges and support for your analysis and interpretations.

The steps for analyzing antecedents and consequences are:

1. List the influences that emerged from the analysis for which there appear to be a causal relationship.
2. Revisit the review of literature to determine whether the analysis of the study supports, or is challenged by, the findings of previous studies.
3. Revisit your data to determine if anything is missing and suggest how your findings may influence the next action research cycle.

As an example, in the Eastview Elementary School study, the concept map (see Figure 6–2) could be expanded to include a mapping of antecedents (causes) and consequences (effects) as an outcome of the analysis. In this example, Jack Reston clearly identified (based on his analysis) that a causal relationship existed between absenteeism and academics (student performance), and absenteeism and discipline (student behavior). Based on these relationships, Jack Reston revisited his review of literature to determine if his data analysis challenged or supported the findings of previous studies. Furthermore, Reston could use these reflections to help formulate the next action research cycle focused on another planned intervention to address absenteeism at Eastview Elementary school.

Displaying Findings

The information you have collected should be summarized in an appropriate and meaningful format that you can share with interested colleagues. To do this, teacher researchers should "think display" as they consider how to convey their findings to interested colleagues. You might use matrices, charts, concept maps, graphs, and figures—whatever works as a practical way to encapsulate the findings of your study. I have also witnessed teacher researchers who have made excellent use of other audiovisual media, such as video recordings and computer multimedia presentations (incorporating text, charts, matrices, audio, and video), to represent their findings. These visual displays of data serve an important function for teachers who wish to share findings and celebrate their insights in a public forum (see Chapter 8 for further discussion). Putting your data into a visual format might also help you "see" new aspects of your data! (See Appendix B for examples of visual displays of data.)

Stating What's Missing

Finally, as part of your full reporting, flag for the consumers of your research what pieces of the puzzle are still missing and identify any remaining questions for which you have not been able to provide answers. Often we find ourselves wanting and needing to provide answers, to move beyond our data with unwarranted assertions that may, in some cases, ultimately lead to embarrassing questions about what we actually did! In keeping with the theme of avoiding premature judgment (arriving at answers to problems without systematic inquiry), the data analysis technique of stating what's missing allows you to hint at what might/should be done next in your quest to better understand the findings of your study. (See Research in Action Checklist 6–1 for a list of data analysis techniques.)

Using Computer Software to Assist with Data Analysis

Increasingly, computer software is being developed to assist with the analysis of qualitative, narrative data. The key word in this sentence is "assist." This software will not do the analysis for you! Novice researchers need to remember that computers alone do not analyze or even code data. They are designed only to help expedite these operations when researchers are working with large bodies of text and other kinds of data. The process of coding, retrieving, and subsequently mulling over and making sense of data remains a laborious process completely controlled by researchers. Even if a computer is used, researchers still must go through the process of punching each code into the data on the computer as they read through their interviews, field notes, and audio and video recordings. Computers are merely handy and extremely fast labeling and retrieval tools. Researchers also must remember that they alone can tell or program the computer to retrieve and count data in specific ways; the machines do not do these tasks automatically. Although computers can enhance and broaden qualitative research analysis, if you are not connected in some way with a research university it is unlikely that you will have access to the software and the expertise of someone to teach you how to use the software.

RESEARCH IN ACTION CHECKLIST 6–1

Data Analysis Strategies

_____ Identify themes.
_____ Code surveys, interviews, and questionnaires.
_____ Analyze an interview.
_____ Ask key questions: who, what, where, when, why, and how?
_____ Do an organizational review of the school.
_____ Develop a concept map.
_____ Analyze antecedents and consequences.
_____ Display findings.
_____ State what is missing.

To help you with your decision about whether to proceed with locating and learning a qualitative data analysis software package, let's review some of the factors that might affect the decision:

- Are you analyzing large amounts (for example, more than 500 pages of field notes and transcripts)?
- Are you adequately trained in the use of the programs?
- Do you have the resources to purchase a program or do you know someone who has the program?
- Do you need to be able to capture specific quotes from a large database? (Adapted from Creswell, 2005, p. 234.)

Three common and popular qualitative data analysis software packages are NVivo 7.0, The Ethnograph v5.08, and HyperRESEARCH 2.7.

- NVivo is designed for qualitative researchers who need to work with complex data, especially multimedia data. More information on NVivo can be found on the QSR International website at www.qsr-ecommerce.com/us/acatalog/ and the DataSense site at www.datasense.org.
- The Ethnograph v5.08 is a program designed to help qualitative researchers work with text files (in any format) and search for and code segments of interest to the researcher. More information about The Ethnograph can be found on the Qualis Research website at www.qualisresearch.com/.
- HyperRESEARCH 2.7 is an advanced software program that allows the qualitative researcher to work with text, graphics, audio, and video sources and to code and retrieve data. More information about HyperRESEARCH (and HyperTRANSCRIBE 1.0) can be found on the ResearchWare website at www.researchware.com.

Remember, computer software will not do the data analysis for you, but it will help retrieve categories from a large amount of narrative (text) data. Given the time (and resources) it takes to learn new software programs, and the relatively modest amounts of narrative data you are likely to encounter as a novice researcher, it is likely that you will resort to using the other "old fashioned" techniques described in this chapter.

Qualitative Data Analysis: An Example

The example that follows is intended to provide a sense of qualitative analysis. A true qualitative study would entail more data analysis than shown here, but the basic ideas represent the process a qualitative researcher would undertake when analyzing data throughout a study.

In this example, the topics under study are the concerns of parents regarding their first child's entrance into kindergarten and the kindergarten teacher's interactions with the students and families. The participants were four parents—three female and one male, representing four families—and the first child in each of the families. The children attend the same school; the kindergarten teacher was also a participant. Data collection procedures included observations and interviews with students, parents, and the kindergarten teacher.

Data analysis would proceed as follows:

1. From the field notes of your classroom observations, you begin to list some common items or topics that you noticed. You recorded in your notes that during classroom instruction, the teacher was using books, videos, and handouts. You also noted that at

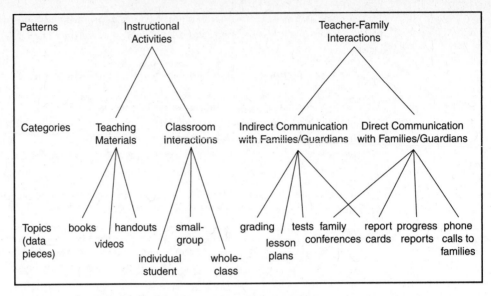

FIGURE 6–3 *Diagram of Category Levels and Organization*

times, instruction was directed toward individual students, sometimes toward the whole class, and sometimes toward students who were working together in small groups.

2. From your interviews with the teacher, you realize that she gave you information about how she communicated with families about the children. You note that she talked about how she indirectly communicates through grading and report cards and how her lesson plans and tests are related to her overall assessment of the students' work. She also mentioned that she talks about report cards directly with families during conferences. Additionally, she communicates with families about their children through progress reports and phone calls.

3. From your initial analysis, you group the individual items or topics together into categories that show how the items or topics are related. For example, as shown in Figure 6–3, you could group books, videos, and handouts under a category called "Teaching Materials." You could group together the ways in which the instruction was carried out—individual, small-group, and whole-class—and label this category as "Classroom Interactions." Using information from the interviews, you could construct the category "Indirect Communication with Families/Guardians" to include grading, lesson plans, tests, and report cards. A category of "Direct Communication with Families/Guardians" could include family conferences, report cards, progress reports, and phone calls to families. Notice that report cards appear in both the indirect and direct communication categories.

4. You organize your four categories into patterns, which are made up of two or more categories. For example, the categories of "Teaching Materials" and "Classroom Interactions" indicate a pattern of "Instructional Activities." The categories of "Indirect Communication" and "Direct Communication" fit together under a pattern of "Teacher-Family Interactions."

You then decide whether you need to collect additional data by interviewing students and parents about their experiences of interacting with the teacher to confirm your categories and patterns.

Analyzing and Interpreting Quantitative Data

Data analysis and interpretation can also involve the use of descriptive statistics to help make sense of your quantitative data. My advice here is simple: Count what counts! If it makes sense to tally and count events, categories, occurrences, test scores, and the like, use an appropriate descriptive statistic. However, do not feel compelled to include elaborate statistical measures simply to add a perceived sense of rigor or credibility to your inquiry. Recall from Chapter 1 that action research is a very different kind of inquiry from experimental research and as such is less concerned with the statistically based claims that scientists make. However, if your research has used quantitative research approaches (for example, survey research, correlational research, causal-comparative research, experimental research, single-subject experimental research, or mixed-methods research) that include quantitative measures, use the appropriate statistics to analyze and interpret your data. Treat statistics as one of an array of many tools that can help teacher researchers gain insight into their data and communicate them efficiently to others.

In this section I will briefly discuss descriptive statistical measures of central tendency (mean, mode, median) and variability (standard deviation). For a more detailed explanation of the appropriate use of these statistics, and of inferential statistics (for example, t tests, analysis of variance, multiple regression, chi square, and other investigative techniques such as data mining, factor analysis, and structural equation modeling), I recommend Gay, Mills, and Airasian (2009). Inferential statistics are data analysis techniques for determining how likely it is that results obtained from a sample or samples are the same results that would have been obtained from the entire population. As stated previously, few (if any) action researchers concern themselves with making claims about the findings of their studies (based on the results obtained in their classrooms) that would generalize to a larger population (for example, all fifth-grade students in the state).

Many readily available computer programs, such as SPSS 14.0 for Windows Student Version and Microsoft Office Excel, may be accessible for computing statistics at your school or university. Remember, there are many excellent math specialists in your school or district, so don't hesitate to call on those resources with questions.

Why Use Descriptive Statistics?

Descriptive statistics give us a shorthand way of giving lots of information about a range of numbers using only one or two numbers. For example, Chapter 4 discussed the use of attitude scales (Likert scales and semantic differentials) to measure students' attitudes and other sources of quantitative data available to action researchers (for example, teacher-made tests, standardized tests, and school-generated report cards). One way to provide a great deal of information about our students' attitudes (as measured by these instruments) is to use descriptive statistics to describe the students' attitudes. For example, we might describe students' attitudes to a new mathematics curriculum (see Chapter 4) by reporting the average response to the following item on a questionnaire:

1. I believe that the problem-solving skills I learn in class help me make good problem-solving decisions outside of school.

SA   A   U   D   SD

By assigning point values—SA = 5, A = 4, U = 3, D = 2, SD = 1—and calculating the average response, we would be able to describe, on average, what children believed about the transfer of problem-solving skills to decisions made outside of school. In other words, the use of a number, in this case an average, conveys a great deal of information about students' attitudes and helps us make sense of our questionnaire data. Without the use of numbers we would be limited to talking about an individual student's response to each question and not in more general terms about the attitudes of all of our students.

Measures of Central Tendency

Simply put, a measure of central tendency is a single number that gives us information about the entire group of numbers we are examining. Three common measures of central tendency are the *mean* (the average), the *mode* (the most frequently occurring score/s), and the *median* (the middle score). In education, perhaps the most common descriptive statistic used by teachers is the mean. It allows us to talk in generalities and to compare how the students in our class have performed "on average" in comparison to other students or over a given time period. As a teacher you have no doubt calculated many averages, but remember: The **mean** (M) is calculated by adding together all of the scores (observations) and dividing by the number of scores.

Mean = The sum of all the scores divided by the number of scores.

For example, you administer a mathematics test with 100 questions to the 30 students in your class. After grading the tests, you award the following scores: 95, 95, 92, 92, 90, 90, 90, 88, 88, 85, 85, 85, 82, 82, 82, 82, 79, 79, 75, 75, 75, 75, 75, 72, 72, 72, 69, 69, 69, 65.

$$\text{Mean } (\bar{x}) = \frac{\Sigma x \text{ (the sum of scores)}}{n \text{ (the number of scores)}}$$

$$= \frac{2424}{30}$$

$$= 80.8$$

The mean is greatly affected by extreme scores, because it is "pulled" in the direction of the atypical values. For that reason, the median is sometimes a better descriptor of the full range of scores. For the most part, though, the mean (or the average) is the easiest, most familiar measure to use.

The **median** (Mdn) is the middle score in a distribution when the scores are ordered from the highest to the lowest. If there is an odd number of scores (say 31), then the middle score (the 16th one) is the median. But in the distribution of the math scores above, there is an even number of scores. To find the midpoint in the distribution when there is an even number of scores, we must add the two middle scores in the rank-ordered distribution and divide by two. In this case, we would add together the two scores that are at positions 15 and 16, and divide by two. In this case it would be scores 82 and 82. Therefore, 82 is the median score.

The **mode** is the most frequently occurring score in a distribution. In the case of these math scores, the mode would be 75, because that score was received by five students in the class. A distribution of scores can have more than one mode (making it bimodal or multimodal) or have no mode at all. The mode is the least useful measure of central tendency in most educational research: It tells us only about the score received most often and doesn't give us any information about the other scores.

Measure of Variability: Standard Deviation

As a teacher, you may have been exposed to standard deviation (SD) but perhaps did not fully understand its meaning. For example, you may have received test scores for your students following administration of a standardized test with individual scores, a class average, and a standard deviation. For our purposes, it is not important to see and memorize the formula for the standard deviation or even to know its origins. It is more important to understand the concepts of variability and standard deviation, to know what they mean, and to recognize when they would be appropriate to use.

A measure of variability tells us "how spread out a group of scores are." The standard deviation is the most important measure of variability for our action research purposes. Whereas the mean is a measure of a position in a distribution of scores (in this case, 80.8 on a scale of 1 to 100), the **standard deviation** indicates the spread of a set of scores around the mean (Gay et al., 2009, p. 223). In essence, the standard deviation helps us to understand approximately how much a particular score deviates from the average score.

As a teacher researcher, I might also be puzzled about whether a relatively large or small standard deviation is "good" or "bad." Perhaps a better way to think of a standard deviation as it relates to our mathematics test scores is in terms of equity. For example, the mean is 80.8 and the standard deviation is 8.59. (I calculated the standard deviation using SPSS Student Version 14.0 for Windows. If you have a larger data set, this is not the kind of calculation you want to do by hand, but for a small data set you can calculate the standard deviation by hand.) If the data set is too large to calculate by hand and you don't have access to SPSS, you can use computer programs such as Excel or a calculator with a statistics function to calculate the standard deviation.

In our example, where the mean is 80.8 and the SD is 8.59, the majority (68% to be precise) of the children scored (roughly) between 72 and 89 (± 1 SD from the mean). In short, most of them probably succeeded on the test, if in fact scoring between this range of scores suggests some kind of mastery of the content. Now, let's compare the standard deviation of 8.59 to a standard deviation of, say, 16. If this were the case, we might conclude that the majority of children scored between 64 and 97. Again the question is one of mastery and whether or not a score of 64 suggests mastery of the content. The larger standard deviation suggests that the children's scores on the math test are more spread out and, hence, leaves us to question the degree to which the children have achieved mastery on the test. For the classroom teacher seeking to confirm mastery of subject matter on a criterion-referenced test (teacher-made test), a higher mean and smaller standard deviation would be a desirable outcome.

All of this leads us to the question, "So how does this help me understand my students' mathematics test scores?" Armed with the knowledge that the average score for the 30 students in your class is 80.8 and the standard deviation of this distribution of scores is 8.59, you can make the following statements:

- On average the children in the class scored 80 on the test.
- Approximately two-thirds of the children in the class scored between 72 and 89 on the test.
- The relatively small standard deviation and mean of 80 suggest that approximately two-thirds of the children achieved mastery of the content that the test covered.

Descriptive Statistics

DEFINITION OF MEASURE	TYPE USED IN ACTION RESEARCH
A **measure of central tendency** is a single number that gives us information about an entire group of numbers.	• Mean (the average) • Mode (the most frequently occurring score/s) • Median (the middle score)
A **measure of variability** tells us how spread out a group of scores is.	• Standard deviation (a measure of distance from the mean that helps us understand approximately how much a *particular* score deviates from the *average* score)

Used in conjunction, the mean and standard deviation can provide you and your colleagues with a great deal of information about the data you have collected if you have determined that it is data that can be counted. See Key Concepts Box 6–1 for some of the uses of descriptive statistics.

An Illustration

In my study of change in the McKenzie School District (Mills, 1988), I administered a survey to classroom teachers. One of the items on the survey focused on the teachers' perceptions of how the district's at-risk program had changed classroom practices. Specifically, teachers were asked to respond to the following statement: To what degree has the at-risk program changed your classroom practice? The survey included an item that required teachers to circle a number between 1 and 5 (1 = no change, 5 = large change). A total of 52 teachers responded to the survey item with the following frequency:

Impact of At-Risk Program on Classroom Practices

	No Change				Large Change
	1	2	3	4	5
Number of Respondents	7(13%)	18(37%)	17(35%)	10(15%)	0(0%)

I used the following descriptive statistics to describe the distribution of teachers' responses:

4,4,4,4,4,4,4,4,4,4,3,3,3,3,3,3,3,3,3,3,3,3,3,3,3,3,3,2,2,2,2,2,2,2,2,2,2,2,2,2,2,2,2,2,2,1,1,1,1,1,1,1

$$\text{Mean } (\bar{x}) = \frac{\Sigma x}{n}$$

$$= \frac{134}{52}$$

$$= 2.58$$

Mode = 2.0 (most frequently occurring score—it occurred 18 times)
Median = 3.0 (the middle score in this distribution of 52 responses)
Standard Deviation = 1.02

However, numbers alone do not tell a complete story. They inform the reader about how a sample responded to a particular item. For example, the analysis of the earlier illustration related to classroom teachers' perceptions of how the district's at-risk program had changed classroom practices is incomplete using only descriptive statistics. To complete my reporting on this item, I included the following representative responses to the question, "To what extent do you think that the at-risk program changed your classroom practices?" The responses were grouped under the categories of "Positive Impact" and "No Impact."

Positive Impact

Reminded me and reinforced the concepts of learning styles and how to provide for them in my classroom.

Having insight to these kids has allowed me to be more sensitive and caring toward them and to act more compassionately.

I am more aware of needs of the "total child" as well as the student.

No Impact

No time to plan and implement all of those ideas!

I feel that the services needed for at-risk students are not available.

I was already using many of the skills.

Have been dealing with at-risk students since becoming a resource teacher so was already aware of the problem.

I believe that I have always been aware of the problem. It's only new at the district level.

The statistical analysis combined with the quotes from the teachers who responded provided me with a good understanding of the teachers' perceptions of the impact the at-risk program had on their classroom practices.

Be Careful about Your Claims

A final caveat: Be careful about how you "interpret" the descriptive statistics that you use to analyze your data and be careful about the claims you make based on a descriptive statistical analysis. Be clear about the limited significance that can be attached to averages and standard deviations. Remember that these statistics are used for description, not for identifying statistically significant relationships that can be generalized to the larger population.

Clearly, this discussion about descriptive statistics is quite brief. My experiences with teacher researchers is that, like me, they are somewhat math phobic and reluctant to incorporate statistics into their studies. But as Pelto and Pelto (1978) remind us:

> In fact, not only humans but also other animals are constantly counting things in the process of adapting to their environments. Basic processes of learning, as described by experimental psychologists, most often imply some kind of counting or measurement that permits an animal (human or other) to distinguish between one condition and another as a relevant stimulus for appropriate action. (p. 123)

If counting things positively contributes to understanding your research or suggests a relationship that warrants further investigation, then use whatever statistic is most appropriate to

TABLE 6–1 Type of mixed-methods designs and data analysis/interpretation procedures

Types of Mixed-Methods Designs	Examples of Data Analysis and Data Interpretation Techniques
Triangulation (quantitative and qualitative data are collected simultaneously)	Quantify qualitative data coding by assigning a number to a code and counting the number times it occurs. Quantitative data are descriptively analyzed for frequency of occurrence. The two data sets are compared.
Explanatory (quantitative data is collected first, followed by qualitative data)	Follow up on outliers (extreme cases). Quantitative data is collected and outliers identified. Qualitative data is then collected on the outliers to increase understanding of these cases.
Exploratory (qualitative data is collected first, followed by quantitative data)	Qualitative data is collected and analyzed and themes identified. The themes are used as the basis for identifying, or developing, an instrument that can be administered to collect quantitative data to measure the identified themes.

Source: Adapted from J. W. Creswell (2005). *Educational Research: Planning, Conducting, and Evaluating Quantitative and Qualitative Research.*

analyze and interpret your data. And, if you are math phobic but still want to examine whether statistics can give you insight into your data, do not hesitate to call on the skills of your critical friends, colleagues, and university professors.

Data Analysis in Mixed-Methods Designs

As I have discussed throughout this chapter, one of the most difficult aspects of any research endeavor is the analysis of data. This problem is showcased when we attempt to analyze quantitative and qualitative data sources concurrently or in sequence and then attempt to find points of intersection as well as discrepancies, as is the case in mixed-methods designs. To refresh your memory, mixed-methods research designs combine quantitative and qualitative approaches by including both quantitative and qualitative data in a single study. Many teacher researchers find themselves including both data sources in their studies, especially when capturing student achievement data. Table 6–1 summarizes the type of mixed-methods research designs and examples of data analysis and data interpretation techniques that teacher researchers can use (adapted from Creswell, 2005). Many of the suggestions in this table build on the information in the quantitative and qualitative analysis and interpretation sections in this chapter and therefore should be familiar to you. (For a comprehensive discussion of mixed-methods research designs see Gay et al., 2009, Chapter 19.)

Qualitative Data Interpretation Techniques

You may wonder, why bother with interpretation, especially since interpretation involves taking risks and making educated guesses that might be off base? According to Wolcott (1994), qualitative (action) researchers must accept "the risks and challenges of the interpretive mode," because in doing so we can "demonstrate to others (and reassure ourselves) that, in spite of their undistinguished origins, our works and the implications to be drawn from them are socially significant" (p. 258). In other words, Wolcott argues for the importance of interpretation because as teacher researchers, our interpretations matter to the lives of our students. In addition, the process of interpretation is important because it can challenge teacher researchers' taken-for-granted assumptions and beliefs about the educational processes they have investigated.

The list of techniques for data interpretation that follow are adapted from Wolcott (1994, pp. 39–46) and Stringer (1996, pp. 87–96) but have been reframed to apply specifically to teacher researchers.

Extend the Analysis

One technique that is low on the data interpretation risk scale is to simply extend the analysis of your data by raising questions about the study, noting implications that might be drawn without actually drawing them. As Wolcott (1994) suggested, "This is a strategy for *pointing* the way rather than *leading* the way" (p. 40, emphasis added). For example, "While it appears as though the teen theater improvisation model positively impacts audience participation, a number of questions are raised by this strategy." In this example from Cathy Mitchell's Teen Theater group's use of improvisation (see Chapter 3), the analysis of data can be extended by raising questions about the intervention that were not asked as part of the original investigation but which may signal the beginning of the next action research cycle.

Similarly, in the Highland Park High School vignette, the research raised questions such as: Is the total elimination of letter and number grades the best way to deemphasize grades? Is there a way to deemphasize grades that requires less paperwork on the teacher's part? What is an appropriate role for students to play in determining their own grades? How can grades be deemphasized while teachers still maintain specific criteria/outcomes for students?

Connect Findings with Personal Experience

Action research is personal business, so it makes sense to personalize our interpretations. For example, you may present your findings with the prelude: "Based on my experiences in conducting this study, this is what I make of it all." Remember, you know your study better than anyone else; after all, it's been conducted in your classroom or school and focused on your students. You have been there for every twist and turn along the way, trying to make sense of discrepant events just when you thought you "had it right." Share your interpretations based on your intimate knowledge and understanding of schools and classrooms and teaching and learning. For example, Deborah South (Chapter 1) had experienced the frustration of working with unmotivated children and the apparent futility of a study skills intervention. When faced with the "So what?" question, she based her interpretation not only on the analysis of data (test scores, surveys, interviews, and observations) but also on the memories and emotions of adolescent off-task behavior—a powerful interpretive lens.

Seek the Advice of "Critical" Friends

If you have difficulty focusing an interpretive lens on your work, rely on your trusted colleagues to offer insights that you may have missed because of your closeness to the work. Offer your accounts to colleagues with the request that they share with you their possible interpretations. For example, the group of teachers at Highland Park High School found that their interpretations were enriched by the multiple viewpoints that came as a result of their collaboration. Remember, these colleagues may be people you have never met face-to-face but with whom you have talked in action research chat rooms on the Internet. Similarly, you may ask your informants (students, parents, teachers, and administrators) for their insights.

But beware! The more opinions you seek the more you will receive, and often these suggestions come with the expectation that you will accept the advice! Over time you will develop reciprocity with a cadre of trusted, like-minded colleagues who will selflessly fulfill the role of critical friends. Take the time to build these relationships and reap the rewards they offer. For example, when Deborah South concluded from her data analysis and interpretation that her study skills class was the "cause" of her students' lack of motivation, her critical friends in her action research class protested that interpretation and provided her with ideas for alternate explanations. What Deborah gained from the feedback of her critical friends was a commitment to change the "intervention" that was being touted as "the solution" to the "unmotivated students" problem in the school.

Contextualize Findings in the Literature

Uncovering external sources as part of the review of related literature is a powerful way for teacher researchers to provide support for the study's findings. Wolcott (1994) suggested that qualitative (action) researchers "draw connections with external authority. Most often this is accomplished through informed references to some recognized body of theory in one's special field, or to the recognized classics, in the tradition of the literature review" (p. 34). Making these connections also provides teacher researchers with a way to share with colleagues the existing knowledge base in a specific area of focus and to acknowledge the unique contribution the teacher researcher has made to our understanding of the topic studied.

Turn to Theory

Let me first offer a modest definition of theory as "an analytical and interpretive framework that helps the researcher make sense of 'what is going on' in the social setting being studied" (Mills, 1993, p. 103). Theory serves a number of important roles for action researchers. First, theory provides a way for teacher researchers to link their work to broader issues of the day. As Wolcott (1994) suggested, "One interpretive tack is to examine a case in terms of competing theories and then proclaim a winner or, more often, attempt some eclectic resolution" (p. 43). Second, "theory allows the researcher to search for increasing levels of abstraction, to move beyond a purely descriptive account" (Mills, 1993, p. 115). That level of abstraction "allow(s) us to communicate the essence of descriptive work to our colleagues at research meetings" (Mills, 1993, p. 115). Last, theory can provide a rationale or sense of meaning to the work we do. As educators we have all been influenced by learning theories that provide a safe haven for our own work. Share the theories that appear to help make sense of your data.

For example, Clem Annice's story of the use of technology to enhance mathematics learning for the students at Billabong Elementary School (Chapter 2) is influenced by theories about how students best learn math. Some of these theories are evident in the references to how students were using technology for "drill-and-kill" activities and how access to calculators was limited because calculator functions had been removed from the computers. The vignette suggests that other theories explain how students best learn math by challenging the "rote learning" theory that appeared well established at Billabong Elementary.

Data Interpretation Techniques

_____ Extend the analysis by raising questions.
_____ Connect the findings with personal experience.
_____ Seek the advice of critical friends.
_____ Contextualize findings in the literature.
_____ Turn to theory.

Know When to Say "When"!

Finally, if you don't feel comfortable with offering an interpretation, don't do it. Be satisfied with suggesting what needs to be done next and use that as a starting point for the next action research cycle. Restate the problem as you now see it and explain how you think you will fine-tune your efforts as you strive to increase your understanding of the phenomenon you have investigated. Wolcott (1994) cautioned, "Don't detract from what you have accomplished by tacking on a wimpy interpretation" (p. 41). (See Research in Action Checklist 6–2 for a list of data interpretation techniques.)

Sharing Your Interpretations Wisely

As educators we have all, at some time, been exposed to what are variously called "fads," "the pendulum swing," the "bandwagon," and so on. Thus, many of us may hesitate to embrace anything new or different that comes our way in schools, calming ourselves with the mantra "This, too, shall pass!" If we, as professional educators, attempt to use our action research findings only to confirm our beliefs and values, then we risk being alienated by our colleagues. Avoid being evangelical about your interpretations, connect them closely to your data and analysis, and share your newfound understandings with colleagues in an appropriate manner.

Summary

Ongoing Analysis and Reflection

1. Action research studies provide teacher researchers with data that can be used formatively and summatively; that is, much of the data collected during the study can be used to positively affect teaching throughout the study.

2. Two questions to guide reflection include:
   a. Is your research question still answerable and worth answering?
   b. Are your data collection techniques catching the kind of data you want and filtering out the data that you don't? (Anderson, Herr, and Nihlen, 1994, p. 155)

3. Although ongoing analysis and reflection is a natural part of the action research process, you should avoid premature actions based on early analysis and interpretation of the data. Action researchers—especially those who are inexperienced—often make rash or impulsive decisions based on limited or no data.

4. The action research process takes time. Teacher researchers must be wary of the lure of quick-fix strategies and patient enough to avoid the pitfalls of basing actions on premature analysis.

The Role of Analysis and Interpretation

5. Data analysis is an attempt by the teacher researcher to summarize collected data in a dependable and accurate manner.

6. Data interpretation is an attempt by the research to find meaning in the data, to answer the "So what?" question in terms of the implications of the study's findings.

7. Put simply, analysis involves summarizing what's in the data, whereas interpretation involves making sense of—finding meaning in—that data.

8. Data analysis and interpretation are critical stages in the action research process that require the teacher researcher to both know and understand the data.

9. One way to proceed with analysis is to follow three iterative, or repeating, steps: reading/memoing, describing what is going on in the setting, and classifying research data.

10. *Reading/Memoing.* The first step in analysis is to read and write memos about all field notes, transcripts, and observer comments to get an initial sense of the data. To begin, find a quiet place and plan to spend a few hours at a time reading through the data.

11. *Describing.* The second step, describing, involves developing thorough and comprehensive descriptions of the participants, the setting, and the phenomenon studied in order to

convey the rich complexity of the research. The descriptions are based on your collected observations, interview data, field notes, and artifacts.

12. *Classifying.* Qualitative data are typically broken down through the process of classifying or *coding;*; the pieces of data are then categorized. A *category* is a classification of ideas or concepts; categorization, then, is grouping the data into themes. When concepts in the data are examined and compared to one another and connections are made, categories are formed.

Qualitative Data Analysis Techniques

13. *Identifying Themes.* One place to start your analysis is to work inductively as you begin to analyze the data: Consider the big picture and start to list "themes" that you have seen emerge in your literature review and in the data collection. Are there patterns that emerge, such as events that keep repeating themselves, key phrases that participants use to describe their feelings, or survey responses that seem to "match" one another?

14. *Coding Surveys, Interviews, and Questionnaires.* One of the most frequent data analysis activities undertaken by action researchers is coding, the process of trying to find patterns and meaning in data collected through the use of surveys, interviews, and questionnaires.

15. *Analyzing an Interview.* Another common form of qualitative data that action researchers analyze is interview data, most commonly in the form of a transcript from the audio recording of the interview.

16. *Asking Key Questions.* Another approach to data analysis involves the use of key questions such as those with which the teacher researcher started the study; they may take form of who, what, where, when, why, and how questions about the educational process.

17. *Doing an Organizational Review.* This approach to data analysis involves focusing on the following features of the organization (e.g., school): vision and mission, goals and objectives, structure of the organization, operation, and problems, issues, and concerns (Stringer, 1996, p. 90).

18. *Developing a Concept Map.* Concept maps are a useful strategy that helps action researcher participants to visualize the major influences that have affected the study (Stringer, 1996). The steps for developing a concept map include the following:
    a. List the major influences that have affected the study of your area of focus.
    b. Develop a visual representation of the major influences (factors) connecting the influences with relationships you know exist (using solid lines) and influences you have a "hunch" about (using dotted lines).
    c. Review the concept map to determine any consistencies or inconsistencies that exist among the influences. This forces you back to your data to see "what's missing."

19. *Analyzing Antecedents and Consequences.* A process of mapping antecedents (causes) and consequences (effects) helps action researchers identify the major elements of their analysis (Stringer, 1996). The steps for analyzing antecedents and consequences are:
    a. List the influences that emerged from the analysis for which there appear to be a causal relationship.
    b. Revisit the review of literature to determine whether the analysis of the study supports, or is challenged by, the findings of previous studies.
    c. Revisit your data to determine if anything is missing and suggest how your findings may influence the next action research cycle.

20. *Displaying Findings.* The information you have collected should be summarized in an appropriate and meaningful format that you can share with interested colleagues. "Think display" as one way to convey your findings.

21. *State What's Missing.* Flag for the consumers of your research what pieces of the puzzle are still missing and identify any remaining questions for which you have not been able to provide answers.

22. *Use Computer Software to Assist with Data Analysis.* Computer software is available to assist with the analysis of qualitative data. This software will not do the analysis for you. It is designed to help researchers who are working with large bodies of text and other kinds of data.

23. Three common and popular qualitative analysis software packages are NVivo 7.0, The Ethnograph v5.08, and HyperRESEARCH 2.7.

Analyzing and Interpreting Quantitative Data

24. Data analysis and interpretation can also involve the use of descriptive statistics to help make sense of your findings. My advice here is simple: Count what counts! If it makes sense to tally and count events, categories, occurrences, test scores, and the like, use an appropriate descriptive statistic.

25. Descriptive statistics gives us a shorthand way of giving lots of information about a range of numbers using only one or two numbers.

26. A measure of central tendency is a single number that gives us information about the entire group of numbers we are examining. Three common measures of central tendency are the *mean* (the average), the *mode* (the most frequently occurring score/s), and the *median* (the middle score).

27. The mean (average) is calculated by adding together all of the scores (observations) and dividing by the number of scores. The mean is greatly affected by extreme scores, because it is "pulled" in the direction of the atypical values.

28. The median is the middle score in a distribution when the scores are ordered from the highest to the lowest.

29. The mode is the most frequently occurring score in a distribution. The mode is the least useful measure of central tendency in most educational research.

30. Standard deviation is a measure of variability that tells us how spread out a group of scores are (Gay et al., 2009, p. 223). The standard deviation is the most important measure of variability for our action research purposes. The standard deviation helps us to understand approximately how much a particular score deviates from the average score.

31. Be careful about how you "interpret" the descriptive statistics that you use to analyze your data and be careful about the claims you make based on a descriptive statistical analysis. Be clear about the limited significance that can be attached to averages and standard deviations.

32. The challenges of data analysis are showcased when we attempt to analyze quantitative and qualitative data sources concurrently or in sequence and then attempt to find points of intersection as well as discrepancies, as is the case in mixed-methods designs.

33. Mixed-methods research designs combine quantitative and qualitative approaches by including both quantitative and qualitative data in a single study.

Qualitative Data Interpretation Techniques

34. *Extend the analysis.* One technique low on the data interpretation risk scale is to simply extend the analysis of your data by raising questions about the study, noting implications that might be drawn without actually drawing them.

35. *Connect findings with personal experience.* Action research is personal business, so it makes sense to personalize our interpretations. Share your interpretations based on your intimate knowledge and understanding of schools and classrooms and teaching and learning.

36. *Seek the advice of "critical" friends.* If you have difficulty focusing an interpretive lens on your work, rely on your trusted colleagues to offer insights that you may have missed because of your closeness to the work. But beware! The more opinions you seek the more you will receive, and often these suggestions come with the expectation that you will accept the advice.

37. *Contextualize findings in the literature.* Uncovering external sources as part of the review of related literature is a powerful way for teacher researchers to provide support for the study's findings.

38. *Turn to theory.* Share theories about teaching and learning that appear to help make sense of your data.

39. *Know when to say "when".* If you do not feel comfortable with offering an interpretation, don't do it. Be satisfied with suggesting what needs to be done next and use that as a starting point for the next action research cycle.

Sharing Your Interpretations Wisely

40. Avoid being evangelical about your interpretations, connect them closely to your data and analysis, and share your newfound understandings with colleagues in an appropriate manner.

Task

1. How will you analyze each data source that you have indicated in your data collection plan? Remember: Don't collect data when you don't know what you are going to do with it. For each data source identified in your data collection matrix identify appropriate data analysis and data interpretation approaches.

Action Planning for Educational Change

This chapter discusses different steps in action planning that help ensure that teacher researchers are able to implement positive educational change based on the insights they gain through action research. **Action planning** basically attempts to answer the question, "Based on what I have learned from my research, what should I do now?"

A Steps to Action Chart is presented to guide teacher researchers through the action planning process. The chart identifies the findings of the study, the recommended action that targets a given finding, who is responsible for specific actions, who needs to be consulted or informed about the findings of the study and the concomitant actions, how to monitor the effects of your actions through the collection of data, a timeline for when the actions and monitoring will occur, and any resources that will be needed to carry out the action. A blank Steps to Action Chart is also included for your personal use.

Finally, this chapter will discuss action planning within the context of challenges that face the teacher researcher and the conditions under which action research and the educational change that follows it can occur.

After reading this chapter you should be able to:

1 Complete an action plan by working through a Steps to Action Chart.

2 Become aware of challenges that confront the action researcher in the action planning process.

3 Become aware of conditions that facilitate educational change in school environments.

4 Become aware of what teacher researchers gain by engaging in action research.

Reflecting on an Absenteeism Policy

JACK RESTON

This vignette is the story of an elementary school principal who modeled the process of action research for his teachers, many of whom were involved in their own action research projects at the same time. Jack's story is particularly powerful because it illustrates the willingness of a school principal to investigate the effect of a policy he had developed. Further, Jack tackled difficult problems facing many teachers and principals: how to keep children in school and the importance of being in school. The result of the study was an action plan that required the change of a district-wide absenteeism policy.

I was selected to serve on a committee of administrators to review current policies concerning students' absenteeism. The task of the committee was to write a new student absenteeism policy, which led to the adoption of a new absenteeism policy and procedure. I recognized throughout this process a need to look into student absenteeism with more depth and understanding, and for this reason I selected the topic of student absenteeism for my action research project.

I initiated my research project with a review of our school's attendance rate profile for the last 5 years. The profile showed little or no change in the attendance rate. This was a concern because I cross-referenced the attendance rate with the funds allocated for various attendance incentives designed to motivate students and could easily see that the dollars spent on incentives were not affecting the attendance rate. I sat at my desk and thought about all my current and past efforts. It was clear that I was not truly passionate about student absenteeism. I had never taken time to clearly understand its causes or researched the best solutions to prevent it. I was passionate about my belief that a child's success in life depends on a solid educational foundation. I was passionate about my belief that students cannot afford to miss class at any time. I was passionate about my belief that absenteeism is a symptom or gauge of a student experiencing failure in school.

I began by asking three questions:

1. What student characteristics are associated with student absenteeism?

2. What are some longitudinal effects of student absenteeism?

3. What are some effective strategies to prevent student absenteeism?

I reviewed current studies, literature, local and national profiles, written surveys, and interviews. I found that absenteeism was highly associated with dropping out of school, academic failure, and delinquency. I learned what students and parents in our school believed about the relationship between school and absenteeism. I concluded that I really did not understand the belief systems of families at risk for poor attendance in school. I conducted a massive survey of students and parents within a four-day period of time. Surveys gathered data concerning such things as respectfulness of students, safety in school, conflict management, discipline, school rules, self-esteem, and academics. In addition, the survey gathered data on mobility rates, volunteerism, and levels of education in parents. The identity of the families surveyed was kept unknown. Instead, the surveys were coded as "at risk" or "not at risk" data.

I collected data from the surveys in three stages. First, each family in the school was mailed a survey. The surveys arrived at the homes of students on a Saturday. Completed surveys were returned to the school prior to 9:00 AM on the following Monday. Second, each student in the entire school was surveyed in their classroom at 9:00 AM on Monday. Third, selected students and parents were interviewed between Monday and Tuesday to collect data similarly gathered on the surveys.

Student teachers from a nearby university and local educators with experience in action research interviewed selected students and parents. The interviews were conducted over the telephone or face-to-face. I compiled all of the data and began searching for a better understanding of at-risk students and parents at my school. I found these people believed the following:

- Other students did not respect them.
- They did not use conflict management skills.
- Adults in the school did not handle discipline effectively.
- School rules are not fair.
- There are behavior problems associated with this group.
- At-risk students perform poorly in academic areas.
- At-risk students in this school are not motivated by rewards such as drawings for prizes and certificates.

This information led to major changes in our approach to improving attendance in school. First, we stopped spending large sums of money for rewards and drawings. Although these are nice things for students, they are ineffective in dealing with the problem of poor attendance. Second, we recognized punitive measures were having little effect on attendance. This led us to the belief that students succeeding in school were more likely to attend school regularly.

We began a concentrated effort to improve the success of students at school both academically and emotionally. This included the use of student/parent/teacher/principal contracts, daily planners for students, individual conferences between the student and the principal every 14 days to review grades and behaviors, better assessments to locate students having academic problems, improved instructional techniques and alignment of curriculum, and more concentrated efforts to improve the self-esteem of students.

In conclusion, I found the following to be true in our effort to improve student absenteeism:

1. Students need to be successful in school.
2. Students need to be connected to the school.
3. Students need friendships with students and adults at school.
4. Students need to develop the skills to deal with life's daily anxieties.
5. The school needs to develop meaningful relationships with the family.

Based on these findings, I worked with teachers and parents to develop quick responses that unite the student, parent, educator, and community in a preventive effort to minimize absenteeism.

To support Kurt Lewin's prophetic statement, "No action without research; no research without action" (cited in Adelman, 1993, p. 8), this chapter discusses how teacher researchers can ensure that action is a natural outcome of their action research efforts. Without action, we have done nothing more than replicate what we set out to avoid—doing research on someone for our own benefit, whatever that may be. But the reward for us all in this process is taking action to improve the educational experiences of our children—action is at the very heart of the action research endeavor.

In Jack Reston's vignette we see a principal and members of the school community (children, parents, teachers, student teachers) who persevered in trying to solve an important problem that faces many schools—how to keep children in school. Reston's action plan identified a number of actions targeted to the findings of the study: developing students' skills to deal with the anxieties of life and school, developing strategies to ensure student success in school, developing meaningful relationships with families, improving instructional techniques and curriculum alignment, using strategies to develop meaningful relationships/partnerships with families, and so on. In the action planning process, Reston had reflected on the findings of the study and what he now understood about the problem of absenteeism. As a result of this reflection, he was better able to plan the next steps in the action research process.

Action planning is a natural next step in the action research process. Using the guidelines in this chapter, you will be able to ensure that the necessary steps are taken to bring your efforts to fruition.

Developing Action Plans

At this phase of the action research process, the teacher researcher is basically trying to answer the following question: "Based on what I have learned from this investigation, what should I do now?" At this point, teacher researchers should reflect on the taken-for-granted assumptions that guided them to the investigation in the first instance and determine what course of action to take next. This reflection allows time for both teachers and administrators to determine what they have learned from their investigations and the related professional literature and to decide on the necessary steps to action.

To facilitate this process, consider using a Steps to Action Chart similar to those shown in Table 7–1 and Table 7–2. (Table 7–1 shows a generic Steps to Action Chart; Table 7–2 shows the Steps to Action Chart created by Jack Reston for his study of student absenteeism.) By working through the steps included on the chart, teacher researchers will have a list of:

- What they learned (findings).
- The recommended actions that target a given finding.
- Who is responsible for specific actions (responsibility).
- Who needs to be consulted or informed about the findings of the study and the associated actions.
- Who will monitor or collect the effects of actions.
- Dates when the actions and monitoring will occur.
- Any resources that will be needed to carry out the action.

Elements of this chart will look familiar to you. Monitoring and data collection efforts will once again involve you in the action research process. In each case, you will focus on a new

TABLE 7–1 Steps to Action Chart

Summary of findings research questions	Recommended action targeted to findings	Who is responsible for the action?	Who needs to be consulted or informed?	Who will monitor/ collect data?	Timeline	Resources
1.0 Research question #1					When will action/ monitoring occur?	What will you need in order to carry out your action?
1.1 Finding #1 1.2 Finding #2		• Teacher • Team	• Teacher • Team			
2.0 Research question #2 2.1 Finding #1 2.2 Finding #2 2.3 etc.		• Department head • Principal • Parents • Students	• Department head • Principal • Parents • Students			

TABLE 7–2 Jack Reston's Steps to Action Chart

Summary of findings research questions	Recommended action targeted to findings	Who is responsible for the action? T – Teacher S – Student P – Principal PA – Parent(s)	Who needs to be consulted or informed?	Who will monitor/ collect data?	Timeline	Resources
1.0 What student characteristics are attributed to student absenteeism?				T, P: 1. Observations 2. Intentions 3. Surveys 4. Test data	Ongoing throughout school year.	None
1.1 Lack of respect	1.1 Model respect for others.	1.1 T, S, P				
1.2 Poor conflict management skills	1.2–1.4 Develop skills to deal with life's daily anxieties.	1.2–1.4 T, S, P, PA	1.2–1.4 PA			
1.3 Lack of self-discipline						
1.4 Behavior problems						
1.5 Poor academic performance	1.5 Improve strategies to develop success in school.	1.5 T, P				
2.0 What are some longitudinal effects of student absenteeism?				T, P: 1. Observations 2. Intentions 3. Surveys 4. Test data	Ongoing throughout school year.	None
2.1 Dropouts	2.1–2.3 Students need to be connected to school. Develop strategies to build a sense of "belonging" at school.	2.1–2.3 T, P, S				
2.2 Academic failure						
2.3 Delinquency						
3.0 What are some effective strategies to prevent student absenteeism?						
3.1 Student/ Parent/ Teacher/ Principal contracts	3.1 Implement contracts.	3.1 S, PA, T, P	3.1 S, PA	T, P: 1. Observations 2. Intentions 3. Surveys 4. Test data	Ongoing throughout school year.	

3.2 Daily planners	3.2 Purchase & use planners.	3.2 P			3.2 $$ for planners
3.3 Diagnostic tools	3.3 Work with district office to administer diagnostic tests.	3.3 P	3.3 District office		
3.4 Self-esteem strategies	3.4 Implement self-esteem curriculum.	3.4 T			
3.5 Improved teaching & curriculum	3.5 Encourage ongoing professional development.	3.5 T, P			3.5 $$ for P.D.

problem, such as "What are the effects of this action on student performance?," and develop specific data collection/monitoring techniques to answer the question. Although not included on the chart, the monitoring/data collection techniques (see Chapter 4) would lead to data analysis and interpretation (see Chapter 6) with findings and further steps to action. Hence, the cycle repeats itself again and again. It may be that you are entirely satisfied with an intervention and that the proposed action is to continue with its implementation. This routinization of instruction still suggests that as a reflective teacher you will continue to collect data—to monitor the effects of your instruction on your students' performance and attitude. At that point, as a self-renewing school faculty or as an individual teacher with a reflective professional disposition, you will continue your systematic inquiry into some other aspect of your practice. (See Research in Action Checklist 7–1 for a list of steps to action.)

Levels of Action Planning

Action planning can occur at a number of different levels within the school: *individual, team,* and *schoolwide,* depending on the scope of the action research effort. Action planning also may take place at a number of these different levels during a single investigation. For example, the problem under investigation may have had a schoolwide focus, such as to determine the effects of an innovative reading curriculum (with an emphasis on constructing meaning) on student performance (as measured by statewide assessment scores and monthly criterion-referenced tests). Participation in the schoolwide effort might also have necessitated that teachers meet in grade-level teams to plan appropriate reading interventions and to analyze regularly collected data. Finally, individual teachers would need to adapt the intervention as appropriate for their own students' needs. In this case, action planning should be undertaken at all levels within the school.

Individual

Typically, **individual action planning** will be characterized by teacher researchers who have worked through an action research cycle as part of a course, licensure, or grant requirement, or by teacher researchers who are undertaking action research as a regular component of their practice. Individual teachers can still work through the Steps to Action Chart (see Table 7–1) and in so doing remind themselves of the steps that need to be taken to implement action and monitor the effects of the action.

In all likelihood, individual teacher researchers will have focused their action research projects and interventions on an issue related to curriculum, instruction, assessment, classroom

Steps to Action

_____ Findings of the research.
_____ Recommended action.
_____ Responsibilities.
_____ Sharing findings with colleagues.
_____ Ongoing monitoring (data collection).
_____ Timeline for action.
_____ Resources.

management, or community involvement. In these areas, the resulting action plan will focus on activities such as:

- *Curriculum development.* Findings of a study related to curriculum development (and implementation) would provide the teacher researcher with specific actions for the next cycle of curriculum development (for example, the inclusion of new and/or revised lessons), additional learning artifacts (resources and materials), and so on. Following the Steps to Action Chart, the individual teacher researcher would be responsible not only for all actions but also for consulting with grade-level colleagues, department heads, district-level curriculum specialists, parents, and the school principal.

- *Instructional strategies.* Findings of a study related to the implementation of new instructional strategies (e.g., cooperative learning, high-level questioning strategies, increase in "wait time," teaching reading across the curriculum, and so on) would provide the teacher researcher with specific actions for the next cycle of developing and implementing any new instructional strategies. Following the Steps to Action Chart, the individual teacher researcher would be responsible for all actions, including consulting with grade-level colleagues, department heads, district-level teaching specialists (for example, a Teacher on Special Assignment [TOSA]), parents, and the school principal. The teacher may identify specific additional professional development activities that need to be undertaken (and budgeted for) prior to the next action research cycle.

- *Assessment strategies.* Findings of a study related to the use of innovative assessment strategies (for example, the Highland Park High School "Emphasizing Learning by Deemphasizing Grades" example in Chapter 6) would provide the teacher researcher with specific actions for the next cycle of implementing an innovative assessment strategy. Following the Steps to Action Chart, the individual teacher researcher would be responsible for all actions, including consulting with grade-level colleagues, department heads, district-level curriculum and instruction specialists, parents, and the school principal.

- *Classroom management strategies/plans.* A common area of focus for beginning teachers (preservice and inservice) is classroom management. Findings of a study related to implementation of a new classroom management plan would provide the teacher researcher with specific actions for the next cycle of teaching. Following the Steps to Action Chart, the individual teacher researcher would be responsible not only for all actions but also for consulting with grade-level colleagues, department heads, district-level curriculum and instruction specialists, parents, and the school principal.

- *Community involvement.* Findings of a study related to community involvement (for example, Jack Reston's vignette at the start of this chapter) would provide the teacher researcher with specific actions for the next cycle of how to improve community involve-

Summary of findings research questions	Recommended action targeted to findings	Who is responsible for the action?	Who needs to be consulted or informed?	Who will monitor/ collect data?	Timeline	Resources

ment in solving local school problems. Following the Steps to Action Chart, the individual teacher researcher would be responsible for all actions, including consulting with grade-level colleagues, department heads, district-level curriculum specialists, parents, the school principal, and probably the district superintendent.

Although the primary audience for the findings from any of these studies is the individual teacher, it is important for teacher researchers to tap into the kind of support networks one will find at universities. As Elliott (1991) suggested:

A small band of isolated teacher researchers can tap into a reflective counter culture in the form of an action-research network which transcends school boundaries and is linked to a teacher education institution. Membership of such a network can provide the kind of cultural resources which strengthen the capacity of aspiring teacher researchers to resist the time pressures operating on them from inside schools. (pp. 66–67)

This networking transcends not only school boundaries, but also global boundaries via participation in online action research listservs and chat rooms. This kind of cyberspace network can strengthen the resolve of teachers who must work in isolation to continue with the process through the action planning stage and into the next revolution of the cycle.

Team

In an era when schools have increasing authority to make decisions about curriculum and instruction, it is common to see teams of teachers, administrators, and sometimes parents working collaboratively on action research projects. Often these groups grow out of networks developed in an action research course among teachers with similar areas of interest and expertise. At other times they grow out of grant requirements for grade-level or discipline-based teams to work collaboratively on a school improvement focus. Regardless of the catalyst for the network, these **teams** all share a common focus at this stage in the action research process—to mobilize their collective energies to move forward with action. This process can be facilitated by working through the Steps to Action Chart and collaboratively determining who has responsibility for what, when, and where. Resolution of any issues that emerge at this stage is critical to the continued success and longevity of the action research team. At this stage the primary audience for the action plan consists of the team members. However, action research teams must seek appropriate ways to transcend the traditional boundaries that have historically seen small teams of teachers burn out without feedback and support from the environments in which they work.

Schoolwide

Schoolwide action research, as the name implies, is about all of the members of the school community working together with a single goal in mind. For example, a schoolwide emphasis on improving reading, writing, or math is a common area of focus in elementary schools. Similarly, and sadly, it is not uncommon to see a high school focus on the effects of a drug and alcohol curriculum on student attitude, understanding, and levels of use. However, the distinguishing feature in these examples is that they have been agreed on by the whole school faculty as the focus for a schoolwide improvement effort that will be driven by the findings of an action research effort. Cooperation, collaboration, and communication are no less important in the action planning phase than they were during the other steps of the process.

The challenge at the schoolwide level is how to actively engage all the participants in goal setting that is integral to the action planning process. There will always be finger pointing and denial, and it will take a skilled facilitator to move a faculty through the Steps to Action Chart if progress is to be made. Do not underestimate the necessity of meaningfully engaging all of the school community in this action planning process, or you will risk perpetual isolation in the world of playground supervision—been there, done that, bought the umbrella!

Action Should Be Ongoing

This discussion about action planning is not meant to suggest that action occurs only at the end of the action research process. The very dynamic nature of teaching necessitates that teachers make many changes to instruction during the course of a day based on the formative feedback (data) collected as an integral part of the teaching process. For example, preservice teachers are often requested to include on lesson plans "Evaluation" statements to the effect of "How will you know if your students have achieved your instructional objectives?" In other words, what data will you collect that informs your post-planning at the end of the day? Often these data are collected intuitively and informally in noninvasive ways. It is such a normative aspect of teaching that we take it for granted. As teachers we have been programmed to collect, analyze, and interpret data quickly and efficiently so we can suggest "findings" and take necessary "actions" (remediation, reteaching, related material, extension activities) that enable learning to proceed in a connected fashion.

The Importance of Reflection

Action planning is also a time for reflection—reflection on where you have been, what you have learned, and where you are going. Action planning and reflection give you an opportunity to identify your individual or collective continuing professional development needs. This reflection is facilitated by the review of the related literature you collected early in the action research process in concert with your own findings. The following questions may also be helpful prompts for reflection:

- What were the intended and unintended effects of your actions?
- What educational issues arise from what you've learned about your practice?

Clearly, these are not questions that elicit quick and easy responses. They urge you to look back at your practice from the enlightened viewpoint of someone who has systematically inquired into the effects of teaching on student outcomes. In undertaking such reflection, you will position yourself to act responsively to the findings of your study. The remaining sections of this chapter will help you to further identify challenges you may face when attempting to implement change and will guide you in meeting those challenges and effecting positive educational change in your school.

Some Challenges Facing Teacher Researchers

As you reflect on the critical steps to action, consider the challenges that all teacher researchers face both when doing action research and when attempting to effect educational change based on the results of their inquiry. If indeed we are going to avoid living out Sarason's (1990) prophecy of "the more things change, the more they will remain the same" (p. 5), then we must be prepared to address these obstacles. These hurdles include a lack of resources, resistance to change, reluctance to interfere with others' professional practices, reluctance to admit difficult truths, the challenge of finding a forum to share what you have learned, and the difficulty of making time for action research endeavors.

Lack of Resources

The scarcity of resources is perhaps the greatest obstacle to action planning you will face. Many excellent action research and change efforts have been blocked by the lack of classroom resources and materials. But by being innovative and remaining energized by what you have learned about your practice, you will find ways to make change happen. This may mean using creativity to solve materials management issues. Don't wait for an administrator, central office person, or philanthropist to offer what you need to be successful. Go after the grants, however small, to fund the resources you identify as critical to the success of your intervention. (See Chapter 8 for further discussion of grant sources available for teacher researchers.) Use the data you have collected, analyzed, and interpreted as a way to build a case for resources that may be presented to Parent-Teacher Associations, district-wide committees, school boards, granting agencies, and so on to make a case for what you need.

Action researchers also need professional as well as material resources. If action research is to become a part of your professional disposition and be continued over time, it must benefit both your own continued professional development and student outcomes. Identification of promising practices will suggest the kinds of professional development you need to seek, either individually or collectively. If your local university or school district can't provide the professional development you seek, use the Internet to find out who does. Again, use your findings to make a compelling, persuasive case for the kind of professional development you need—not what someone else thinks you need.

Resistance to Change

Any type of change, however small, may be viewed as threatening by some. After all, the status quo is familiar and comfortable. But the era of schools that refuse to innovate is past. The ever-changing social and political environment in which we live necessitates that teachers become sophisticated instructional leaders and decision makers who have the skills to empower students and other individuals in their learning communities. Participation in and support of the action research process is critical if there is to be a shift in the culture of schools to the reflective practitioner culture of the self-renewing school. Living the commitment to a dynamic school culture as opposed to living the traditional "advocate of constraint" persona will go a long way toward revitalizing an individual school's culture and bringing about positive change.

For example, Jack Reston's investigation of the effect of the school/district policy on absenteeism showed that attendance rates had remained the same despite costly student incentives that were an integral part of the policy. Once he realized that the current intervention was having no impact, Jack knew he had to take responsibility for trying to change the system to make Eastview Elementary School an environment where all children (especially those at risk for absenteeism) would want to come to school. That meant changing even fundamental things, such as the way administrators interacted with students and the amount of time he spent with them individually. In doing so, he overcame several factors, including the institutional resistance to change.

Reluctance to Interfere with Others' Professional Practices

Unfortunately, there seems to be a prevailing cultural value in schools of "Don't mess around in someone else's professional practice"—especially if you are not invited. The dilemma here for the teacher researcher arises from a conflict between the desire to persuade colleagues to experiment with or embrace new practices that have been shown via action research to have positive effects and a "respect for the professional expertise of colleagues and their right to exercise authority within the confines of their own classroom" (Elliott, 1991, p. 59).

Often teacher researchers faced with this dilemma back away from their investigations and change efforts to "keep the peace" with colleagues. However, if we are to learn from our own and others' professional practice, we must be willing to set aside the traditional protection of each other's classrooms and to embrace as a community of learners the proposed action plan that emerges from our research.

How you approach this professional collaboration with other teachers in your school is as important as trying it at all. It is critical to the success of your action research and change efforts, particularly at the schoolwide level, not to have alienated yourself from others by appearing to be a member of some "enlightened elite" who now knows all of the answers to the problems that affect students' inability to do well on statewide assessments! You will have gone a long way to revitalizing the professional disposition of teaching if you have been able to nurture your own and your colleagues' understanding of the problems you have investigated and built a teamwide commitment to implementing action based on your findings. Collaboration can help break down these stubborn professional barriers.

Reluctance to Admit Difficult Truths

If we view action research and action planning as one way to empower teachers, we should also be aware of the increased accountability these efforts place on teacher researchers. We can't have it both ways: If we want the authority to make the changes we have recommended based on our action research findings, then we must be prepared to look into the mirror and face what we see. After all, if each of us has the power to make the most important decisions in our schools—that is, the ones that have the greatest impact on students—then we must also not abdicate responsibility when things don't go our way. If what we learn is that, despite our best efforts and intentions, our interventions have not succeeded, then we must be prepared to look objectively at the data and make new recommendations for change in our quest to provide the best education possible for our students.

For example, Deborah South (Chapter 1) had hoped to find in her action research project that the group of "unmotivated" students in her study skills class would respond positively to her instruction and guidance. Instead she noticed an alarming and demoralizing trend: Students' grades were dropping. Deborah had to wrestle with this "difficult truth" and carefully consider her own responsibility for the students' performance before coming to a conclusion about the best way to effect change to benefit these "unmotivated" students.

Finding a Forum to Share What You Have Learned

The potential for an action plan to serve as the catalyst for reflective conversation between professionals is limitless. Elliott (1991) argued that such data sharing "promotes a reflective conversation and is at the heart of any transformation of the professional culture" (p. 60). However, an open conversation about what the data from the study suggest (analysis and interpretation) and how these findings have been transformed into a proposed action plan will not always be an easy one.

What is needed is a forum (local, national, or global!) for teachers to share their accounts and a recognition by the profession that change-oriented action research is an important part of the professional competencies of being a teacher. For example, some preservice teacher preparation programs are incorporating action research into their requirements. Individual schools are providing teachers with opportunities to showcase their action research skills as part of an annual teacher evaluation cycle; state and federal grants incorporate action research as part of the instructional improvement cycle; school-based decision-making teams are embracing an action research model to guide their school improvement efforts; and state teacher-licensing agencies are incorporating action research into continuing license renewal requirements.

Although teacher researchers typically have not published their findings, the sharing of teacher researchers' stories has also been facilitated by Web-based action research sites. Teachers can now use a global forum to share their stories, the actions they have taken based on their research, and what they have learned in subsequent action research cycles. (These online journals include *Educational Action Research, Networks, Action Research International,* and *Action Research Electronic Reader.*) The sharing of action plans and what teacher researchers learn in the process is critical to the emerging teacher-as-researcher culture. (See Chapter 8 for practical guidelines for "getting the word out.")

Making Time for Action Research Endeavors

We have already discussed the challenge of making time for action research in your busy daily schedule. Just when you thought the action research cycle was over and you are ready to return to "just teaching," you are thrust back into the process with further reflection about the actions suggested by the findings of your study and the who, what, and when of the next cycle.

"You mean I need to take more action and monitor its effects? But I don't have the time to do one more thing!" This exasperated call for putting the brakes on the process is not uncommon or unreasonable. By the time you have arrived at action planning, you may be all but spent and happy to claim that the status quo is working just fine. If you fall into this category of teacher, I would suggest that you follow your instincts. Allow yourself time to reflect and plan at a bearable pace. You are no good to the students in your care if you are burned out. (As the parent of a child in eleventh grade, the last thing I want is my child's teacher all worn out from a year of doing action research!) The goal is to evolve to the point where action and research become a part of your professional life, but not at the expense of the energy that you need to be vital, creative, and exciting in your daily teaching. After all, if the action research process cannot be normative and undertaken without adversely affecting your primary focus of teaching children, then it *should not be done*.

On the other hand, if you have arrived at the action planning phase with renewed energy and enthusiasm for your work, if you are committed to implementing a locally contextualized innovation that you believe will contribute to the well-being of the students in your care, and if you have maintained a clear sense of direction, mission, and purpose, then move forward in the process and share your stories by whatever medium you can! It will be your stories of success and being a lifelong learner that will change the culture of teaching. These are intimate changes that cannot be forced on any of us from outside—they must come from the passion within.

Regardless of international, national, state, and local trends and initiatives, the individual teacher researcher's ability to resolve the issue of time constraints will ultimately determine whether action research is routinized into the classroom. However, if we as professionals cannot find time to do the work associated with it, then action research will be discarded on the dust heap of other promising educational initiatives.

Facilitating Educational Change

The goal of action research is to enhance the lives of students and teachers through positive educational change. We have just discussed several common challenges that teachers face when attempting to effect educational change based on action research findings. In addition to being prepared to address those challenges, you can help create an environment that is conducive to change. The following are eight conditions that facilitate educational change (adapted from Fullan, 1993; Miller & Lieberman, 1988; Sarason, 1990).

Teachers and Administrators Need to Restructure Power and Authority Relationships

The first condition for fostering action research and encouraging educational change is that teachers and administrators need to restructure power and authority relationships. Power relationships in schools have the potential to empower or underpower action planning efforts. **Power** is not being used in a pejorative sense here—teacher researchers have the potential to harness the collective power of their colleagues, including administrators, to bring about meaningful change through a democratic, liberating, and life-enhancing process. For this to happen, participants in the action research process must be prepared to ask the hard questions related to implementing action based on the findings of the study: What is the recommended action? Who is responsible for doing what? Who needs to be consulted or informed? How will the effects of the implementation be monitored? When will tasks be completed? What resources are needed?

Asking these questions invariably leads to discussions about who has the final decision-making power in the school. In an era of school-based decision making, it is likely that a team of teachers, parents, students, and administrators will have the authority to answer action planning questions and to make decisions. However, whether your school has a professional or a bureaucratic model of school-based decision making in place will determine the amount of influence you will have individually or as a team. According to Conley (1991), the bureaucratic model emphasizes the formal authority of administrators to delegate responsibilities to subordinates, to formulate rules to govern subordinate behavior, and to implement centralized control, planning, and decision making. In contrast, the professional model emphasizes the professional discretion and expertise of teachers in diagnosing and addressing student needs, with an aim to provide teachers the rights they expect as professionals.

Power should be seen as an investment, not as a means of controlling people. According to Miller and Lieberman (1988), "If we look at power this way, teachers and principals can hold leadership roles, and, working together, they can help the schools build a professional culture" (p. 653). This view emphasizes a reflective practitioner culture that empowers rather than underpowers teachers.

Deborah South was empowered, for example, to make changes to the study skills program for unmotivated students based on what she learned from her action research study. Jack Reston was empowered to change the absenteeism policy for his school and to recommend changes to the district's absenteeism policy based on his new understandings of what worked and didn't work for keeping children in school. Viewed in this way, power was an investment in the quality of the educational experiences of many children.

Both Top-Down and Bottom-Up Strategies of Change Can Work

In effecting educational change, both top-down and bottom-up strategies of change can work (Hord, Rutherford, Huling-Austin, & Hall, 1987). **Top-down strategies** can be thought of as changes that are mandated by school/district/state administrators without giving teachers an equal voice in the decision-making process (bureaucratic model). Alternatively, **bottom-up strategies** can be thought of as change that is driven by teachers when given the authority to make decisions (professional model). The debate over whether top-down or bottom-up efforts at change produce the greatest effects has flourished for many years. Fullan (1993) concluded, "What is required is a different two-way relationship of pressure, support and continuous negotiation" (p. 38), such as a continuous discourse between administrators and teachers involved in a collaborative action research project.

For example, the teachers at Highland Park High School worked collaboratively with the school's assistant principal and involved him in the team's action research activities. In this respect, there was obvious support from the school's administration for the action research effort. Alternatively, the teachers at Billabong Elementary School (Chapter 2) were quite resentful that the principal had mandated a math text for the school without consulting teachers in the process.

Teachers Must Be Provided with Support

Additionally, teachers involved in change efforts brought about by action research must be provided with support. Support for teachers in their endeavors ideally would come from all quarters: students, other teachers, the school administration, students' families, government officials, and so on. For example, Jack Reston's investigation into absenteeism could not have occurred had it not been for the support of the parents, teachers, and student teachers (who helped with interviews). Deborah South relied heavily on the emotional support of her critical friends in the action research class when she shared the analysis and interpretation of her study of unmotivated students.

Every Person Is a Change Agent

Both individual and collective efforts are critical to successful change, and every person has the potential to be a change agent. The action research vignettes in this book illustrate the potential for change to happen at the individual, team, and schoolwide levels. But perhaps the key point of all these examples is that it took the desire of an individual teacher or principal to initiate the action research process and to effect positive educational change based on the findings. As Fullan (1993) reminds us, "Each and every teacher has the responsibility to help create an organization capable of individual and collective inquiry and continuous renewal, or [change] will not happen" (p. 39).

Change Tends Not to Be Neat, Linear, or Rational

Equally important, those involved in action research must recognize that change tends not to be neat, linear, or rational. Consider as an example the work of Cathy Mitchell and the Duct Tape Theater (Chapter 3). Although Cathy was able to confirm that her objective of making teen theater a more meaningful experience was sound, she also recognized that the approach of interactive improvisation did not have the desired effects. The audience did not respond to the "Violence Improv" scene as she expected and, as a result, her action research project did not provide her with the tidy solutions she hoped for. Although recommitted to her goal, Cathy is still faced with figuring out new ways to make teen theater a more meaningful experience. For Cathy, the processes of action research and change will be recursive and cyclical.

Teacher Researchers Must Pay Attention to the Culture of the School

A sixth condition is that teacher researchers must pay attention to the culture of the school. Change efforts should always be viewed in the context of the culture of the school and classroom in which the action research effort is being conducted. For example, until Jack Reston investigated the effectiveness of his school's absenteeism policies, it was assumed that the current reward system of drawings and certificates was effective. Instead, he found that the reward system made no difference for at-risk students. As a result, he tried to isolate what intervention would make a difference to these children. He used surveys and interviews to attempt to thoroughly understand the culture, values, and belief systems of the families of children at risk for absenteeism. Based on his findings, he was able to recommend meaningful changes to the school's policy on absenteeism that specifically responded to the needs of this group, especially their need to feel connected to the school.

The Outcome of Any Change Effort Must Benefit Students

A somewhat obvious condition for doing action research and effecting educational change is that the outcome of any change effort must benefit students if it is to be continued. Action research can provide a method for recording, measuring, and analyzing the results of an educational practice or intervention. For example, the data collected by James Rockford in his study of the effectiveness of keyboarding software on the class word processing rate provided conclusive evidence that the keyboarding software being tested was very effective and that time spent on computers at schools was critical. These persuasive data gave James confidence in the benefits of this educational intervention and supported his recommendation that teachers take students to the computer lab every day, monitor keyboarding habits, and see that each student received a minimum of ten minutes of practice per day.

Being Hopeful Is a Critical Resource

Finally, being hopeful is a critical resource if teachers are to perform action research and stay the course of change. Recall the words of Cathy Mitchell, whose teen theater action research project was described in Chapter 3:

The most important part of this project is that I felt renewed energy for my work. Last year at this time I was busily seeking a replacement for myself and announcing to everyone that I wasn't going to direct teens anymore. I didn't even consider that there was a problem that could be addressed and remedied. It feels really good to expect something to happen in my working life as a result of the research and reflection that I myself have done.

As a result of her action research inquiry, Cathy has created a powerful resource for herself—the hope that she will discover new ways to make her work meaningful for teens. Even though she once felt like quitting, she writes that this new hope is powerful enough to sustain her through future change efforts.

For educational change to be successful, all those involved must be optimistic about the results of the transformation. (Of course, they also need to be realistic: Being hopeful is not the same as being naïve.) Reform efforts can sometimes generate negative emotions and a sense of hopelessness because the individuals involved may be on the defensive from external attack or part of small groups of reformers suffering burnout (Fullan, 1997). But if we are going to make progress with reform efforts, we have to weather the negative emotions to succeed.

At the action planning stage of the action research process, you may again have to confront negative emotions from other stakeholders in the process. This is a critical turning point in the action research process: You can easily adopt the position that this is a lost cause, or you can rely on the most critical resource any of us have—*hope*. Individually, we all must take a stand on whether our investigations have yielded findings that warrant taking action. If we have done a good job, we should have collected findings that are trustworthy and true. Reflect on the hope you felt when you first began your project, then use that hope to sustain you through the action planning process. "Being hopeful and taking action in the face of important lost causes may be less emotionally draining than being in a permanent state of despair" (Fullan, 1997, pp. 231–232).

Recognize that we can do little to really change how a colleague thinks, acts, and feels—we must all answer to ourselves and the search for self-efficacy that comes with being a professional educator. If any of us reach a point in our professional lives when we feel that we can no longer make a difference or no longer struggle in the face of adversity (limited time or resources, for example), then it is probably time to try another professional calling. In education, whether it's a lack of chalk, paper, or RAM for the computer, none of us have ever had a blank check to finance the time and resources we think we need to be the best we can be. But what sets us apart from other professionals is the belief that we can make a difference in children's lives, with or without the resources.

Schools are complex social settings, and those of us who have taught at a number of different schools know how they can differ from community to community. You are in the best position to know what lessons you can apply from this broad discussion of educational change to your own situation. But we can all learn from each other's experience by sharing our stories. Whenever possible, share your action research stories with others. In doing so, you will help revitalize the professional disposition of teachers.

What Do Teachers Gain Through All of This Work?

If you are now living this process, perhaps in a quiet, unassuming way, what follows will validate your work as a professional—contribute to your sense of self-efficacy—for it is within that we all find the rewards that teaching has to offer. Returning to our earlier discussion about critical/postmodern perspectives of action research, you will recall that what we believe as a professional community and what we as individual teacher researchers have gained through all of this work has systematically guided us to action.

Having invested a great deal of time and energy into investigating the taken-for-granted relationships and practices in your professional life, you have now arrived at the point where the "rubber meets the road." Will you really initiate action and continue the process? If you answer in the affirmative, you have gone a long way toward embracing some of the tenets of a socially responsive approach to research: You have engaged in a democratic process that has encouraged the participation of your colleagues. The process has been equitable, with the participants all having one voice. The experience has been liberating and has freed you from accepting with blind faith something that may have been forced on you. Finally, the experience has been life enhancing for you as a professional and for the students who will benefit from your teaching.

For me, the ultimate payoff for teacher researchers who have stuck with the process, have learned and internalized the action research skills, and are now committed to action and self-renewal is the belief and knowledge that those who are the real beneficiaries of your work are the students in your care. There can be no argument against this powerful and altruistic goal.

Summary

Developing Action Plans

1. Action planning is an effort to answer the question, "Based on what I have learned from my research, what should I do now?" Without action, we have done nothing more than replicate what we set out to avoid—doing research on someone for our own benefit, whatever that may be. But the reward for all of us in this process is taking action to improve the educational experiences of our children—action is at the very heart of the action research endeavor.

2. To facilitate the action planning process consider using a Steps to Action Chart that addresses issues related to what you as a teacher researcher have learned (findings), what recommended action targets a given finding, who is responsible for specific actions (responsibility), who needs to be consulted or informed about the findings of the study and the concomitant actions, how you will monitor the effect of your actions by collecting data, on what dates the actions and monitoring will occur, and what resources will be needed to carry out the action (see Tables 7–1 and 7–2).

3. Action planning can occur at a number of different levels within the school: individual, team, and schoolwide.

4. Individual action planning is done by teacher researchers who have worked through an action research cycle and can still work through a Steps to Action Chart, and in so doing, remind themselves of the steps that need to be taken to implement action and monitor the effects of the action.

5. Team action planning is most commonly done by teams of teachers, administrators, and sometimes parents working collaboratively on action research projects. An action research team shares a common focus at this stage in the action research process—to mobilize their collective energies to move forward with action.

6. Schoolwide action research is about all of the members of the school community working together with a single goal in mind. The challenge at the schoolwide level is how to actively engage all the participants in goal setting that is integral to the action planning process.
7. Action planning, at all levels, is also a time for reflection—reflection on where you have been, what you have learned, and where you are going. Action planning and reflection give you an opportunity to identify your individual or collective professional development needs.

Some Challenges Facing Teacher Researchers

8. Some of the challenges faced by action researchers who seek to implement positive educational change include: lack of resources, resistance to change, reluctance to interfere with others' professional practices, reluctance to admit difficult truths, difficulty of finding a forum to share what you have learned, and lack of time for action research endeavors.

Facilitating Educational Change

9. Eight factors for facilitating educational change in a school environment are: (1) teachers and administrators need to restructure power relationships; (2) both top-down and bottom-up strategies for change can work; (3) teachers involved in change efforts brought about by action research must be provided with support; (4) every person is a change agent; (5) those involved must recognize that change tends not to be neat, linear, and rational; (6) teacher researchers must pay attention to the culture of the school; (7) the outcome of any change effort must benefit students to be continued; and (8) being hopeful is a powerful resource.

What Do Teacher Researchers Gain Through All of This Work?

10. The ultimate payoff for teacher researchers who have stuck with the action research process, have learned and internalized the action research skills, and are now committed to action and self-renewal is the belief and knowledge that those who are the real beneficiaries of your work are the students in your care. There can be no argument against this powerful and altruistic goal.

Tasks

1. Develop an action plan based on your action research findings and present it using the Steps to Action Chart format.
2. How would you apply what you have learned about the challenges of implementing educational change to overcome potential obstacles that you may encounter in taking action?

8

Writing Up
Action Research

There is little point to writing up qualitative research if we cannot get anyone to read what we have to report, and no point to research without reporting.

(Wolcott, 2001, p. 7)

Perhaps one of the most difficult tasks confronting teacher researchers is finding the time and inclination to commit to paper what they have learned about their area of focus. For university researchers who live in a "publish or perish" world, the motivation to write up and publish their research is far more extrinsic. However, teacher researchers are more concerned about the pressures and complexities of daily classroom life—after all, their number one priority is the planning, implementation, and evaluation of engaging learning experiences for the children in their classrooms.

Yet, teacher researchers can help fellow teachers as well as themselves by writing about action research in a prescribed way—in an organized report. Think of this last step as helping to close the gap that has historically existed between research and practice (something alluded to in Chapter 1 with the work of Mary Kennedy). It is important to be familiar with a form that is most commonly accepted for publication in journals and certainly for satisfying traditional university course requirements.

There are two primary motivations for writing up your action research:

1. The act of writing helps each of us better understand the story we are trying to tell.
2. A written account provides us with a permanent, accessible record for our professional and personal use.

Many of my students find themselves writing not by choice but by mandate (you may well be in the same situation!). In fact, some of you may see the very act of writing up your studies as unpleasant . . . just one more term paper to complete, another hoop to jump through. On the other hand, you may not mind writing but still may be frustrated by some of the nuts and bolts issues associated with writing and finding an audience for your work. Read on! I can't guarantee that the outcome of your writing journey will be publication in a prestigious journal or book, but I can guarantee you that if you invest the time and energy into writing your research story, you will at least benefit your students as well as give yourself the opportunity to have it read by like-minded folks. And what could be more altruistic than helping other teachers help their students? What's that saying about if a tree falls in the forest and nobody hears it, did it make a sound? The same is true for writing up our research efforts. If you don't share your stories, how will anyone know you ever did anything that contributed to the teachers' body of knowledge?

After reading this chapter you should be able to:

1. Describe the value of writing about action research.

2. Utilize strategies for writing about action research.

3. Describe guidelines for submitting your action research write up for publication.

Before our discussion about formally writing about your action research, we need to discuss the value of writing up your action research experience and findings.

Why Should I Formally Write about My Action Research?

Perhaps one of the most difficult concepts I have to "sell" to teacher researchers is the importance of "writing up" their research efforts; they struggle to see the value of it. These teachers are focused on understanding the impact of what they do in classrooms and on how and what their students learn. In short, these professional teachers are committed to improving their own practice but do not necessarily see the purpose of sharing what they have learned with a wider audience. Often teacher researchers have declared to me:

I developed my action plan based on what I learned. . . . I am making a difference in my own classroom for my own kids. What does it matter if somebody else reads about what I did and learned?

Writing up what I have done and trying to publish the story is not rewarded or recognized as important by my school and district. Why bother if nobody cares?

Again, this is a difficult argument to win when one argues on the basis of giving back to the profession and contributing to the knowledge base, and blah, blah, blah! Yet, as members of a profession, we have to get beyond the point that writing up research is something that is done by academics in ivory towers.

The value in writing up your research is that the process of writing requires the writer to clarify meaning—to choose words carefully, thoughtfully describe that which is experienced or seen, reflect on experiences, and refine phrasing when putting words on a page. You may learn something important about your students and their learning—something you may have missed had you not considered your words on the page—as you formally write about your research. Furthermore, the act of putting information on paper for your peers necessitates honesty, accuracy, clarity, and thought, thereby encouraging you to create a better product than if you had simply made a mental note of your action research as you left school at the end of the day. So, keep this reason in mind as you engage in this writing phase of your research:

- *Clarification.* Writing your research requires clarity and accuracy of expression. Writing about your research activities encourages thought and reflection, and perhaps creates new questions that are resolved, a process which shapes and completes your research.

Other reasons to write up your research include:

- *Validation.* Publishing your research and the feedback you will receive from your reviewers and readers will validate who you are as a professional educator and what you do.
- *Empowerment.* Reflecting on your practices through writing will empower you to continue to challenge the status quo and be an advocate for your children.
- *It is Generative.* Writing is a generative activity that culminates in a product, something tangible that you can share with colleagues, supervisors, and parents.
- *Accomplishment.* Writing up your research will provide you with a sense of accomplishment. It is both humbling and exciting when colleagues read your work and compliment you on your accomplishments!

Format and Style

Format refers to the general pattern of organization and arrangement of the research report. The number and types of headings and subheadings to be included in the report are determined by the format used. Style refers to the rules of grammar, spelling, capitalization, punctuation, and word processing followed in preparing the report. Formats may vary in terms of specific headings included, and research reports generally follow a format that parallels the steps involved in conducting a study. For example, although one format may call for a discussion section and another format may require a summary or conclusions and a recommendations section (or both), all formats require a section in which the results of the study are discussed and interpreted. All research reports also include a condensed description of the study, whether it be a summary of a dissertation or an abstract of a journal article.

Most colleges, universities, and professional journals either have developed their own required style manual or have selected one that must be followed. Check with your instructor about the style used in your institution. Do this before beginning writing, because rearranging a format after the fact is tedious and time consuming. One such manual, which is increasingly being required as a guide for theses and dissertations, is the *Publication Manual of the American Psychological Association*, also called the APA style manual (currently in its sixth edition). If you are not bound by any particular format and style system, the APA style manual is recommended, as it is the most widely accepted academic format and style system used by colleges, universities, and journals. In addition to acquiring and studying a copy of the selected manual, it is also very helpful to study several reports that have been written following the same manual. For example, look at existing action research write ups to get an idea of format and what is expected. To the degree possible (e.g., with respect to tables, figures, references, and student examples of tasks) this text you are reading reflects APA guidelines, as does the following discussion. Are you sold on the idea of writing? If so, let's forge ahead with examining an example of an action research article.

Sample Annotated Action Research Article

The following research article is reprinted here so that you may examine the general structure and components of written action research. I hope that you will refer to this example frequently as you write your first action research report. Just as you've been trained to observe your students, be observant as you read the following article and consciously note the various components of this written report: the headings, some of the phrases that are characteristic of particular sections of the write-up, and the meaning of each section. As you will soon see (or perhaps you came to this realization earlier), the organization of an action research write-up is not rocket science. In fact, the sections that follow predictably mirror the core chapters of this book and the Steps in the Action Plan: the Area of Focus Statement, Research Questions, Review of Literature, Data Collection, Data Analysis, and the Action Plan. (Look at the Table of Contents of this book—look familiar?)

Now that you've seen a sample of something you might produce, let's discuss some nuts and bolts ideas on writing up action research.

Catchy Title
→

"Come to My Web (Site)," Said the Spider to the Fly: Reflections on the Life of a Virtual Professor

Geoff Mills

This paper was presented at the Third Conference of the Self-Study in Teacher Education Practices group at Herstmonceux Castle, East Sussex, England, July 2000, and is included in the proceedings for the conference.

Abstract

Intervention or Innovation
→

The purpose of this paper is to share the results of a 2-year study that focused on the effects of teaching action research via a web-based class. In a market-driven economy in which many universities now find themselves, web-based delivery of education classes has become increasingly popular. This paper will share the findings of a study that looked at the experiences of teaching and learning action research in a web-based environment.

Introduction

In recent years, Oregon universities have moved to decrease the amount of "satellite" time associated with distance learning classes and to increase the amount of support made available to students "on-line." As a result of the Learning Anywhere, Anytime Project (LAAP) grant by the Oregon University System, the Education Department at Southern Oregon University is pioneering the development and implementation of completely web-based graduate classes in education. This paper is based on my experiences of teaching a web-based version of action research for two terms in 2 consecutive years.

Context
→

The Action Research course is a 10-week introductory, graduate level class focused on the development, implementation, and evaluation of action research. One of the goals of the web-based class is to maximize the interaction between the instructor and the students, and among the students. In order to encourage this interaction, students "post" their responses to weekly tasks as well as respond to other students in the class. Additionally, the class utilizes a listserv and a discussion board (chat room). In order to complete the course, students are required to write a review of related literature, respond to weekly postings and tasks, and complete an action research project. Students register for the class and request a copy of the required text by calling a toll-free number or registering on-line. The course is based around the text *Action Research: A Guide for the Teacher Researcher* (Mills, 2000) and is supplemented with PowerPoint presentations that can be downloaded from the course web site. A complete overview of the class can be accessed at the following URL using the password "research" to enter the class: http://www.collegecourse.com/sou/ed/ed519/.

Action research involves teacher researchers in a four-step process that includes the following: identifying an area of focus, data collection, data analysis and interpretation, and action planning. In doing action research, teacher researchers have developed solutions to their own problems and as such are the authoritative voices as to what works in their particular settings. They exhibit a professional disposition that is encapsulated in their willingness to challenge the taken-for-granted assumptions that influence their daily instructional practices. By modeling the action research process for my graduate education students, I believe that I am able to nurture the development of a teacher researcher professional disposition and, in some ways, to demystify the process. My students are able to witness the development of an emerging action research project that involves them in the data collection process. They are also able to see a teacher who is committed to improving his own teaching through the use of an action research model. For many of my students, this is a revelation in itself—that someone who teaches at a university would actually want to improve his practice! Therefore, this paper is structured using the action research conceptual framework I use to teach action research (see Figure below).

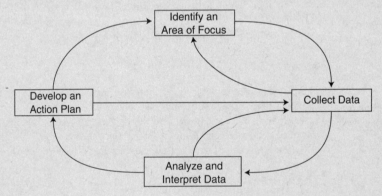

Area of Focus Statement

Area of Focus Statement

———▶

The purpose of this study was to describe the effects of web-based instruction in a distance learning action research class on student outcomes and attitudes. This area of focus statement satisfies my central tenets of action research in that it involves teaching and learning, is something that is within my locus of control, is something I feel passionate about, and is something I would like to change or improve (Mills, 2000, p. 27).

Research Questions

———▶

Research Questions

1. What is the effect of web-based instruction on students' communication with each other? With the instructor?
2. How do students' learning styles affect their success in a web-based class?
3. How do on-line resources meet students' needs to access course materials?

Review of Related Literature

Literature Review ⟶

As an expatriate Australian, I am positively predisposed to distance learning. As a young teacher in a small rural "outback" town in Australia, my only option for continuing my education was via correspondence education. In the United States, correspondence education is not widely accepted as an acceptable form of education by those of us working in universities. But why is this the case when other developed countries (like Australia!) have wide acceptance of distance learning via correspondence? I believe that this issue gets to the heart of the propositions many of us hold about effective pedagogy, whether it is in a live or web-based learning environment, and provides the framework for the related literature to be considered here.

There is a dearth of literature that addresses what is for me one of the most critical aspects of classroom learning environments—the nature and quality of the interaction between teachers and students, and between students with other students. This pedagogical concern can be viewed in broader terms to include "the identification of learning goals, philosophical changes in teaching and learning, reconceptualization of the teacher's role, evaluation of student and instructor, and the stimulation of interactivity" (Schrum, 1998, p. 56). In order to foster interaction in a virtual classroom, Berge (1999) points out that teachers must utilize interactions of a synchronous (communication occurs in real time) or asynchronous (technologically mediated in time) nature. I taught my action research class based on an asynchronous model—students who registered for the class could take it anywhere, anytime—although they were encouraged to follow a 10-week outline of tasks and activities. Similarly, the class was characterized by asynchronous communication—there was never the expectation that the class would meet in "real time" or with any face-to-face interaction. But as I will discuss later in this paper, this kind of communication provided me with a significant challenge in the way I developed rapport with my students. Levin (1997) characterizes this challenge in the following way:

> I can neither see the puzzlement in an online learner's eyes or the "aha" twinkle when a student gets the point. One of the attractions of asynchronous computer mediated communication also poses another challenge: anytime, anywhere, but alone. If you believe as I do that learning should be viewed as the social construction of meaning and knowledge, then this isolation poses a stiff challenge to learning. Online learning is conducted largely within text. (p. 6)

As you will see, I find this inability to see the twinkle of my students' eyes a drawback in my ability to develop a rapport and understanding of the complex worldviews they bring to the learning environment. However, there is little evidence in the literature to suggest that students of web-based instruction (WBI) classes perform differently compared with traditional classes.

Teachers and students who participate in WBI classes appear to hold somewhat contrasting views of the distance learning experience that are challenging to reconcile. For example, faculty are consistently concerned about the quality of the teaching/learning experience and the degree of interactivity that occurs. Alternatively, students are generally positive about the experience and report that the convenience of this medium meets the needs of the nontraditional (distance learning) student who balances work, family, and study (Daugherty & Funke, 1998). The same study reports that faculty perceptions of WBI can be categorized as follows: lack of technical support, lack of software/adequate equipment, lack of faculty/administrative support, the amount of preparation time required to create and grade assignments, and student lack of knowledge and resistance to the technology. Alternatively, students tend to acknowledge the utility of the Internet and the "discovery" learning that occurred through the use of Internet resources and, according to Daugherty and Funke (1998), "appeared genuinely impressed by the variety and quality of the learning materials offered via the Web" (p. 30). In an earlier study, Harasim (1987) reported an even greater list of perceived advantages of on-line learning, from an increased interaction in quantity and intensity to motivational aspects related to text-based communication (p. 124). Students value being able to communicate in a text-based environment to a far greater degree than they would in a traditional live class—a finding that is supported in my own study and to which I will speak later in this paper.

Data Collection

Qualitative data collection techniques were used as the primary research methods for this study. However, the traditional ethnographic technique of "participant observer" was limited to written communication and postings at the course listserv and discussion board (chat room). The only time I met with students "face-to-face" was in the rare instance when a student drove to the university to talk to me, or when I interviewed the students at the end of the course. There was never an opportunity to observe the students in their own learning environments at home (where all of the students "attended" the course).

Data Sources

Data Collection

- *Surveys*—Students filled out surveys throughout the class in order to provide insights into their experiences during the term in which the class was taught and follow-up surveys during which time they reflected on their experience in the class and its application to their regular teaching environment.

- *Interviews*—Following the surveys, students were invited to meet with me to further discuss their experiences throughout the class. As Agar (1980) suggests, information from interviews can serve as the "methodological core" against which observational data can be used to "feed" ongoing informal interviews. The interviews can best be categorized as informal ethnographic interviews that allowed me to inquire into the experiences of the students in the on-line class and to follow-up on comments individual students had made in response to survey items.

- *Matrix*—All of the listserv postings were printed and analyzed in terms of the number of postings and the types of communication that were occurring. This constant "lurking" on the Web was a valuable data source.

- *Artifacts*—Students submitted final action research projects in "display" form, which varied from multi-media presentations posted to the course's web page to audio and video presentations with accompanying poster boards.

Data Analysis and Interpretation

The following themes emerged from the analysis of the surveys, interviews, observations, and students' projects.

Theme

The Frequency and Type of Communication

The frequency and types of communication varied considerably throughout the length of the course. Frequently, students reported being "overwhelmed" with the volume of e-mail that was an integral part of the weekly class participation. Although not every e-mail required a response from the instructor, like the students in the class, I found the daily task of responding to e-mail quite daunting.

Theme

The Benefits and Drawbacks of Listserv Communication

Students considered the benefits of listserv communication as follows:

- Comfort level of being able to give feedback in an on-line setting. Many students expressed high levels of satisfaction with being able to give and receive feedback without feeling pressured to "talk" in class.

- Frequency of responses individual students received appeared related to their area of focus and the frequency of responses they made to other students in the class, that is, if the content area was something a number of students had in common, they tended to gravitate toward each other. The matrix of frequency and kinds of responses indicated that quiet students received less feedback on their projects.

Students considered the drawbacks of listserv communication as follows:

- The overwhelming volume of e-mail messages. It did not appear to matter whether there were 10 or 20 students registered in the class—both groups described the volume of e-mail as "overwhelming."

- Delay in receiving feedback. Some students expressed frustration with not receiving "immediate" feedback from the instructor and/or colleagues in the class.

- Lack of nonverbal cues. A number of students requested that we "post" digital photographs so that we could "put a face with a name. " There appeared to be interest in getting to know each other but a virtual classroom environment was not the ideal setting for establishing rapport.

Related to the use of the listserv and e-mail was the use of a discussion board (chat room) during the second offering of the class. My intent in implementing the discussion board was to cut down on the frequency and total number of e-mail postings. However, the use of the chat room appeared to cause more problems than it solved due to technical problems of access to the discussion board. Students were given the option of using one communication network or the other. Ultimately, this did not work and caused a division in the class that challenged the continuity of the communication among all students.

Themes

Learning Styles and Traits for Success in a Web-Based Class

The completion rate for students in the first offering of the class was 50% and increased to 63% in the second offering. I believe that this completion rate raises questions about matching students' learning styles with the medium of instruction. For example, my traditional "live" offerings of this action research class average about an 85% completion rate. The majority of students (70%) indicated that if traveling distance to the university was not a factor, they would have preferred a "live" class.

On-Line Resources

Students indicated a high level of satisfaction with the availability and quality of on-line resources available on the Internet. However, there were some students who expressed concern about the "black hole" of time that accompanied searching for materials on the Web. Similarly, students who were new users ("newbies") expressed concern about the amount of time it took for them to acquire the skills to search the Internet in an effective and efficient manner.

Action Plan

⟶

Action Plan

Based on the themes that have emerged from this study, I plan to make the following changes in the future offerings of my web-based, distance learning action research:

- Restructure the class tasks so that the interaction between students, and between the students and the instructor, are manageable. Any future use and implementation of the chat room strategy would have to come with an assurance that **all** students would be able to access the discussion board. This is critical for effective communication—perhaps the one aspect of a web-based learning environment that is critical to success.

- Learning styles—Although there appears to be a dearth of literature that discusses the importance of students' learning styles as they relate to web-based learning, I believe that it is critical that students are somehow screened in order to determine the likelihood that they will succeed in a virtual classroom environment. For example, in future offerings of the class I will interview all students prior to giving permission to register for the class to determine their comfort level with (a) the use of computers and the Internet, and (b) their comfort level with being an independent, "self-starter" learner who can work on tasks in a relatively self-directed fashion. I will try to identify an instrument that can assist with this task and for which there is predictive validity.

- On-line resources—I will continue to explore the use of on-line resources to facilitate independent teacher research, such as supporting students' efforts to retrieve copies of journal articles, which is an otherwise expensive activity.

- Rapport building—In order to build rapport with my students, and between students, I will include an interactive, face-to-face communication facilitated by distance learning technologies. Rapport may also be facilitated by the use of cameras mounted on the top of computers. Finally, I will incorporate the use of a dial-up teleconference during which time students can present their term projects. For example, students could "post" their projects to the listserv, which could then be downloaded prior to a designated class session. Using a toll-free university phone tree, students could participate in a teleconference and be able to scroll through each other's projects during a presentation. All of these strategies will function to facilitate the development of rapport and decrease feelings of isolation.

Final Thoughts

As I mentioned earlier, I am positively predisposed to distance learning modalities. I believe that it addresses issues of equity and access to education for all. This is particularly true at my university, which provides services to many teachers working in rural communities.

However, with spiraling tuition costs, many of these teachers also question whether or not they are getting "value for money" when they choose to learn in isolation. Do equity and access equal good pedagogy? How is it that on-line courses maintain the integrity of a graduate education? What characteristics distinguish an on-line course from a correspondence course? This study has raised more questions for me than it has answered. I am challenged by the opportunities that current distance learning modalities offer and strive to balance issues of equity and access against quality. Ultimately, perhaps, the responsibility for choosing to learn via an on-line environment rests with the learner. Similarly, the responsibility for overcoming some of the inherent problems associated with teaching in an on-line environment must rest with the teacher. Through the implementation of an action research approach, I have reflected on the limitations of teaching in a web-based environment and am committed to address them in future class offerings.

References ⟶

References

Agar, M. (1980). *The professional stranger: An informal introduction to ethnography.* Orlando, FL: Academic.

Berge, Z. (1999). Interaction in post-secondary web-based learning. *Educational Technology, 39*(1), 5–11.

Daugherty, M., & B. L. Funke. (1998). University faculty and student perceptions of web-based instruction. *Journal of Distance Education, 13*(1), 21–39.

Harasim, L. (1987). Teaching and learning on-line: Issues in computer-mediated graduate courses. *CJCE, 16*(2), 117–135.

Levin, D. (1997). *Institutional concerns: Supporting the use of Internet discussion groups.* ED 416481.

Mills, G. E. (2000). *Action research: A guide for the teacher researcher.* Upper Saddle River, NJ: Merrill.

Schrum, L. (1998). On-line education: A study of emerging pedagogy. *New Directions for Adult and Continuing Education, 78,* 53–61.

Rituals and Writing

One of my favorite books on writing is Howard Becker's *Writing for Social Scientists: How to Start and Finish Your Thesis, Book, or Article* (1986). As Becker points out, many writers hold certain irrational rituals as necessary precursors to the act of writing:

> From one point of view, my fellow participants (in the writing workshop) were describing neurotic symptoms. Viewed sociologically, however, those symptoms were magical rituals. According to Malinowski (1948, pp. 25–36), people perform such rituals to influence the result of some process over which they think they have no rational means of control. (p. 3)

A survey of friends and colleagues suggested the following magical rituals were powerful predictors of successful writing sessions. How do they compare with your own?

- Writing can only occur between the hours of 7:00 AM and 12:00 PM.
- At least six sharpened pencils and a yellow legal pad must be in place next to the computer.
- Writing can only be done longhand using a blue pen and white legal pad.

- The house must be clean before writing starts.
- Everything must be in order (materials, lighting, soft music, etc.) before writing can commence.

Establishing a Writing Routine

There is no easy way around the pragmatic issue of time—writing takes time and we never have enough time to do all that we have to do, professionally and personally. The only advice I can offer here is to somehow make writing part of your professional life and responsibility. Capture the minutes and hours where they fall—before school, after school, preparation periods, cancelled faculty meetings, failed parent conferences, and professional development days. Argue for the time as part of your faculty meetings and professional development days . . . and be prepared to ante up when asked to share the outcome of your efforts.

I know of no other way besides attacking personal family time to get my writing done. In the short term, our loved ones will put up with "I need to stay home and get this writing (or grading, lesson planning, or test development tasks that teachers take home) done. You go ahead and enjoy the movie (dinner, picnic, hike, river rafting, skiing). " We could all fill in the blank based on our professional life as a teacher.

However you make it happen, I am assuming that there will come a time when you sit down in front of a keyboard, or with a blank pad of paper, and start the task of writing up your action research. I can picture you now—pencil in hand, keyboard at the ready—poised to pen the story of your action research! Go to that place for a while. Get ready to write!

In the spirit of sharing tips for successful writing, see Figure 8–1 for some tips on what *not to do*. You might identify with some of these.

On a more practical note, here are some guidelines for writing and editing:

- Write at the same time every day, a time when you know you won't be disturbed.
- Write up your story as though you're sending an e-mail to a friend. Pretend that your friend needs it explained in simple terms.

- Think about all the things at school that I need to do before tomorrow.
- Scan my desk to see if someone has left me a note about a meeting, sports practice, birthday party that I need to go to NOW.
- Check my voicemail.
- Check my e-mail.
- Check my checkbook to see if it is balanced.
- Call my wife/child/colleague/friend/enemy to see what they are doing.
- Walk down the hallway to see if I can find someone to talk to.
- Dream about winning the lottery.
- Make an appointment to see my dentist.

FIGURE 8–1 *Geoff's Tips for Being Able to Avoid Writing*

- Tell a story as you write. Most teachers are good storytellers. Whether it is telling third graders about Columbus's voyages, how chicks hatch in an incubator, or an embarrassing incident that occurred "way back when" when you were in school, teachers are compelling storytellers who can capture the imagination of their students. This is true regardless of the content matter. These skills can be transferred to the way in which we share our action research stories. And I do not use the term *storyteller* in a pejorative sense here—storytellers can still employ rigor in their work.
- If you're having trouble getting started, "write it the way you talk. " The editing can come later. Tell your story with an audience of colleague teacher researchers in mind and the words will flow naturally. If you get hung up on writing for a larger "academic" audience, the words will not come easily and sentences may be stilted and formal. There is also no reason to use big words.
- Organize your thoughts around an outline and tell your story in a way that stays true to the facts of your study. Make it coherent and make sure your story flows.
- In the early stages don't worry too much about how well the text reads or whether it is full of grammatical errors. Write without consideration for grammar, syntax, or punctuation—just write. Concentrate on getting the story out. Look for progress, not perfection.
- Write whatever comes to mind. Then go back and hunt for what you are really trying to say—it's there.
- Have you ever thought to yourself, "I wish I had done that differently"? Writing is like that, and then you get to do it differently—editing your own work is a delight. Write boldly and then say it again—better.
- Writing, then editing, then rewriting, and then reediting clarifies thoughts into a coherent package. Even a gem needs to be mined roughly, cut ruthlessly, then buffed.
- Nobody knows my work better than I do. Writing is an exercise in learning about your own work. I'm always surprised how much better I know it when I've discussed it with my computer a few times.
- Edit after you have all your thoughts on paper. I may be a poor writer, but I am a fast writer! I churn out words faster than you can imagine. The problem is they take a lot of editing, wordsmithing, revising, rethinking, and replacing along the way. What you see here is not my first draft—or my last. It also has benefited from the collective wisdom and skills of a development editor, copy editors, people with Ph.D. degrees in English and Literature, and friends who are pretty good writers. In short, as readers of research we should not hold ourselves to unrealistic expectations of grandeur. Any of us can write well given the time, effort, and assistance needed to produce "good" writing. Set realistic expectations for yourself somewhere between "The first draft is the last draft! " and "This will never be perfect—I'll just stick with it for another few years!"
- If you accept that your first draft is not your last draft, living with mediocre text becomes easier to accept. Put another way:

The only way I can get anything written at all is to write really, really sh__ first drafts. . . . All good writers write them. This is how they end up with good second drafts and terrific third drafts. (Lamott, 1994, cited in Wolcott, 2001, p. 55)

I am sure that you can add to these lists with your own rituals and tips. My advice to you is consistent with the advice I once gave to my third-grade students when teaching them to play the recorder: "Make as much noise as you want to for the next two minutes. Get it out of your system. When the time is up we will focus on playing the music on the page. Go ahead and blow!" A suggestion: Write down your avoidance list and stick it next to wherever it is that you write. Check it occasionally, but get the behaviors out of your system. Consider it therapeutic and try and catch yourself being "good," that is, staying on task with your writing. Think of a little reward system (if you are somewhat extrinsically motivated like me, that is). Here are a few things I "treat" myself to when I have dedicated myself to some writing time (not in order of preference): a run, time to play with my son and wife, something sweet (you know, some sugar to help with the fatigue!), an adult beverage, food, sleep, or all of the above.

Now that you have identified your avoidance techniques and treats, let's get down to the business of writing: structure, how to submit the write-up to a journal, using a consistent style, and assessing content. Later we'll discuss article length, choosing a title, getting feedback, and final editing.

An Outline for an Action Research Report

Review the following list. Does it look familiar?

PEARSON
myeducationlab

Go to the Assignments and Activities section of Topic #6, *Reporting Action Research*, in the MyEducationLab for your course and complete the activity titled "Outlining the Report." In this activity, you will have an opportunity to review the relationship between an outline and a report.

- Area-of-focus statement ("The purpose of this study was to . . .")
- Related literature
- Defining the variables
- Research questions
- Description of intervention or innovation
- Data collection
- Data considerations (issues of validity, reliability, and ethics)
- Data analysis and interpretation
- Action plan (e.g., "Steps to Action Chart")

This is the basic outline I have used with teacher researchers for many years and it has proved to be a valuable approach. You may need to adapt the structure of your article to fit your audience. This outline is not set in stone—a statement that will no doubt be supported by your own professor (if you are taking a class), school (if you are writing up your action research as part of an evaluation model), or journal editor (if you are submitting your story to an action research journal). Nevertheless, this outline is a useful way to start organizing your thoughts about your story. Later in this chapter, you will see a rubric of essential elements to include in your report and points to consider for each of the items in this list.

Other Structures in Action Research Reports

As an alternative to using this outline, you can look at the "Notes for Contributors" or "Author Guidelines" in action research and teacher research journals that you might want to target for publishing your story. These sections provide guidelines for authors to consider before submitting work to the journal's editor or editorial board. For example, *Networks*, an online action research journal, offers the following guidelines for submissions:

When submitting a contribution, please indicate the section for which your submission is intended.

- full-length articles (normally 2,000–3,500 words). These will typically report a completed investigation or offer a critical review of a number of investigations that share a common theme or topic.
- shorter articles and notes (about 300–750 words). These might describe work in progress, raise issues arising from such work, or discuss general issues related to methodologies, ethics, collaboration, etc.
- book reviews (about 750–1000 words). These will typically provide a sense of the main arguments and presentation style of the author. In addition, reviews will take the perspective of a critical friend in terms of the author's assumptions, arguments and evidence, drawing, where possible, on other work on the same topic or issue.
- resources for teacher-research. These notices will keep teacher-researchers informed of upcoming events, opportunities, and resources.

Submission Preparation Checklist

As part of the submission process, authors are required to check off their submission's compliance with all of the following items, and submissions may be returned to authors that do not adhere to these guidelines.

1. The submission has not been previously published, nor is it before another journal for consideration (or an explanation has been provided in Comments to the Editor).
2. The submission file is in Microsoft Word, RTF, or WordPerfect document file format.
3. All URL addresses in the text (e.g., http://pkp.sfu.ca) are activated and ready to click.
4. The text is single-spaced; uses a 12-point font; employs italics, rather than underlining (except with URL addresses); and all illustrations, figures, and tables are placed within the text at the appropriate points, rather than at the end.
5. The text adheres to the stylistic and bibliographic requirements outlined in the Author Guidelines, which is found in About the Journal.
6. The text, if submitted to a peer-reviewed section (e.g., Articles), has had the authors' names removed. If an author is cited, "Author" and year are used in the bibliography and footnotes, instead of author's name, paper title, etc. The author's name has also been removed from the document's Properties, which in Microsoft Word is found in the File menu. (Visit the journal at http://journals.library.wisc.edu/index.php/networks.)

Similarly, *Educational Action Research* calls for contributions from practitioner researchers (in fields varying from education to nursing, medicine, and other "social settings") with the following guidelines:

Two kinds of papers are particularly welcome: (1) accounts of action research and development studies; and (2) contributions to the debate on the theory and practice of action research and associated methodologies. Readability and honest engagement with problematic issues will be among the criteria against which contributions will be judged. The journal can be construed as carrying out, through its contributors and reviewers, action research on the characteristics on effective reporting, and the Editors will, therefore, welcome exploratory forms of presentation. (Notes for Contributors)

As a teacher researcher reading these guidelines, you are probably struck by one overriding feeling—anxiety! What is meant by "honest engagement with problematic issues" anyway? And how will it be judged? What are the criteria? To take this anxiety one step further, let's look at who the people are who publish in journals. My hunch is that 99% of articles published

Journal Name	Publisher	Address	E-mail or Web Site	Phone Fax	Description
Networks: An Online Journal for Teacher Research	University of Toronto	NA	www.oise.utoronto.ca/ctd/networks/	NA	An online journal that provides a forum for teachers working in classrooms (elementary–university) to share their experiences and learn from each other. Also publishes book reviews and discussions on current issues in teacher research.
Reflective Practice	Carfax	Carfax Publishing Taylor & Francis Ltd 325 Chestnut St. 8th Floor, Philadelphia, PA 19106 USA	www.tandf.co.uk enquiry@tandf.co.uk	(800) 821-8312 (US & Canada) Fax: (625) 821-2940 (US & Canada)	A refereed journal "about and for the enhancement of practice through reflection." Articles are focused on the connections between reflection, knowledge generation, practice, and policy.
Educational Action Research	Triangle Journals	Triangle Journals Ltd P.O. Box 65, Wallingford, Oxfordshire OX10 04G United Kingdom	journals@triangle.co.uk www.triangle.co.uk	NA	A refereed journal that publishes accounts of action research in education and across the professions. Also provides a forum for dialogue about current action research issues.
Action Research International	Southern Cross University	NA	www.scu.edu.au/schools/gcm/ar/ari/arihome.htm	NA	A refereed journal of action research that seeks to publish papers about the integrated theory practice of action research. Papers may be a work in progress, a completed study, a theoretical paper, or a book review.

FIGURE 8–2 *Action Research Journals*

(and probably submitted) to **refereed journals** (a fancy way of saying that more than one "qualified" person reads the submission) are by teachers teaching and researching in higher education. However, this does not mean that it must continue to be that way, and I have been delighted with the teacher researcher articles published in *Networks*, a journal that seems to live up to its billing as being a journal by teachers and for teachers. (For a comparison of action research journals that you may want to target for publication see Figure 8–2.)

So, what do these "Notes to Contributors" and my outline have in common? Is there a rubric that will help me decide whether I am meeting the publication's benchmark? Unfortunately, there is no easy answer to this conundrum. I have a drawer full of rejection letters for what I thought were "reader friendly" journal articles that addressed an "issue of significance"! I also know "published" academics who, despite their reputation and experience, still manage to get rejected on occasion. Of course, this is the magic of the **blind review** process, a practice by which articles submitted for publication are presented to reviewers without name and institutional affiliation to avoid bias. The editorial board wants to ensure that the article is accepted on its merit, not the author's reputation. Therefore, let me offer the following modest advice for attending to contributors' notes.

General Guidelines for Submissions to Journals

- *Attend to the context of your study.* Craft a narrative that guides your audience to the site at which your study occurred. For example, let's compare a good and bad context narrative from the sample paper " 'Come to My Web (Site), ' Said the Spider to the Fly. "

Good example: "As a result of the LAAP grant by the Oregon University System, the

Education Department is pioneering the development and implementation of completely web-based graduate classes in education. This paper is based on my experiences of teaching a web-based version of action research for two terms in consecutive years."

Poor example: "This study is based on my experiences of teaching a web-based class on action research."

The good example provides the reader with information about the setting (a university), the audience (graduate education students), the length of the study (two terms in consecutive years), and that the course development and implementation was funded by a grant (Learning Anywhere, Anytime Project grant). This brief statement provides the reader with helpful information about the study that is otherwise overlooked (in the poor example).

- *Use a clear, reader-friendly writing style.* Don't try to model your writing after the kinds of articles you have read in prestigious research journals. Be realistic in your goal and write using the same voice that you use to tell the story of your research to your colleagues. (See the guidelines for writing listed earlier in this chapter.)
- *Peruse the journals you are considering* for your submissions and notice the structure and writing style of the researchers whose work has been accepted and published.
- *Include a brief description of what you did.* Attend to issues related to data collection, analysis, interpretation, and data collection considerations (e.g., validity, reliability, ethics).
- *Write in an honest, open manner.* Don't try to hide behind jargon and don't make statements that you can't substantiate. Let your data speak for themselves. In other words, what is the gist of what your data show? Say it. Remember what Kennedy (1997) said (see Chapter 1) about teachers not reading research because it is not accessible. Now is your chance to explain it as if you were discussing it over coffee with a colleague or with your Uncle Fred who may not know about your research. Make it understandable.
- *Keep readers' attention.* If you are like me, you read something that is "published" and make a judgment like "Not bad," "Engaging," "Pretty bad," or "I'll give it another few pages before I put it in the round file." For whatever reason, we intuitively know what will keep our attention. For example, I read fiction books, not textbooks, for pleasure. Indeed, these are different genres and we should not be surprised by the fact that we are engaged in reading bestseller novels and not academic writings. (I joke with my non-teacher friends that I know a good cure for insomnia—and its title starts with Action Research!) But does enjoyable, engaging reading (and, hence, writing) have to be mutually exclusive from academic writing? Consider writing up your teacher researcher studies in a way that makes them engaging for you and your audience.
- *Follow a style* (e.g., American Psychological Association [APA] style) used in action research journals.

Perhaps the underlying lesson here is that if we have a story to tell, and a compelling way in which to tell it, then there is a good chance that an editorial board will agree with you!

Choosing a "Journal" Style

Teacher researchers often ask me what "convention" they should follow when writing a term paper or preparing an action research study for publication. There is no simple answer to this. I usually suggest one of the following approaches:

- Choose an article from the journal you are targeting for your write-up and follow the conventions used by the author. Rationale: If the journal published the article using the conventions contained therein, then the editor will probably accept your mirroring of it!
- Follow the conventions outlined in the *Publication Manual of the American Psychological Association* (sixth edition), also known as the APA style manual. For those of us trying to publish in education journals, it is the most widely accepted style to follow.

At the risk of trying to oversimplify a 412-page style manual, the list below suggests conventions that you should attend to in your writing. And remember, if in doubt, go to the *Manual* itself or visit the APA style website at www.apastyle.org. I offer this as a simple reminder of the conventions that most often plague my teacher researcher colleagues.

APA Publication Manual Conventions

Punctuation

- *Period*. Use a period to end a complete sentence.
- *Comma*. Use a comma between elements in a series of three or more items.
- *Semicolon*. Use a semicolon to separate two independent clauses that are not joined by a conjunction.
- *Colon*. Use a colon between a complete introductory clause and a final explanatory phrase or clause.
- *Dash*. Use an em-dash (—) to indicate only a sudden interruption in the continuity of a sentence.
- *Quotation marks*. Use double quotation marks to introduce a word or phrase used in an ironic comment, to set off the title of an article or chapter, or for a direct quotation of less than 25 words.
- *Parentheses*. Use parentheses to set off structurally independent elements, for citations, and to introduce abbreviations.

Preferred Spelling

- *Merriam-Webster's Collegiate Dictionary* is the standard spelling reference for APA journals and books. (Consult www.apastyle.org for current information.) For example, appendix, appendices; criterion, criteria; phenomenon, phenomena; curriculum, curricula *or* curriculums.
- *Check part of speech*. write up (verb), write-up (noun).
- *Hyphenation*. Refer to the dictionary to determine if you should use a hyphen. For example, is follow-up or followup the correct form to use?

Abbreviations

- APA prefers that authors use abbreviations sparingly.

Reference Style

- *Periodical*. Mills, G. E. (1999). Teacher research and the professional disposition of teaching. *New England Mathematics Journal, 31*(2), 5–17.
- *Book*. Mills, G. E. (2000). *Action research: A guide for the teacher researcher*. Upper Saddle River, NJ: Merrill Prentice Hall.

- *Online reference.* Hansen, L. (2000). The inherent desire to learn: Intrinsically motivating first grade students. *Networks, 4*(2). Retrieved January 15, 2002, from www.oise.utoronto.ca/nctd/networks.
- Six or more authors in a reference, use "et al."

This listing of APA editorial style cannot really summarize a 138-page chapter on editorial style! Once you identify the journal you are going to target for publishing your work, find out the preferred editorial style for your manuscript. Consult the complete APA style manual for specific details. However, most of the teacher researchers with whom I work struggle with simple issues related to punctuation, spelling, and references. To this end I offer the guide above—for everything else, go to the source.

Self-Assessing Your Write-Up

The following rubric (Figure 8–3) may be one way of self-assessing whether your write-up is ready to be sent to a journal for consideration. If you rank yourself with 3s on all of these categories, you are probably ready to submit your article for publication. What follows is an example of how the rubric was applied to the article "'Come to My Web (Site),' Said the Spider to the Fly."

Assessing an Article Using Rubric Criteria

In the following outline I have self-assessed my article reprinted in this chapter using the criteria in the rubric.

a. *Organization and Use of Conventions—3.* The article complies with an acceptable format and uses correct grammar, spelling, and punctuation.
b. *Area of Focus—3.* The article includes a clear area of focus statement: "The purpose of this study was to describe the effects of web-based instruction in a distance learning action research class on student outcomes and attitudes."
c. *Data Collection—3.* The article includes a clear statement outlining the data sources used for the study: surveys, interviews, matrix, and artifacts. This section might have been improved by including a data collection matrix (see Chapter 4).
d. *Review of Literature—3.* The article includes a succinct literature review that is directly related to the area of focus. Specifically, the review focused on the challenges of synchronous and asynchronous components of online courses. This section might have been strengthened by the use of subheadings to guide the reader, or by the inclusion of a literature matrix (see Chapter 3).
e. *Context—3.* The article provides the reader with a context for the study and how it is related to the Learning Anywhere Anytime Project grant.
f. *Writing Style—3.* I wrote it so it must be good, right?! The narrative is reader friendly.
g. *Action Plan—3.* The article includes an action plan that clearly outlines the next steps in the search for excellence in online teaching and learning. There is a clear connection between the data and the suggested future changes.

After you've completed the second draft of your write-up, consider each of these points to assess whether you are ready to share your work with others.

Category	1	2	3
A. Organization of Conventions	• Write-up does not follow any format • Many errors in grammar, spelling, and punctuation	• Write-up partially follows a format • Grammar, spelling, and punctuation are generally accurate	• Write-up follows a format • Grammar, spelling, and punctuation are free of errors
B. Area of Focus	• There is no clear area of focus for the study • Research questions are vague (e.g., "Is on-line learning good?")	• The area of focus is too broad or too narrow • Research questions are poorly written (e.g., "What is the effect of on-line learning?")	• There is a clear area of focus statement ("The purpose of this study was to . . .") • Research questions are clear and appropriate (e.g., "What are the effects of web-based instruction on student outcomes?")
C. Data Collection	• Few data sources are evident • Data sources do not match the research questions	• Multiple data sources are evident • Data sources roughly match the research questions	• Multiple data sources are evident and there is an attempt to triangulate the data • A variety of data sources is used • Data sources match the research questions
D. Review of the Literature (Refer to Chapter 2 "Writing a Review of the Literature" for suggestions about writing this section)	• There is no attempt to connect the study to existing research	• Five recent sources (within the past 3 years) are cited • One or more sources that do not relate to the study are cited • One or more sources are incorrectly cited	• Five or more recent sources are cited • Irrelevant sources are not cited • Citations are made correctly, per APA style or another style required for the audience
E. Context	• No context for the study is provided	• Context is provided but is vague	• Context is well-written and provides the audience with a clear understanding of where the study was conducted
F. Writing Style	• Narrative is hard to read	• Narrative uses headings that guide the reader • Writer uses jargon	• Narrative is clear, coherent, and reader friendly • Evidence is provided to support statements (e.g., see reprinted research paper in this chapter)
G. Action Plan	• There is no action	• Components of the action plan are missing or incorrectly stated • There is not a clear connection between data analysis and the action plan	• There is a clear connection between the findings of the study and proposed changes in practice (e.g., an action plan may start with the following: "Based on the themes that have emerged from this study, I plan to make the following changes. . . .")

FIGURE 8–3 *Action Research Write-Up Rubric*

Integrating Teaching, Research, and Writing

Classroom teachers face a stressful challenge every day—they must inspire children in their classes for eight hours each school day. And, of course, the day doesn't end there—there is always planning, grading, perpetual cleaning of the classroom, organizing, creating, professional development, and parent-student-teacher conferences. No wonder that teacher researchers express concern about finding time to write.

So, if writing is not a way of life for teacher researchers, what advice can I offer that may help encourage and nurture writing? Let's assume for one moment that you have a story that you *want* to tell; then the issues become finding the time to tell the story to an interested audience and finding enjoyment in committing the story to words. So, as a teacher researcher, how can I find the time to write a story that I want to share with like-minded teacher researchers?

I believe that the secret lies in the ability to integrate teaching, research, and writing. For the teacher researchers with whom I have worked, the secret to writing has been a commitment to integrate the writing as part of their daily routine. It usually does not mean committing a large block of time to writing, but every little bit helps, especially when it is done on a daily basis. What follows is a list of creative strategies that teacher researchers have used to make time for writing.

- *Journal Writing Time.* Many teachers provide their students with dedicated class time to journal each day. Teacher researchers will often use this time to write their research. Furthermore, teacher researchers who practice this often tell me that if they model writing for their children during "journal time, " children are more likely to spend the time writing! Keep your journal or legal pad within easy reach in or on top of your desk. Your observations should be fresh, so ideally you should jot down conversations or classroom observations while you're in school.
- *"Down Time" in School.* In rare cases, teacher researchers are able to carve out writing time by committing a planning period, a supervisory study hall, a period that might be freed up by student teachers or art and physical education specialists, or library time to writing. And although I would not recommend that teachers always leave their students during these times, it can be an effective way to find some writing time during the contract day.
- *Professional Development Days.* Many school districts have collective bargaining agreements that allow for a day per term for teacher professional development. Teacher researchers can negotiate with their building administrators to use some of this time for writing. This argument can be enhanced when teacher researchers incorporate action research as a component of their annual evaluation process.
- *Vacation.* A commitment of one day during each vacation period on the school calendar can make huge inroads into the writing task. I know many teachers who take a day out of each vacation period to simply clean their classroom. Writing could become the new "cleaning" or "catching up" priority.
- *Time Dedicated to Grant Writing.* Grants from professional organizations, such as the International Reading Association and the National Council of Teachers of Mathematics, may be used to fund release time for the purpose of writing and publishing teacher research. The Teacher as Researcher Grants of the International Reading Association support classroom teachers in their inquiries about literacy and instruction. Grants will be awarded up to (US) $5,000, although priority will be given to smaller grants (e.g., $1,000 to $2,000) in order to provide support for as many teacher researchers as possible. Completed applications must be received by January 15 each year (www.reading.org/association/awards/

research_teacher_as_researcher.html). Similarly, the National Council of Teachers of Mathematics (NCTM) through the Mathematics Education Trust (MET), awards the Edward G. Begle Grants—Classroom-Based Research Grants for Grades K–12 Teachers. The purpose of this grant is to support and encourage classroom-based research in precollege mathematics education in collaboration with college or university mathematics educators (www.nctm.org/about/met/begle.htm). NCTM also offers K-8 Preservice Teacher Action Research Grants (www.nctm.org/resources/content.aspx?id=15479). The purpose of this grant is to provide financial support for action research conducted as a collaborative by university faculty, preservice teacher(s), and classroom teacher(s) seeking to improve their understanding of mathematics in K–8 classroom(s).

How Long Should the Write-Up Be?

This is always a burning question for teacher researchers who are required to write up their action research projects in order to earn academic credit. My answer, "It depends, " is usually not very helpful. It depends on the scope of the study, the kind of research that was conducted, the audience, the time allowed for writing, what the professor has stated in the syllabus, or what the "Notes to Contributors" for the targeted journal suggests.

For Submission to a Journal

Let's assume that you are targeting a journal for your write-up. The average length for a journal article typically is 2,500 to 3,500 words. I suspect that this is about twice the length of an average "term paper" (approximately 6 to 10 double-spaced, $8\frac{1}{2}$" $\times$ 11" pages). Again, don't worry about length. I know how overwhelmed I felt when I received the contract for the first edition of this book that stated it would be approximately 90,000 words! I couldn't conceive of the idea that I had 90,000 words to say on the topic, but like any teacher, I found that talking (and writing) about the focus of my writing, in this case action research, was easier than I had thought. If you break the task down into pieces of manageable length (as per an outline or table of contents), the task becomes less overwhelming.

For Distribution to Local Colleagues

The length of your write-up will also depend on your audience. For example, for colleagues in your school you may want to keep it to an "executive summary" of a page or two. Similarly, if you are sharing your study with a school board, principal, or PTA, then a brief summary probably is appropriate. However, if you are developing a paper that will be presented at a professional development seminar or conference, you might think about something along the lines of 1,000 to 2,000 words in length. Ultimately, you are the best person to decide whether you have included enough context and detail in the write-up so that you can affirmatively answer the question: "What happened in this study?" If in doubt, err on the side of detail rather than be criticized for providing readers with an incomplete picture.

Seeking Feedback

I would recommend that you seek feedback from trusted friends and colleagues, with one caveat: Be careful what you ask for because you will get it! Interpretation: If you ask someone for feedback, they will probably give it to you; however, you may not like what they have to say and not know what to do with it! The feedback I receive from my family and friends is, "Why do you want to spend your leisure time writing and not playing with us? " I have a few trusted colleagues who work with me and who also teach action research. I know that when I ask them for feedback that they will be brutally honest with me. Similarly, I will often ask my students for feedback on my writing (in an anonymous, nonthreatening way)—after all, they are the audience with whom the success or failure of the text rests.

The point here is simple: Different audiences will give you different kinds of feedback that, if taken seriously, will ultimately result in a better outcome. This process is no more evident than in the development of a commercial textbook such as this one. The publishers use folks who are experts in grammar and content experts who check the content validity of the material in an effort to get it right. But for teacher researchers, seeking feedback should be a far more pragmatic activity. You will know your study better than anybody else; therefore, you provide your own content validity to your write-up. The feedback you will seek is more along the lines of:

- Does the write-up provide a complete picture of the research?
- Is the write-up reader friendly?
- Is the write-up engaging?
- Will someone (besides loved ones!) want to read it?

I offer one last suggestion here: Do not expect your friends and colleagues (and professors, for that matter) to do your editing for you. Before you send them a draft, make sure that you have attended to the basic editorial needs of grammar and punctuation. Otherwise you run the risk of focusing their attention on the structure of the narrative rather than the story itself.

What's in a Title?

When it comes to giving your write-up a title, I would suggest that you be somewhat creative. I think that we all probably underestimate the power of the title for attracting our readers. After all, if we can't get folks past the title, there is probably little chance that they will get into the story that follows. The following examples are illustrative of the importance of titles and the roles they play:

It's Memorable!

I have a friend who reads applications for competitive grants. His advice to me about successful grant writing has been this: Make sure you have a catchy title or acronym—something that the reader will remember. Now, I don't want to suggest that grant readers are so shallow as to be solely attracted to a title; however, folks are attracted to engaging titles and are more likely to pick up a text or journal article if their curiosity is piqued by the title. Of course, you are probably thinking, "Oh sure, what does this guy know? He came up with a really engaging title for his book! " I remember discussing the title with my friend and mentor Harry Wolcott. He suggested that I write down all of the descriptors that would convey the content of the book and try to organize them in a way that is engaging. With a textbook, or journal article for that matter, you need a title that will also be found by a keyword search, such as on ERIC. I remember asking friends for advice and receiving suggestions like: "Lights, Camera: Action Research!" I also think that I have written some pretty good conference papers that utilized catchy titles, such as the article reprinted in this chapter, " 'Come to My Web (Site),' Said the Spider to the Fly: Reflections on the Life of a Virtual Professor," "Talking Heads and Techno-Pages: Reflections on the Development of a Graduate Distance Learning Program," and

"Herding Cats and Nailing Jello: Reflections on Being a Dean of Education." You may also notice that I have a habit of using a colon in my titles. I tend to use a catchy opening and follow the colon with a subtitle that clarifies what the paper is about. I like to have fun with titles and hope that my readers will find them fun as well—enough fun so that they will at least pick up the report in the first place.

It Provides a Focus

The other more practical purpose that a title can serve is to provide a focus for your writing. For example, the title for my article was both memorable and a focus for my writing. Specifically, the subtitle "Reflections on the Life of a Virtual Professor" kept me on track during the writing. That is, I was constantly reminded that I was writing about what it was like to be a "virtual professor. " However, it may also be that the title changes during the write-up—a fact that reflects the writer's better understanding of the meaning of the study.

Polishing the Text

Let's assume that you have made it to the point where you are ready to submit your write-up for publication or presentation and you want to take one last shot at making the text as tight as possible. Wolcott (2001) provides a useful analogy to help with this process:

> Some of the best advice I've ever found for writers happened to be included with the directions for assembling a new wheelbarrow: Make sure all parts are properly in place before tightening. (p. 109)

I've never assembled a wheelbarrow, but if my experience with assembling a barbecue grill is anything to go by, I can relate to the analogy. The directions for the barbecue were quite explicit: "Ensure assembly is complete before igniting."

To apply the assembly metaphor to our polishing task, be sure to take the time to carefully read the narrative (instructions!) and attend to all details. Working with the narrative and getting it ready for publication is not the time to be in a hurry. You have endured many days, weeks, and months of doing action research. You are close to meeting your personal and professional goal and want to get the text off your desk (or hard drive). Now is not the time to be foolhardy and to try and light the barbecue before all the pieces are correctly positioned and tightened! Take time to do a word-by-word edit and delete unnecessary words and "excessive anythings" (Wolcott, 2001, p. 116).

In this chapter I have provided some simple suggestions for getting the word out. There is no substitute for perseverance and perspiration when it comes to writing. Your commitment to getting your word out and the positive impact it will have on your students and colleagues is the ultimate reward.

Summary

1. There are two primary motivations for writing up your action research:
   a. The act of writing helps each of us better understand the story we are trying to tell.
   b. A written account provides us with a permanent, accessible record for our professional and personal use.

Why Should I Formally Write about My Action Research?

2. Other reasons to write up your action research include: clarification validation, empowerment, it is a generative activity, and accomplishment.

Format and Style

3. Format refers to the general pattern of organization of the research report. Formats may vary in terms of specific headings included, and research reports generally follow a format that parallels the steps involved in conducting a study.
4. Style refers to the rules of grammar, spelling, capitalization, punctuation, and word processing followed in preparing the report.
5. Most colleges, universities, and professional journals either have developed their own required style manual or have selected one that must be followed.
6. One of the more popular style manuals is the *Publication Manual of the American Psychological Association*, also called the APA style manual (currently in its sixth edition). Additional information about the APA style manual can be found at www .apastyle.com.

Rituals and Writing

7. There is no easy way to get around the pragmatic issue of time when it comes to writing. One suggestion to overcome this issue is to somehow make writing a part of your personal and professional life.
8. Practical tips for writing include:
   a. Write at the same time every day, a time when you know you won't be disturbed.
   b. Write up your story as though you're sending an e-mail to a friend. Pretend that your friend needs it explained in simple terms.
   c. Tell a story as you write.
   d. If you're having trouble getting started, "write it the way you talk."
   e. Organize your thoughts around an outline and tell your story in a way that stays true to the facts of your study. Make it coherent and make sure your story flows.
   f. In the early stages don't worry too much about how well the text reads or whether it is full of grammatical errors. Write without consideration for grammar, syntax, or punctuation—just write. Concentrate on getting the story out. Look for progress, not perfection.
   g. Write whatever comes to mind. Then go back and hunt for what you are really trying to say—it's there.
   h. Write boldly and then say it again—better.
   i. Writing, then editing, then rewriting, and then reediting clarifies thoughts into a coherent package. Even a gem needs to be mined roughly, cut ruthlessly, then buffed.
   j. Nobody knows my work better than I do. Writing is an exercise in learning about your own work.
   k. Edit after you have all of your thoughts on paper.
   l. If you accept that your first draft is not your last draft, living with mediocre text becomes easier to accept.

An Outline for an Action Research Report

9. An outline for an action research report may include the following headings:
   - Area-of-focus statement
   - Related literature
   - Defining the variables
   - Research questions
   - Description of intervention or innovation
   - Data collection
   - Data considerations
   - Data analysis and interpretation
   - Action plan

Other Structures in Action Research Reports

10. As an alternative to using the outline suggested in this text, you can also look at the "Notes for Contributors" or "Author Guidelines" in action research and teacher research journals that you might want to target for publishing your story.
11. A refereed journal is a journal in which articles are reviewed by a panel of experts in the field and are thus seen as more scholarly and trustworthy than articles from nonrefereed or popular journals.
12. The blind review process is a practice by which articles submitted for publication are presented to reviewers without name and institutional affiliation to avoid bias.

General Guidelines for Submissions to Journals

13. Attend to the context of your study.
14. Use a clear, reader-friendly writing style.
15. Peruse the journals you are considering for your submissions and notice the structure and writing style of the researchers whose work has been accepted and published.
16. Include a brief description of what you did.
17. Write in an honest, open manner.
18. Keep readers' attention.
19. Follow a style used in action research journals, for example, the Style Manual of the American Psychological Association.
20. The following rubric may be one way of self-assessing whether or not your write-up is ready to be sent to a journal:
    a. Organization and use of conventions
    b. Area of focus
    c. Data collection
    d. Review of Literature
    e. Context
    f. Writing style
    g. Action plan
21. The secret to writing lies in the ability to integrate teaching, research, and writing. Creative strategies that teacher researchers have used to make time for writing include:
    a. Journal writing time
    b. "Down time" in school

      c. Professional development days

      d. Vacation

      e. Grant writing to secure funding to support writing time

22. The length of the write-up depends on the intended audience. Journals are typically 2,500–3,500 words, while summaries of projects to be shared with colleagues might be in the 1,000–2,000 word range.

23. Different audiences will give you different kinds of feedback that, if taken seriously, will ultimately result in a better outcome.

24. A title should be memorable for the reader and provide a focus for the writer.

25. Be sure to take the time to carefully read the narrative and attend to all details. Working with the narrative and getting it ready for publication is not the time to be in a hurry. Take time to do a word-by-word edit and delete unnecessary words.

Tasks

1. Develop a list of your personal writing rituals and how they help (or hinder!) your writing.

2. Develop an outline for your action research write-up that includes the headings provided in this chapter with an accompanying brief descriptive statement that captures what you will include in each section.

3. Review the "Notes for Contributors" for the following journals and decide which journal you will submit your action research report to: *Networks: An Online Journal for Teacher Research, Reflective Practice, Educational Action Research*, or *Action Research International*.

4. Develop a writing schedule for the development of your write-up and stick to it!

Evaluating Action Research

Whereas Chapter 7 showed teacher researchers how to ensure that action is planned with consideration of the findings of the study and the potential obstacles to implementing change, and Chapter 8 described the writing process and suggestions for how to "get the word out," this chapter addresses the criteria for evaluating action research reports in terms of area of focus, research questions, locus of control, data collection, ethics, reflective stance, action, the relationship between action and data, and format. A published journal article is included at the start of the chapter for evaluation.

After reading this chapter you should be able to:

1 Identify criteria for evaluating the quality of action research.

2 Apply the criteria for evaluating action research to a published article and/or your own action research project.

"Let's Talk": Discussions in a Biology Classroom: An Action Research Project

PENNY JUENEMANN

Introduction

Action research has provided me with the opportunity to engage in professional development enabling me to reflect upon my teaching and determine whether I am living up to my values. In this action research project I have been studying how my teaching has changed in order to facilitate meaningful discussions in the classroom, and I have been assessing how these changes impact my students. The motivation for this study came from my desire to have students make connections between what they already know and new knowledge they encounter in biology. By reflecting upon my teaching I discovered that I was doing most of the biology related talking. As an undergraduate we discussed the importance of a student-centered classroom and when I graduated I was confident that I would always be a student-centered teacher. It has been almost ten years since I received my undergraduate degree and I haven't always lived up to that value. By increasing my ability to facilitate meaningful discussions I hope to swing the pendulum back to the students. I teach biology to all tenth grade students and believe that it is important that students are able to make connections between biology content we cover in the classroom and the world around them. By engaging in more discussions I believe students' learning will become more meaningful.

Context

During the 2003–2004 school year at Two Harbors High School I taught five sections of 10th grade biology, one section of 12th grade Advance Placement biology and one section of 11th and 12th grade physics daily. Each class had approximately 22 students except AP biology, which had 8 students. My action research focused on my 10th grade biology students.

Research Questions

How will incorporating more meaningful discussions into my biology classroom affect my teaching and the ability of students to learn?

Sub-questions

1. How do I need to change my teaching to facilitate more meaningful discussions in my biology classroom?
2. Will having more meaningful discussions allow students to learn content at a higher level?
3. Will having more meaningful discussions help students make connections between biology content and the world around them?
4. Will having more meaningful discussions increase students' ability to make informed decisions regarding socially and/or ecologically significant issues?

Theoretical Framework

This paper is about my journey as a teacher through action research. Action research is a process by which teachers attempt to study their problems scientifically in order to guide, correct and evaluate their decisions and actions concerning their teaching and learning. Action research requires the researcher to be reflective of his or her practice. Through action research the researcher is striving to live his or her values in the classroom.

I feel it is important for students to make connections between what they already know and what we learn in class. To acquire a deep understanding of complex ideas (meaningful learning), students need to make connections between what they know and new knowledge that they encounter. Such an epistemology is referred to as constructivism. One of the first philosophers to explain constructivism was Piaget. The idea can be traced back even further to Giambattista Vico in 1710 who proclaimed, "To know means to know how to make." He substantiates this notion by arguing that one knows a thing only when one can explain it (Yager, 2000, p. 44).

Through better discussions, students can develop a better understanding of the content being covered in class. Lord (1994) suggests that "By attempting to explain what one knows about a topic to someone else, explainers test the fit of their understanding. Similarly, while trying to understand what a colleague is saying, listeners question and challenge their own understanding and try to fit the material into their already established cognitive foundations" (Lord, 1994, p. 346–347).

Students must talk about what they are doing, relate it to past experience and then apply it to their daily lives. By discussing topics that are relevant to students' lives, but also topics that contain the biological concepts students are required to know, students will construct their knowledge in a meaningful way. By monitoring these discussions, teachers can obtain immediate feedback. If one student is incorrectly explaining material aloud to another, the teacher can do immediate re-teaching. More optimistically, teachers can also give immediate praise.

Early on in my project I realized that it would be important to ask good questions and monitor student responses and cognition. There are three domains of learning: cognitive, affective and psychomotor. In 1956, Benjamin Bloom defined the cognitive (the mental process or faculty of knowing) domain for educators (Henson, 1993, p. 124). He developed a taxonomy for categorizing questions, objectives, or responses. His six categories can be divided into two groups, low order and high order. The low order categories are the simplest and the least demanding, whereas high order categories require greater understanding and are thus more demanding. Low order categories are knowledge and comprehension. High order categories involve application, analysis, synthesis, and evaluation. Asking higher-order questions challenges students to think while promoting learning, as higher-order questions require students to process information in ways associated with greater comprehension and understanding. In order for me to stimulate meaningful discussions, I need to ask questions of a higher order on Bloom's taxonomy. Simple knowledge-based questions elicit little discussion. Another important concept regarding questioning is

wait time. It is recommended to wait three to five seconds after asking a question, and again after the response, in order to give students a chance to think and formulate a high-order response. A third important consideration in questioning is the use of Socratic dialogue. In Socratic dialogue, teachers respond to students' questions with questions. It is also very important that students ask questions. "If we want to engage students in thinking through content we must stimulate their thinking with questions that lead them to further questions" (Elder, 1998, p. 298).

After monitoring discussions for about a month, I discovered that the make-up of the group conducting the discussion is important as people learn in different ways. The main learning styles are visual, auditory, and kinesthetic. Visual learners learn best by seeing, auditory learn best by hearing and talking, and kinesthetic learners learn best by doing. People can possess any combination of these learning styles, but often times one is dominant. Through discussions with a critical friend, I decided to try grouping students heterogeneously by their learning styles. Later on, after reading more literature, I discovered that many teachers have had success grouping their students heterogeneously by ability. I then tried arranging my students heterogeneously by learning style and ability in an attempt to improve discussions.

Another path my action research has taken me on is cooperative learning. Cooperative learning models also recommended that groups be arranged heterogeneously. In a study conducted on cooperative learning at the college level the researcher said, "We experienced first hand that homogenous teams are a prescription for disaster in a cooperative learning driven course . . . It is important for students from different backgrounds to work together and learn from each other's perspectives and strengths" (Trempy, 2002, p. 32). To facilitate meaningful discussions, students need to work together cooperatively. This practice was reinforced by the results of a questionnaire I gave my students in which they stated that participation was important for quality discussions to take place. To address this concern, I began using some cooperative learning techniques. Cooperative learning is an approach that encourages students to collaborate with each other to achieve common learning goals. According to Johnson and Johnson (1985) one of the main elements of cooperative learning is "individual accountability," where every student is responsible for contributing to the group. This can be done by assigning and checking individual contributions to the group, assigning roles or jobs to every member, randomly quizzing every member over the material, and/or giving individual tests. Another essential element is "positive interdependence" when students feel they need each other in order to complete the task successfully. According to Holubec (1992), cooperative learning is also a style that leads toward higher-level thinking. When students are working together and discussing the material, they will work beyond the lower-order questions. Within discussion groups, students need to accept and learn from each other's opinions, strengths and contributions. In Lotan's research she found that students can be empowered by this type of group work, "Group-worthy tasks require students to share their experiences and justify their beliefs and opinions. By assigning such tasks, teachers delegate intellectual authority to their students and make their students' life experiences, opinions and points of view legitimate components of the content to be learned" (Lotan, 2003, p. 72).

The affective domain, which addresses students' attitudes and values, is also important in the classroom. Part of my research examined socially and/or ecologically significant issues, with the hope of encouraging moral growth in my students, helping them become more aware of their values and to allow them to make connections between biology and the world around them (between new and preexisting knowledge). In addition to making necessary connections, hopefully students will improve their critical thinking skills. Woodruff explains how discussing these issues can increase students critical thinking skills, "Ethical thinking is neither a matter of pure intellect nor of gut feelings and prejudices. What is important here is one's reasoning and critical thinking skills. Thus, by strengthening and expanding these skills, the student will be able to view our ever-changing biological world from a new perspective, and not be limited by the past or previous belief-systems" (Woodruff, 1992, p. 2).

In summary, through my action research and my desire to be more of a constructivist teacher, I have found it necessary to research good questioning skills, higher-order learning, learning styles, and cooperative learning.

Changes in My Teaching Practices

The main focus of my research is on small group discussions, as that is where more students can participate in a more comfortable environment. Though I didn't have a defined method of research as I began, I collected and analyzed data and made what I thought were appropriate changes in my teaching as I progressed through my action research. The following is a list of changes that I made.

1. I increased the number of discussion opportunities in my classroom.
2. I administered a learning style inventory then arranged students into groups heterogeneously based on their learning style and later on arranged students heterogeneously by learning style and ability.
3. I increased the number of high-order questions. Throughout my research I tried to ask higher-order questions according to Bloom's taxonomy in hopes that students would increase their higher-order responses. When preparing discussion questions I referred to Bloom's taxonomy. Also, I tried to keep myself from directly answering a student's question but to guide them to their own understanding through an increase in Socratic dialogue.
4. I used more cooperative learning techniques. From the first questionnaire that I gave students I discovered that students wanted everyone to participate more, including themselves. I used roles or jobs within a group, the numbered heads together technique, the round robin technique, and the jigsaw technique. In the numbered heads technique, the students were numbered off within a group and told that I would randomly pick a person from their table to answer a question. They must work together to make sure everyone understands the topic. The round robin technique is when each group has one paper and it is passed around the table for everyone to contribute to. I used this technique to review the plant kingdom. Students were instructed to make a dichotomous key as a group going around the table until the key was finished. The jigsaw method uses two groups, a 'home' group (their original group) and the 'jigsaw' group. First students start in their home group to discuss the issue, then they break into their jigsaw group (students are numbered within their home group-then all like numbers get together to make the jigsaw group). Last, students return to their home group

to share information they collected. While using cooperative learning groups I had a student mention that discussions should be "worth more" referring to points) and it was suggested by a colleague to have students evaluate each other on their participation. In response to this I developed a rubric for students to evaluate each other on their participation.

5. As a way to involve students in discussions, I designed and facilitated discussions on socially and ecologically significant issues. Ten of the twenty discussions focused on socially and/or ecologically significant issues. Some discussions involved scientific articles. First, students read the articles and answered questions independently. Then they discussed their answers to the articles using a cooperative learning technique. Another type of activity I used was dilemma cards for example 'Deer Dilemma' modified from an activity in Project Wild where students had to respond to the ecological impacts that the growing deer population has in our environment and design a solution as a group. I used the jigsaw method for this activity.

6. Another way to involve students in discussions was by having them design and carryout labs as a group. I provided them with the question and with some guidelines; guided inquiry. Four of the twenty planned discussions were designing labs.

Data Collection and Analysis

Data collection for this study came from several sources. To analyze this data I read through my journal on a regular basis, analyzed student questionnaires, discussed results with my validation team while searching for themes within the data.

Teacher Journal

While reflecting on my journal entries I was able to verify the need for this action research project. In an early entry I was concerned about 'down time,' students not engaged and a couple months later was very excited about initiating a good discussion. Reading journal entries helped guide my teaching.

Student Questionnaires

Students responded to two questionnaires. The greatest benefit from the first questionnaire was that students let me know that participation was critical for

CHART 1 Triangulation of Data				
	Data Collection Techniques			
Research Questions	**1**	**2**	**3**	**4**
How do I need to change my teaching to facilitate more meaningful discussions in my biology classroom?	Teacher Journal	Student Questionnaire	Student Interviews	Lesson Plan Book
Will having more meaningful discussion allow students to learn content at a higher level?	Audiotape of discussions	Student Questionnaire	Unit Tests	
Will having more meaningful discussion help students make connections between biology content and the word around them?	Audiotape of discussions	Student Questionnaire	Student Interviews	
Will having more meaningful discussions increase students' ability to make informed decisions regarding socially and/or ecologically significant issues?	Student Questionnaire	Mock situations where students use their biology knowledge and skills to address a social or ecological problem.	Student Interviews	

CHART 2 Analysis of Biology Test

Date	Test name	Point total for higher-order question/total point	% of points from higher-order questions	Number of tests analyzed	Students' average score on higher-order questions	% of points earned for higher order questions
9/12/03	Microscope and Scientific Method	10/47	21%	111	6.7	67%
10/10/03	Eukarya Test	13/60	22%	95	8.1	62%
10/29/03	Animal Kingdom	7/22	32%	107	5.4	78%
11/11/03	Bacteria and Viruses	4/22	18%	99	2.6	65%

group work success. One open-ended question on the questionnaire was: What can I (the teacher) do to improve discussions in the classroom? 8% of the students responded that I should make sure everyone participated. In the second open-ended question: What can you (the student) do to improve discussions in the classroom? 46% of the students responded that they should participate more. Also, from this first questionnaire, I noticed that students want to make connections between what we are doing in biology and the world around them. Two students made this comment, "Have things we may run into later in life." One student seemed to be aware of the benefit of discussions to constructivism, "Have a weekly class discussion that involves not only what we learned but what we know."

In the second questionnaire I noticed that students were still concerned about participation but they noted several instances when discussions were better because everyone participated. For example, with the round robin virus articles a student said, "Everyone participated because they had different information." And with the deer dilemma some student comments were: "It got everyone involved and participating." "We had to decide something as a group." "We had good conversations." From the second questionnaire I also noticed that students enjoyed discussing socially and ecologically significant articles. A student said, "We shared our point of views and opinions on the article. So I learned others' thoughts on the article."

In summary, the questionnaires helped guide me in my research by showing how important it was to the students that everyone participates. I also discovered that students feel it is necessary to make connections between the biology content and the world around them

and that they felt that by engaging in these discussions helped them to do that.

Unit Tests

When analyzing my tests I used Bloom's taxonomy to determine if questions were low or high order questions. Then I studied the students' responses to determine the percent of points earned on the higher order questions. The purpose was to see if increases in discussions would lead to more points earned on higher order questions throughout my research.

From this data I can conclude that I still need to work on writing higher-order questions. I believe the content type influences the amount and type of questions that are asked.

Audiotapes of Discussions

On seven different occasions I audiotaped discussions. Using Bloom's taxonomy I categorized the discussion questions that I designed prior to the discussions and questions that developed during the discussion. When I audiotaped more than one group I averaged the number of high or low-order questions.

From this graph I can see that I have increased the number questions that I am asking and I have increased the amount of high-order questions that I am asking. However, because this graph combines different types of activities, I graphed the difference between high-order and low-order questions in graph 2.

As indicated by this graph I am making progress towards asking more high order questions compared to low order questions over time.

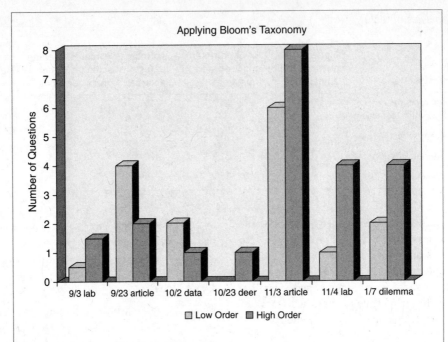

GRAPH 1 An evaluation of teacher questions

GRAPH 2 Change in higher order questions

Student responses from the audiotapes were also categorized using Bloom's taxonomy.

Again it is important to note that the six discussions in these graphs are from different types of activities. 9/3 and 11/4 are when students designed and conducted their own labs within their discussion group. On 9/3 students had chosen their discussion groups and on 11/4 they were arranged heterogeneously by ability and learning style. 9/23 and 11/3 students read articles and answered questions independently and then discussed their answers. On 11/3 they answered their questions using the numbered together cooperative learning technique. On 10/2 students were analyzing data from a lichen field study. On 10/23 students solved the deer dilemma. On 1/7 students responded to an ethical dilemma based on articles they read about stem cell research.

I graphed the difference between high-order and loworder questions from 3 in graph 4.

I was excited when I unexpectedly noticed that students had more high-order responses to low-order responses when they were involved in student-centered activities. The three positive bars are from designing their own experiments and from the deer dilemma. Even though I increased the number of higher-order questions with the antibiotic article on 11/3/03, students responded with a higher number of low-order statements. However, I can also see that as discussions have increased, there is more being said during the discussions.

Student Interviews

From the student interviews, I found that students believe and appreciate that I am trying to get everyone involved but two of the four were still concerned that everyone doesn't always participate. In response to the question "What do you like about my teaching?" one student seemed to recognize that discussions help her make connections, "You teach from the book but then we do other things and we discuss them. It sticks really well. When I first read the chapter I think I'm never going to remember but after while it all clicks together and by the end it's stuck in my brain." Three of the four students felt that having roles during discussions helped improve the participation and one felt that it worked really well in the deer dilemma. All four students

felt that grading students on their participation would improve discussions. Three of the four students felt that discussing socially or environmentally significant issues was meaningful to them. I asked the following question: We discussed a couple of socially or environmentally controversial issues—the deer population and the antibiotics—how do you feel about discussing these types of issues—is it meaningful to you? One student responded, "I like to discuss them because it gives you more understanding of the world around you. Cause like I never knew there were so many antibiotic resistant bacteria. I learned a lot from that. And then with the deer it gave me different perspectives because I'm not the deer hunting type so it gave me a different perspective of where people are coming from. And it is something you could relate to in your life." A second student responded, "Oh yeah I take what I think of it and then with the deer you gave us the things that we had to be, the thing that you gave me was not what I was originally thinking so it made me think in their point of view which was a lot better than just staying focused on my point of view."

Results

As a result of this study many themes emerged. In the following chart I will triangulate the themes that emerged with the data that was collected.

How do I need to change my teaching to facilitate more meaningful discussions in my biology classroom?

With the goal of facilitating meaningful discussions in my classroom I have been more systematic when designing discussion groups and using more cooperative learning techniques. I have been more thoughtful when designing questions and have required students to be more responsible for their role within their discussion group. I have been focusing more on topics of concern to our society. The numbers of discussions that students participated in are greater this year than in the past. Students are doing more guided inquiry activities then in the past. With the greatest challenge, I have increased the number of higher order questions that I ask.

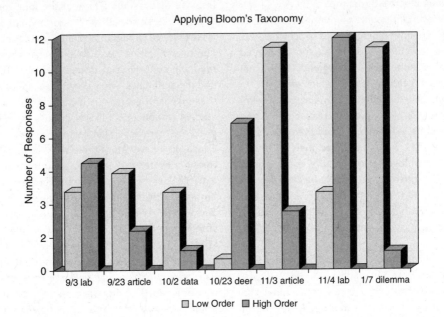

GRAPH 3 An evaluation of student responses

GRAPH 4 Change in higher order responses

Theme	Data Source	Data Source	Data Source
Increase in discussion opportunities.	Lesson Plans	Teacher Journal	Student Questionnaire
Increase in cooperative learning techniques.	Lesson Plans	Teacher Journal	Student Interviews
Increase in higher order questions being asked of students.	Audiotapes of discussions	Unit Test	Teacher Journal
Increase in authentic learning through discussion of socially and ecologically significant issues.	Lesson Plans	Audiotapes of discussions	Teacher Journal
A more student centered classroom.	Audiotapes of discussions	Student Interviews	Teacher Journal

Will having more meaningful discussions allow students to learn content at a higher level?

From analyzing the audiotape transcriptions the length of student discussions has increased over time; however, this could be due to the type of discussion. Depending on the type of activity, students increased the number of higher order responses made during discussions. Student-centered or student directed activities seemed to elicit higher-order responses. From student responses to a questionnaire 77% of my students believe discussions help them learn biology content. I was unable to see any changes in my students' test scores by analyzing points they earned on higher order questions. Throughout the course of this project lower ability students have increased their participation. This could be the result of a variety of factors such as the heterogeneous grouping, maturity, the increase in discussions and/or other factors.

Will having more meaningful discussions help students make connections between biology content and the world around them?

Yes. Having meaningful discussions does help students make connections between biology content and the world around them. One piece of data to support this result is from an audiotape transcription of a discussion on an article about using hydrogen produced from algae as a fuel source. The question was: Why would you want to fuel your car with pond scum? One student responded, "So we reduce carbon dioxide." Another student in the same group responded, "And we don't need to borrow it (oil) from foreign countries." The article does not discuss nor had we discussed in class where our fuel supply currently comes from. The deer dilemma clearly helped students connect biology to the world around them because many of my students hunt and there were a lot of varying strong opinions. But as students said on the questionnaires and in interviews, they found it valuable to role-play a perspective other than their own. It was rewarding to learn from parents that students were discussing these issues at home.

Will having more meaningful discussions increase students' ability to make informed decisions regarding socially and/or ecologically significant issues?

From the second questionnaire 74% of my students felt that discussing socially and ecologically significant issues will help them make informed decisions. From the interviews I discovered that it is through these types of issues that students are really able to make the connections between biology and their life. These issues provide the hook that gets students interested in the topic of study. From interviews students agreed that it is a good idea to discuss these issues and they are glad that they are informed.

Conclusions

To achieve meaningful learning, I have also considered the four commonplaces: teacher, learner, curriculum and governance.

Teacher

Through action research I have become a more reflective teacher. I have studied my teaching and used the data I collected to guide my actions while continuing to collect data for self-evaluation. Throughout my pilot study conducted last year, and my current project, action research has connected me to my students. It is their feedback combined with my journal that I have used to make changes in how I teach!

Because of this project I am living closer to my values. One of the main motivations for this study was to help students make connections. I have gained a lot of satisfaction hearing students say that discussions have helped them connect biology to their world.

My classroom is a more student-centered environment; I am more learner-sensitive and constructivism is taking place as I am facilitating more meaningful discussions. By monitoring students' discussions, I listen more, detecting misconceptions and giving students immediate feedback. I learn from my students.

Action research has given me a systematic way to make changes in my classroom and determine if those changes are worthwhile. I will continue to facilitate meaningful discussions and use action research as a tool to evaluate the impact these discussions are having on my students and myself.

Learner

Students are talking about science more in the biology classroom! These discussions give students the opportunity to share their knowledge and beliefs, which deepens their understanding through actively discussing and listening. In the course of these discussions students have acquired meaningful learning. Through cooperative learning techniques, students began helping each other in a productive way. Students can learn more in a group than individually. We are more together than alone.

Curriculum

This project has not required much change in the biology curriculum. We studied the same topics while I used articles and/or activities to compliment these topics. Any extra time these discussions take is worth it, because when students can discuss what they know it reinforces their learning and makes them active learners.

Governance

Currently, the state of Minnesota is in the process of developing a new set of standards, which at this time looks like biology will have to cover an even broader range of topics. As teachers are asked to cover more material in the same amount of time, it becomes more difficult to set up a learning environment that is conducive to meaningful learning. I am confident that student discussions will be integral to the meaningful learning of these new standards.

Discussion

Action research has given me the opportunity to study my profession in a systematic way. The part of action research that has always been most appealing to me is the opportunity to live closer to my professional values. McNiff says, "Another difference of action research is that it has an explicit value basis. Your intention as an action researcher would be to bring about a situation that was congruent with your value position." I have long believed that students need to visualize that what they are studying fits into the broader scheme of life. Through constructivist methodologies students can connect what they know and what they have experienced to new pieces of information. Through this action research project I have been able to live closer to my values as I facilitated discussions and that helped students make the biology knowledge fit their prior experiences. Through these discussions students are able to learn content at a higher level because they are discussing the issues, formulating the information into their own words. I believe students need to think critically about the world around them, by studying and discussing social and ecological issues students are better able to relate these important issues to the biology content they are being exposed to.

The journey we make is not alone—the teacher and the student must both be active participants. Through this project I have learned a lot from my students and myself. This has been the most important lesson of action research; that I can effectively make changes in my teaching profession if I reflect on my own thoughts and the thoughts of my students.

Bibliography

Council For Environmental Education. (2000). *Project Wild K12 Curriculum & Activity Guide.*

Elder, L. and R. Paul. (1998). The Role of Socratic Questioning in Thinking, Teaching, and Learning. *Clearing House*, 71(5), 297–301.

Henson, Kenneth, T. (1993). *Methods and Strategies for Teaching in Secondary and Middle Schools*, 2ed. New York, Longman.

Holubec, E. J. (1992). How Do You Get There From Here? Getting Started With Cooperative Learning. *Contemporary Education*, 63(3), 181–184.

Johnson, D.W., R.T. Johnson, E. J. Holubec, & Roy, P. (1985). Circles of Learning: Cooperation in the Classroom. *Association for Supervision and Curriculum Development.*

Lord, Thomas, R. (1994). Using Constructivism to Enhance Student Learning in College Biology: *Journal of College Science Teaching*, 23(6), 346–348.

Lotan, Rachel, A. (2003). Group Worthy Tasks. *Educational Leadership.* March. 72–75.

McNiff, Jean., P. Lomax, & Whitehead, J. 1996. *You and Your Action Research Project.* London, RoutledgeFalmer.

Novak, J.D. & Gowin, D.B. (1984). *Learning How To Learn.* Cambridge, Cambridge University Press.

SchoolNet Grass Roots Program. (2003). *GrassRoots Taxonomy of Thinking Skills.* Retrieved October, 2003, from http://www.schoolnet.ca/grassroots/e/project.centre/shared/Taxonomvy.asp.

St. Edward's University Center for Teaching Excellence. (2001). *Bloom's Wheel.* Retrieved October 2003, from http://www.easykayaker.com/school/reading/bloom.html.

Trempy J.E., Siebold W.A., & Skinner, M.M. (2002). Learning Microbiology Through Cooperation: Designing Cooperative Learning Activities that Promote Interdependence, Interaction, and Accountability. *Microbiology Education*, 3(1), 26–36.

Yager, Robert E. (2000). The Constructivist Learning Model. *The Science Teacher* 67(1), 44–45.

Woodruff, Brian. (1992). Woodrow Wilson Biology Institute.

Note: From "'Let's Talk': Discussion in a Biology Classroom: An Action Research Project" by P. Juenemann, 2004, *AR Expeditions*, http://arexpeditions.montana.edu. Reprinted with permission.

It is unlikely that by the time you have arrived at this point in the book you will have actually been through the full action research cycle and will be ready to immerse yourself in the next cycle. It is likely, however, that you are currently engaged in the process, perhaps collecting data, undertaking early analysis, monitoring the appropriateness of your data collection, and so on. As the title suggests, this chapter is about evaluating action research. And although it may be premature, given the stage you are at in the process, to discuss its critical evaluation and "public debut," it is appropriate to consider some of those issues now, and how they impact your view of your own research and the published research of others.

Knowing how to conduct research and how to produce a research report are valuable skills, but as a professional you should also know how to consume and evaluate research. Anyone who reads a newspaper, listens to the radio, or watches television is a consumer of research. Many people uncritically accept and act on medical and health findings, for example, because the findings are presented by someone in a white lab coat or because they are labeled "research." Very few people question the procedures utilized or the generalizability of the findings. You have a responsibility to be informed about the latest findings in your professional area and to be able to differentiate good from poor research when investigating a topic. A researcher critically evaluates each reference and does not consider poorly executed research.

To evaluate a research study competently, you must have knowledge of each component of the research process. Your work in previous chapters has given you that knowledge. In this chapter, then, we discuss the criteria on which to evaluate an action research report.

General Evaluation Criteria for Educational Research

Many research studies have flaws. Just because a study is published does not necessarily mean that it is a good study or that it is reported adequately. The most common flaw is that the author has failed to collect or report information about data-gathering procedures, such as tests, observations, questionnaires, and interviews. Other common flaws in a study itself include weaknesses in the research design and inappropriate or biased selection of participants; flaws in the report include failure to state limitations in the research and a general lack of description about the study. Watching for these problems is part of being a competent consumer of research reports; the problems also highlight common pitfalls to avoid in your own research.

At your current level of expertise, you may not be able to evaluate every component of every study. However, you should be able to detect a number of basic errors or weaknesses in research studies. You should, for example, be able to detect obvious indications of researcher bias that may have affected qualitative or quantitative research results. For example, a statement in a research report that "the purpose of this study was to **prove** . . ." should alert you to a probable bias. Remember, we don't start a study in order to *prove* anything but rather to better understand our area of focus.

As you read a research report, either as a consumer of research keeping up with the latest findings in your professional area or as a producer of research reviewing literature related to a defined problem, you should ask and answer a number of questions about the adequacy of a study. The answers to some of these questions are more critical than the answers to others. An inadequate title is not a critical flaw; an inadequate research plan is. Some questions are difficult to answer if the study is not directly in your area of expertise. If you specialize in reading, for example, you are probably not in a position to judge the adequacy of a review of literature related to anxiety effects on learning. And, admittedly, the answers to some questions are more subjective than objective. Whether a study was well designed is pretty clear and objective; most quantitative researchers would agree that the randomized posttest-only control group design is a good design. On the other hand, the answer to whether an author used the most appropriate design, given the problem under study, often involves a degree of subjective judgment. For example, the need for a pretest may be a debatable point; it depends on the study and its design.

Despite the lack of complete agreement in some areas, most professionals recognize that evaluation of a research report is a worthwhile and important activity. Major problems and shortcomings are usually readily identifiable, and you can formulate an overall impression of the quality of the study. Moreover, you should be able to transfer the skills you need to evaluate published research to the evaluation of your own research. In the sections that follow, I list for your consideration evaluative questions that can be applied to action research. This list is by no means exhaustive, and as you read it, you may very well think of additional questions. You may also note that not every criterion applies equally to both quantitative and qualitative research studies.

Criteria for Evaluating Action Research

As discussed in Chapter 1, action research conducted in school settings is research done *by* and *for* teachers and students, not research done on them. As such, the methods for doing action research and the methods for sharing action research are uniquely suited to its special purposes. Given these distinctions, what are the criteria for evaluating action research? Each of us who accepts the responsibility of being a self-governing professional must apply some or all of the criteria for evaluating the quality of the action research accounts that we encounter.

Criteria for Evaluating Action Research

_____ **Area of focus**—Does the area of focus involve teaching and learning?

_____ **Research questions**—Does the researcher state questions that were answerable given the researcher's expertise, time, and resources?

_____ **Locus of control**—Was the area of focus within the researcher's locus of control?

_____ **Data collection**—Did the researcher use appropriate data collection techniques (qualitative and/or quantitative) to answer the study's research questions?

_____ **Ethics**—Did the research face any ethical challenges? If so, how were they resolved?

_____ **Reflective stance**—In what ways has the action research effort contributed to the researcher's reflective stance on the ways teaching and learning are viewed?

_____ **Action**—Did the outcomes of the study lead to action?

_____ **Action-data connection**—How is the proposed action connected to the study's data analysis and interpretation?

Based on a number of evaluative schema, I have devised a list of criteria and questions, shown in Research in Action Checklist 9–1, to help you evaluate your own action research efforts and the efforts of others. These questions are intended to capture the essence of the multitude of evaluation criteria described earlier in the chapter and to bring together the criteria for the action research process described throughout the book.

Applying Action Research Evaluation Criteria

In this section I will apply the action research evaluation criteria listed in Research in Action Checklist 9–1 to this chapter's opening vignette, "Let's Talk": Discussions in a Biology Classroom: An Action Research Project," by Penny Juenemann.

Area of Focus

PEARSON
myeducationlab

Go to the Building Research Skills section of Topic #7, *Evaluating Action Research*, in the MyEducationLab for your course and complete the activity titled "Evaluating Action Research." As you work through the learning unit, consider components of good research reports.

Ideally an action research study conducted by a teacher should have an area of focus that involves teaching and learning, is within the teacher's locus of control, and is something the teacher feels passionate about and would like to change or improve. Some of these characteristics are difficult to evaluate based on reading an action research account. For example, how do we know the researcher is passionate about the area of focus and that it is something that she would like to change or improve upon? However, when reviewing the article presented at the beginning of the chapter, you can see that Juenemann's focus is on her own biology classroom ("How will incorporating more meaningful discussions into my biology classroom affect my teaching and the ability of students to learn?"). Juenemann makes a strong connection between her area of focus and the context that led her to the desire to have students make connections between what they already know and the new knowledge they encounter in her biology classroom. Juenemann also connects her area of focus to a strong theoretical framework based in constructivism and cooperative learning principles.

A poor-quality research article lacks clarity of focus, or it has an area of focus that narrows the focus a bit, but does not address a specific teaching and learning intervention, for example, "How do biology students learn?" A research question such as this does not provide the researcher with the required level of specificity related to a specific teaching and learning intervention. The word *focus* suggests clarity, and an area of focus that lacks clarity does not provide the action researcher with the guidance necessary to implement a study.

Research Questions

Research questions breathe life into the area of focus statement and help provide a focus for the action researcher's data collection plan. These questions should provide the researcher with a workable way to proceed with the research. When reviewing the Juenemann article you can see that she lists the following research questions:

1. "How do I need to change my teaching to facilitate more meaningful discussions in my biology classroom?"
2. "Will having more meaningful discussions allow students to learn content at a higher level?"
3. "Will having more meaningful discussions help students make connections between biology content and the world around them?"
4. "Will have more meaningful discussions increase students' ability to make informed decisions regarding socially and/or ecologically significant issues?"

These questions clearly link to the area of focus and strongly suggest sources of data needed to determine the effectiveness of an instructional intervention.

In contrast, a poor-quality research article would include questions that did not relate to the area of focus and specifically to teaching and learning. For example, a poor-quality study might ask, "How do higher-level analysis and application questions enable students to be better citizens?" While an interesting question, it would be impossible for an action researcher to "measure" what it means to be a good citizen.

Locus of Control

By definition, an action research area of focus and research questions must be answerable and in the teacher researcher's locus of control. For example, Juenemann states, "My action research focused on my tenth-grade biology students." A poor-quality action research article would include an area of focus and research questions that are outside of the teacher researcher's locus of control, for example, "My action research focused on my teaching partner's eleventh-grade physics students." Clearly, Juenemann's teaching partner's eleventh-grade physics students would be outside of her locus of control! It is a common pitfall for a teacher researcher to overly broaden the scope of the research to include data sources that are outside of the teacher's locus of control, in this case, to compare tenth-grade biology student performance against student performance in other areas of study.

Data Collection

When reviewing an action research report, you should carefully consider the appropriateness of the sources of data the teacher researcher has identified. Will these data sources provide the teacher researcher with the information necessary to answer the research questions? For example, if the teacher researcher was studying the impact of a specific teaching intervention on student achievement on statewide assessment tests, did the teacher researcher collect test scores and analyze the results using appropriate descriptive statistical analysis? Similarly, if the teacher researcher was studying the impact of a classroom management intervention on student attitudes towards school, did the teacher researcher use a semantic differential to measure student attitude changes along with individual and/or focus group interviews? The Juenemann article lists the following data collection sources: teacher journal, student questionnaires, unit tests, audiotapes of discussions, student interviews, and the teacher's lesson plan book (see Chart 1: Triangulation of Data). These data sources can be matched to the four research questions in the study and also allowed Juenemann to triangulate her findings. For example:

Research question 1. How do I need to change my teaching to facilitate more meaningful discussions in my biology classroom? Data sources: teacher journal (based on observations of student discussions in class), student questionnaire, student interviews, and lesson plan book.

Research question 2. Will having more meaningful discussions allow students to learn content at a higher level? Data sources: transcriptions of audiotapes of discussions, student questionnaire, and unit test results.

Research question 3. Will having more meaningful discussions help students make connections between biology content and the world around them? Data sources: transcriptions of audiotapes of discussions, student questionnaire, and student interviews.

Research question 4. Will have more meaningful discussions increase students' ability to make informed decisions regarding socially and/or ecologically significant issues? Data sources: student questionnaire, social problem simulation, and student interviews.

Juenemann's research report would have been of inferior quality if she had included any data sources that did not contribute to her understanding of her research questions. For example, collecting data about another teacher's tenth-grade biology class would not have been relevant to Juenemann's study. This kind of data would be outside of Juenemann's locus of control and would not provide any insights in to the effectiveness of her own teaching of biology.

Ethics

When reviewing an action research article, the reader should be sensitive to any possible ethical challenges faced by the researcher. For example, were students' individual test scores made public in a manner that would have resulted in student embarrassment and ridicule? While Juenemann does not address any specific ethical challenges that she faced conducting the study, it appears as though student scores were only shared as group data, thus protecting individual students from being identified. There is no indication that Juenemann experienced any problems related to the confidentiality and anonymity of her students. Juenemann's research report would have been unacceptable had she violated any of the ethical tenets of conducting action research, for example, had she specifically singled out students by name and test score.

Reflective Stance

Ideally an action research study results in the researcher adopting a reflective stance on the ways teaching and learning are viewed. Juenemann was very clear about the impact of the action research process on the way she views teaching and learning when she states,

Through action research I have become a more reflective teacher. I have studied my teaching and used the data I collected to guide my actions while continuing to collect data for self-evaluation. Action research has connected me to my students. It is their feedback combined with my journal that I have used to make changes in how I teach!

Juenemann's article would have been of an inferior quality if she had failed to discuss how the action research process had impacted her classroom practices.

Action

As Kurt Lewin reminds us, "No action without research; no research without action" (cited in Adelman, 1993, p. 8). Ideally an action research study should lead to action by the teacher researcher. In Juenemann's article, several statements make it clear that the outcomes of the research led her to take action: "My classroom is a more student-centered environment." "I am more learner-sensitive and constructivism is taking place as I am facilitating more meaningful discussions." "By monitoring students' discussions, I listen more, detecting misconceptions and giving students immediate feedback." Juenemann's research report would be of inferior quality had it failed to discuss how she is taking action based on what she learned about her teaching and her students' learning.

Action-Data Connection

Juenemann clearly links data analysis to her actions in the section of her research titled "Data Collection and Analysis." For example, she states, "The questionnaires helped guide me in my research by showing how important it was to the students that everyone participates." "When analyzing my tests I used Bloom's taxonomy to determine if questions were low or high order questions. . . . From this data I can conclude that I still need to work on writing higher-order questions." Juenemann also does an excellent job of visually displaying her data (see graphs 1–4) to provide the reader with a clear connection between her data and the actions embedded in the research project. Juenemann's research report would have been of inferior quality had she failed to connect proposed actions to the analysis of data.

This Is Just the Beginning!

It should come as no surprise that I suggest toward the end of this book that now is really the beginning of your work. At this point, you have invested considerable time and energy reading about action research, learning how to do action research, locating action research within the broader framework of socially responsive research, developing your own action research efforts, clarifying an area of focus, establishing data collection techniques, undertaking data analysis and interpretation, and formulating an action plan through the use of a Steps to Action Chart. In short, you have done much work in a relatively short amount of time.

But now comes the real test of any educational innovation. Can it become a critical component of your regular, ongoing teaching practice? If you have found ways to overcome the potential obstacles to incorporating action research into the reflective practice stance you now have, you are well on your way to living the life of a reflective teacher researcher. Living this professional life, in the ways described here, can enable us to change the culture of schools so that we can once again evoke the faith and confidence of our communities in our schools and in our profession of teaching.

We can all think of reasons why we shouldn't be incorporating action research into our craft culture—most notably because we are challenged by the impediments of time and resources. However, if you believe in what you are doing, you will find a way to make it happen. Call me an idealist if you will, but I am constantly impressed by the positive nature of teachers who, faced with adversity and challenges, are able to find ways to make a positive difference in children's lives. Make no mistake, that is what this action research journey has been about.

Armed with your knowledge, skills, values, and attitudes about action research, the work now begins as you routinize the practice and continue to monitor the effects of your innovations on students' learning, openly accepting the credo for professional practice and living the life of a lifelong learner. What you are learning about your practice will ultimately enhance the lives of the children in your care. If you are now motivated to continue with the action research process, one next logical step is to "Get the word out!"

Summary

Criteria for Evaluating Action Research

1. *Area of focus*—Does the area of focus involve teaching and learning?
2. *Research questions*—Does the researcher state questions that were answerable given the researcher's expertise, time, and resources?
3. *Locus of control*—Was the area of focus within the researcher's locus of control?
4. *Data collection*—Did the researcher use appropriate data collection techniques (qualitative and/or quantitative) to answer the study's research questions?
5. *Ethics*—Did the research face any ethical challenges? If so, how were they resolved?
6. *Reflective stance*—In what ways has the action research effort contributed to the researcher's reflective stance on the ways teaching and learning are viewed?
7. *Action*—Did the outcomes of the study lead to action?
8. *Action-data connection*—How is the proposed action connected to the study's data analysis and interpretation?

Task

1. Apply the criteria for evaluating action research to your own action research report.

Action Research in Action

A Case Study of Curtis Elementary School and an Article Critique

This appendix includes a case study of Jonathan Stewart, a fifth-grade teacher at Curtis Elementary School. This account of Jonathan's study of the effects of an "altered curriculum" on student achievement in reading follows the framework for action research outlined in this text and includes a critique using criteria for judging action research from Chapter 9. The case is offered not as an ideal for action research but rather as yet another example (this time, a more detailed one) of what action research looks like in practice. This case also illustrates how action research can be embedded into the culture of a Professional Development School (PDS) through cooperative work between public school and university faculty.

After reading this appendix you should be able to:

1. Describe what good action research looks like in practice.

2. Apply the criteria for evaluating action research to the case study of Jonathan Stewart at Curtis Elementary School.

3. Discuss how you will represent your own action research projects.

The Setting: Curtis Elementary—A Professional Development School

Curtis Elementary School is a small K–5 urban elementary school with 256 children and 12 teachers. Located in the Pacific Northwest town of Cedarwood (population 18,000), Curtis Elementary was built in 1949. The limitations of the structure became evident when the school, like others in Cedarwood, received a grant to purchase computers for each classroom. The result—the school needed to be rewired to cope with the extra strain on the electrical system! The building is also considered to be "at risk" in the event of an earthquake and regularly undergoes structural inspections. A new wing was recently added to the school to house music and drama classes. The school also has an extensive playground that abounds with activity during the school day and a soccer/softball field that is used by community groups (such as the YMCA) for after-school sports.

For the most part, the teachers and principal have been working at the school for an average of ten years and all report high levels of satisfaction with the teaching/learning environment. Curtis Elementary boasts a high level of parental involvement in school activities and a supportive Parent-Teacher Association as well as a supportive community. This support manifests itself in regular school-sponsored field trips, materials to enhance the curriculum (in particular computer software), and teacher appreciation luncheons.

The demographics of the school are as follows: 256 students, 12 classroom teachers, and 10 certified support personnel. The ethnic backgrounds of the students are Native American (2%), Hispanic American (4%), African American (5%), Asian American (5%), and White (84%). All of the teachers are White and most of them live in Cedarwood. Some of the teachers have children who attend the school.

The general socioeconomic status of the community is revealed by the fact that 27% of the students are eligible for "free or reduced lunch," making the school eligible for federal Chapter One funding.

The principal has been at the school for 15 years and is highly respected by the teachers, children, and parents for his leadership, particularly through a period of embedding technology in the school to improve teacher productivity and enhance curriculum. The principal is described by his teachers as being "caring, thoughtful, and an educational leader," and he facilitates many of the decisions affecting curriculum and instruction through a consensus, school-based decision-making process. The principal has also worked closely with faculty from the local university in areas of program development and student teacher selection and placement in public schools in the region.

Curtis Elementary is a **Professional Development School (PDS)**, or "partner" school, with the local university. PDSs (analogous to teaching hospitals in the medical profession) are based on the following principles:

- **Reciprocity**—Mutual exchange and benefit between research and practice.
- **Experimentation**—Willingness to try new forms of practice and structure.
- **Systematic inquiry**—The requirement that new ideas be subject to careful study and validation.
- **Student diversity**—Commitment to the development of teaching strategies for a broad range of children with different backgrounds, abilities, and learning styles.

PDSs such as Curtis Elementary are "settings for teaching professionals to test different instructional arrangements, for novice teachers and researchers to work under the guidance of gifted practitioners, for the exchange of professional knowledge between university faculty and practitioners, and for the development of new structures designed around the demand of a new profession" (Holmes Group, 1986, p. 67). In PDSs, experienced teachers help teach and induct new members into the profession. In doing so, these experienced teachers also continue their quest to become better teachers themselves.

Curtis has used its PDS relationship with the university to drive school improvement efforts through action research. The partnership has created a synergistic relationship of public school teachers, preservice teachers, and university professors who can complement each other's skills. These are not research projects developed by professors to study teachers and children. They are collaborative, systematic, long-term efforts focused on improving teaching and learning. They are activities that can ultimately enhance the lives of children in classrooms. What follows is a description of the action research process as experienced by one teacher during a year at Curtis Elementary.

The Area of Focus: Constructing Meaning in Reading

The educators at Curtis Elementary have collectively agreed to make reading instruction a priority. As a team, they have decided that the general focus for action research efforts at Curtis Elementary will be on how children construct meaning in reading and how teachers can enhance student learning. After many collaborative discussions and reconnaissance activities, the members of the action research teams determined the school's area of focus would be: What is the effect of an "altered curriculum" on student performance? They defined an altered curriculum as an individual teacher's changes in what reading was taught and how it was taught based on professional development activities focused on constructing meaning in reading.

These decisions (and others like them) were based on reflective conversations like this one held at the weekly early morning faculty meetings at the beginning of the year:

Principal: As you know, I've been working for the past few weeks trial-running interview questions and strategies with students in grades 3, 4, and 5. From these interviews, it's clear that children use a variety of techniques for constructing meaning in their reading.

Teacher 1:   One of the things I've been sitting here thinking about is the difference for our students between reading fiction and nonfiction.

Principal:	I think that you're right. I wonder what this means for the way that we teach children to construct meaning in their reading.
Teacher 2:	I read some research recently that indicated that children construct meaning by connecting what they are reading to other concepts they have learned.
Teacher 3:	That's real similar to what happens in mathematics when children construct meaning. They link their new knowledge to existing knowledge.
Principal:	Let me share with you one more story from a third grader. It appears as though she felt unable to trust her guesses about what was happening in the story, but she also gave me a vivid example of how she used visualization to construct meaning. I think that some of these examples point to how children use prior knowledge and context to construct meaning.
Teacher 4:	It makes me think about how we create opportunities for students to create meaning in all of the different strategies I use in my classroom. But to be honest with you, while the information you have collected from the interviews with the students is so rich, I think that it's unrealistic to expect us to interview all of our students.
Principal:	I think that you're right about that, which is why I think we should involve our preservice teachers in data collection. It will also satisfy a university course requirement for them. But I do think that these data are very rich and can help us understand how our students create meaning and what the effects of our reading strategies are on increasing their ability to construct meaning.

Reviewing the Literature

A subcommittee of the teachers conducted a review of literature. They consulted sources already present in the school: professional journals, teachers with advanced preparation in reading, and faculty from the university. They also accessed literature via the Internet through the AskERIC Service for educators and the AskERIC Q&A service (askeric@askeric.org). A list of sources provided by ERIC for teachers at Curtis Elementary is shown in Figure A–1.

Creating an Action Plan

To guide them through their year-long action research projects, the teachers created action plans in conjunction with the principal. These action plans were used to guide and document the teachers' action research projects. Fifth-grade teacher Jonathan Stewart's action plan looked like this:

Creating Meaning in Reading

JONATHAN STEWART

I am concerned about the ability of students in my classroom to construct meaning as they read. I teach fifth grade and feel that in my teaching of reading I have resorted more to emphasizing volume (the number of books children read) than to creating meaning (whether or not children really understand what they are reading). I guess that by the time children come to my fifth grade class I have started to take for granted that they already know how to read and how to create meaning from what they read. As last year's statewide assessment scores indicated, I (and other teachers in this school) need to challenge the assumption that older children have already developed the skills to read and create meaning by the fifth grade. Therefore, the purpose of this study is to describe the effect of an "altered curriculum" on student achievement in reading.

Defining the Variables

As a whole faculty we defined an altered curriculum as an individual teacher's changes in how reading was taught based on professional development activities focused on constructing meaning in reading. Student performance was defined as the scores children earned on statewide assessment tests and teacher-made tests administered regularly during the year.

Research Question

What is the effect of an altered curriculum on student performance?

Intervention

The reading intervention that I implement in my class will be developed on the basis of the professional development activities we engage in as a faculty. I anticipate

---

Web Sites

- ERIC Clearinghouse on Reading, English, and Communication
  http://www.indiana.edu/~eric_rec
- Reading for Meaning
  http://www.sasked.gov.sk.ca/docs/ela_mean.html
- Vocabulary Instruction and Reading Comprehension
  http://www.indiana.edu/~eric_rec/ieo/digests/d126.html
- Reading Comprehension Instructional Strategies—Elementary Level
  http://www.indiana.edu/~eric_rec/ieo/bibs/rdcompel.html
- How to Improve Reading Comprehension
  http://www.marin.cc.ca.us/~don/Study/7read.html

Readings

- Barrentine, Shelby, et al. (1995). Reading mini-lessons: An instructional practice for meaning centered reading programs. Grand Forks, ND: Center for Teaching and Learning, University of North Dakota.
- Cote, Nathalie, et al. (1995). Children's use of prior knowledge and experience in making sense of informational text. Paper presented at the annual meeting of the American Educational Research Association, San Francisco, CA. April 18–22, 1995.
- Cothern, Nancy B., et al. (1990). Using readers' imagery of literacy characters to study text meaning construction. *Reading Research and Instruction, 30* (1), 15–29.
- Dugan, JoAnn-Rubino, & Bean, Rita M. (1997). Side-by-side reading: Scaffolding meaning-making through literature discussions. Paper presented at the annual meeting of the American Educational Research Association, Chicago, IL. March 24–28, 1997.
- Hass, Christina, & Flower, Linda. (1988). Rhetorical reading strategies and the construction of meaning. *College Composition and Communication, 39* (2), 167–183.
- Keene, Ellin Oliver, & Zimmermann, Susan. (1997). *Mosaic of thought: Teaching comprehension in a reader's workshop.* Portsmouth, NH: Heinemann.
- Kucer, Stephen L. (1985). The making of meaning: Reading and writing, as parallel processes. *Written Communication, 2* (3), 317–336.
- Langer, Judith A. (1986). Reading, writing, and understanding: An analysis of the construction of meaning. *Written Communication, 3* (2), 219–267.
- Mosenthal, Peter B. (1987). Research views: Understanding meaning in reading. *Reading Teacher, 41* (2), 206–209.
- Oded, Brenda, & Stavans, Anat. (1994). The effect of "false" schema activation on the construction of meaning. *System, 22* (4), 497–507.
- Rowell, Jack A., et al. (1990). The construction of meaning from text: Possible effects of different reading strategies. *Educational Psychology: An International Journal of Experimental Educational Psychology, 10* (1), 39–55.
- Tierney, Robert J. (1990). Redefining reading comprehension. *Educational Leadership, 47* (6), 37–42.
- Wangberg, Elaine G. (1983). Instructional strategies for implementing a reading for meaning approach. *Reading Horizons, 23* (4), 259–262.

Figure A–1 *Sources Provided by ERIC for Teachers at Curtis Elementary* that these activities will include a renewed emphasis on comprehension skills and diagnostic techniques and a greater understanding of exactly how children create meaning from what they read. I am also hoping that the literature will reveal some promising practices that I might consider for use in my classroom.

Membership of the Action Research Group

All of the teachers in the school have adopted the same action research goal for the year. However, we are working individually with the specific interventions that we feel are most appropriate for the students in our individual classrooms.

Negotiations to Be Undertaken

The principal fully supports the action research process and will use individual teacher's documentation of the process and classroom observations of teaching as major components of the annual teacher evaluation cycle. I will need to negotiate my individual action research project with the principal, especially if I need to purchase any resources.

Timeline

- *Summer*—Search ERIC for literature. Do professional reading. Attend professional development activities offered by the university. Take graduate class in reading.
- *Fall*—Work with other teachers to determine appropriate professional development opportunities. Develop the specifics of my "creating meaning" reading intervention. Develop data collection strategies and collect some baseline data.
- *Winter–Spring*—Implement intervention and collect data. Meet regularly with colleagues to discuss the effects of the intervention.
- *Spring*—Analyze and interpret data and present findings to the faculty during an action research celebration. Plan the next cycle in the action research process.

Resources

- Paid non-contract time during summer to work on reviewing the literature.
- Support to attend summer institute on reading.
- Tuition reimbursement for cost of graduate credit.

Data Collection Ideas

- Interviews with students in my class.
- Observations during reading activities.

- Statewide assessment scores.
- Regular collection of student work.

Following the summer activities, Jonathan developed a formal data collection plan that included multiple-choice activities, cloze activities, and oral storytelling activities, as outlined below.

Data Collection

During the school year I will use three different sources of data to help me "see" how my fifth graders are able to construct meaning when interacting with given passages of printed text. These data sources will include:

1. Multiple-choice, comprehension/recall activities using reading passages from grade levels 3 through 6.
2. Cloze procedures involving the students in the oral reading of a passage, at grade level, on Paul Bunyan, in which they will orally supply missing words from the text which complete the meaning of the passage.
3. Reading and retelling of a passage, at grade level, about the Bermuda Triangle (to name one example), in which the students will be allowed to read the passage as many times as they wish and to write/draw a retelling of the passage in their own words.

Data Analysis and Interpretation

Obviously, the only way I have of "knowing" that my students have reacted favorably to the curriculum and instruction changes used to implement my vocabulary focus on constructing meaning from the written work is to witness those students as they read, write, and interpret those same written words, both in context and individually. For the sake of brevity, I will simply share one situation that I have seen this year relating to each of the goals of increased vocabulary and meaning.

In the middle of a total group reading of *Thunder Cave* by Roland Smith, I was stopped by the class to recognize just how important it was that Jake, the young hero of the story, had been said to have handed a "folded" letter to a foreign official as part of a visa request process. This carried great meaning to me in that they had to realize (construct meaning) that, since the letter was to have come from his father in Africa and that he had just forged the letter on his own computer only blocks away, the insight to fold the letter rather than just bring it in flat was absolutely necessary for the story to hold credibility to both the official and the reading audience. (Note: When my class brought this passage up to the author, who visited our school in person, he had to admit he had never thought about it in quite that much detail, but he was glad that he had done it correctly by their critical standards of reading!)

During our annual Storytelling Unit this year, it was specifically brought to my mind by several of my 25 students, as they were "learning by heart" their tell-able tales, that some words used by the re-tellers of the chosen tales you just "had to memorize to use well" or the meaning of the story would change. As one student put it, "If they (the audience) can't understand that her venomous personality was snake-like, then I'll just have to add a line that lets them know that she really behaved like a snake and even looked like one at times." (Note: One student asked to be allowed to perform the same story she had done last year in fourth grade because she felt that this year she really understood what the story was about and could tell it in a more believable way.)

Student writings and rewritings show how they are constructing meaning either as a response to something they have already read or in thinking about how they want their readers to react to what they have put down on paper. For example, the following student dialogue evolved between a classmate and a peer proofreader and captures the essence of creating meaning:

> "Charlie, how badly is this guy supposed to be hurt in this part of the story?"
>
> "Not too bad. He's just got a cut on his forearm from the knife and it's bandaged up already."
>
> "Then don't you think that gushed is a little strong for the way the blood was coming out of the bandage? Maybe it should be ooze or seep?"

When the children are having the discussions, asking the questions, and making the clarifying statements with each other, the teaching is invisible and at its highest level. Words weave wondrous webs!

Of the various factors of meaning construction I observed through the use of the data collection techniques, the most striking to me was the pivotal importance of each student "knowing or not knowing" the meaning of the vocabulary used in the story—not just the words "at grade level" that are the basic glue for the verbal presentation, but rather the "extended or specialized" terms that truly gave personality, character, and depth to the writing. Especially through the cloze procedure I was able to witness, with my own ears, the mental processing that some readers could, and others could not, employ to generate a meaningful and appro-

priate word choice to continue, complete, and in many cases, enrich a pre-initiated idea.

I was most aware of my students' reactions to and use of heightened vocabulary to increase their construction of meaning through three different activities:

1. Students recognize through a word replacement activity that it is very difficult to maintain the meaning of a well-written passage or sentence if you are trying to replace certain specifically selected words in that segment.
2. Students have "voiced" the feelings and mental pictures brought forth in their minds by different passages, both read and listened to, during various curricular reading assignments.
3. Student writing samples demonstrate how well they absorb and use different writing styles, voice, and word selection to create a more interesting, engaging, and detailed piece of writing.

The Findings

Based on my data analysis and interpretation, I will present the following findings of my study of the effects of an altered curriculum on student achievement to the other teachers and the principal:

- A high level of the skills and knowledge developed in professional development settings transferred to my classroom practice.
- Students understand the difficult nature of word replacement in activities where they try to replace words and maintain the meaning of a passage.
- As students have learned to create meaning during reading, they can discuss the feelings and mental pictures evoked by the passage.
- Students' ability to create meaning of what they read is also evident in their abilities to create interesting, engaging, and detailed writing of their own.

Action Planning

Though I have long been a person who loves to play with words and understands their massive power, I have never really tried to pass on that idea of literal word power. I plan to continue to emphasize looking for, reading, discussing, understanding, and employing the added power that well-used vocabulary can create in both oral and written expression.

My focus on vocabulary reinforcement will be extended through the following areas of reading and written expression with my students: group novels, published poetry, current events magazines, storytelling collections, student-created stories, narratives, opinion papers, descriptions, research papers, and oral presentations.

I plan to use the following in-class techniques to monitor, modify, and evaluate the impact and effectiveness of my vocabulary intensification efforts: observations of student learning, reflections with students (oral, written, individual, and group), and continued assessment using the data-gathering techniques mentioned earlier (multiple-choice activities, cloze activities, and oral storytelling activities). Students will also make regular journal entries recording their own observations of how different wording has affected their construction of meaning.

I have already implemented several teaching and curriculum changes as a result of this action research project. One helpful technique was my asking students to look up certain vocabulary words from novel selections, to know the meaning of the word as it was used in the selection, and then to try to replace the word with another word or phrase that maintained the flow and intent of the chosen sentence. Students are already finding out why the author chose a particular word for the intent of the sentence.

I am sure that as I start the next cycle of action research I will be "constructing meaning" of my own about how children construct meaning. The constant inquisitive nature of my fifth-grade learners will ensure that we are continually thinking together about our reading and how to improve ourselves. (See Table A–1.)

On-Line Resources

Throughout the year, I visited the following on-line sites to research the literature, check for promising practices and current trends within the professional organizations in the area of reading, and discuss my action research work-in-progress with other teachers across the nation:

- ERIC—I used the AskERIC Q&A service to conduct an electronic search of the literature related to my area of focus.
- Association for Supervision and Curriculum Development (http://odie.ascd.org).
- International Reading Association (http://www.ira.org)—The IRA offers grants to support teacher research (up to $5000) through their Teacher as Researcher Grants. I also discovered that the IRA homepage had links to their Research and Policy Division and links to upcoming research conferences and meetings.
- PARnet—I visited the PARnet website (http://www.parnet.org) to see if any other teachers were working on similar action research projects.
- Arlist—I subscribed to the action research listserv and monitored conversations.

Sharing the Findings

The faculty at Curtis Elementary met once a month for regular professional development activities related to the "creating meaning in reading" area of focus. Most of these activities were held after school and culminated with a dinner discussion at a restaurant or a faculty member's house. These forums for discourse are embedded in the culture of Curtis Elementary and are funded by the school's professional development fund.

Evaluating Action Research

Now, let's take a few moments to apply the criteria for evaluating action research (from Chapter 9) to Jonathan Stewart's action research project. Before proceeding with this activity, take a few minutes to write down your reactions to the study and whether you think that it is "good" action research.

1. *Area of focus*—Does the area of focus involve teaching and learning?

   Jonathan provided the reader with the context to his study, explained why it was that the teachers at Curtis Elementary School wanted to focus on how children construct meaning in reading, and described how in his own classroom an "altered (reading) curriculum" can enhance student learning.

2. *Research questions*—Does the researcher state questions that were answerable given the researcher's expertise, time, and resources?

   Jonathan's study involved one specific question that was answerable given his expertise, time, and resources: "What is the effect of an altered curriculum on student performance?" Jonathan

TABLE A–1 Jonathan Stewart's Steps to Action Chart

Summary of findings research questions	Recommended action targeted to findings	Who is responsible for the action? T – Teacher S – Student P – Principal PA – Parent(s)	Who needs to be consulted or informed?	Who will monitor/collect data	Timeline	Resources
1.0 What is the effect of an altered curriculum on student performance?					Ongoing throughout school year.	
1.1 High level of transfer of P.D. skills and knowledge to classroom practice.	1.1 Continue to monitor transfer of P.D. skills and to modify and evaluate vocabulary intensification efforts.	1.1 T	1.1 T, P	1.1–1.4 Multiple-choice activities. Cloze procedures.		1.1 $$ for P.D. and tuition reimbursement.
1.2 Students' understanding of word replacement strategies was high.	1.2–1.4 Continue to implement strategies that improve students' abilities to create meaning in their reading and writing.	1.2–1.4 T, S	1.2–1.4 T, P, S, PA	Retelling passage/story activities.		1.2–1.4 $$ for curriculum materials.
1.3 Students were able to create meaning during reading and to discuss feelings and mental pictures.				Student journal writing.		
1.4 Students were able to create meaning through their own writing.						

operationally defined his "altered curriculum" intervention and how he was going to measure its impact on student performance.

3. *Locus of control*—Was the area of focus within the researcher's locus of control?

Although part of a schoolwide focus on how children construct meaning in reading, Jonathan's focus was clearly on the performance of the children in his classroom and how his "altered curriculum" impacted the children in his care.

4. *Data collection*—Did the researcher use appropriate data collection techniques (qualitative and/or quantitative) to answer the study's research questions?

Jonathan used the following appropriate data collection techniques to answer his research question:

- Interviews with students in his class.
- Observations during reading activities.
- Statewide assessment scores.
- Regular collection of student work.

5. *Ethics*—Did the research face any ethical challenges? If so, how were they resolved?

There is no evidence to suggest that Jonathan was confronted by any ethical challenges during the conduct of his action research study.

6. *Reflective stance*—In what ways has the action research effort contributed to the researcher's reflective stance on the ways teaching and learning are viewed?

Jonathan's professional disposition now appears to embrace a reflective stance and shows a willingness to continue with the action research process to monitor the impact of his intervention during the next year.

7. *Action*—Did the outcomes of the study lead to action?

Jonathan implemented a reading curriculum that enhanced vocabulary development through reading and written expression activities involving group novels, published poetry, current events magazines, storytelling collections, student-created stories, narratives, opinion papers, descriptions, research papers, and oral presentations. Students also incorporated regular journal entries, recording their own observations of how different wording has affected their construction of meaning. Furthermore, Jonathan will continue with his reading intervention as it was originally developed, but he is open to incorporating any new promising practices that emerge from his continued professional development opportunities. Jonathan will also add to his data collection strategies the use of journal writings in which students reflect on how they create meaning in reading.

8. *Action-data connection*—How is the proposed action connected to the study's data analysis and interpretation?

Jonathan's narrative includes some references to data that informed his decision making, including observations of students as they read, write, and interpret written words in context; multiple-choice comprehension/recall activities; cloze procedures involving oral reading tasks; and writing, drawing, and retelling passages from stories. The data presented in Jonathan's case suggest a strong action-data connection. That is, Jonathan's proposed actions are connected to the data he collected, analyzed, and interpreted.

Final Thoughts

We have now been through the full cycle of the action research process. We have read about the historical antecedents and theories that underpin action research. We have read about (and ideally, put into practice) each of the four steps in the process. We have read action research vignettes that breathe life into the process and demystify what action research might look like in practice. We are now ready to move on to the next action research cycle.

Action research is a process, but it is also a way of thinking and being. Becoming a teacher researcher means making a commitment to continually reflect on the way things are in our classrooms and schools and striving to learn what we can do to make them better. Your decision to do action research—your commitment to this way of thinking and being—contributes to the revitalization of the teaching profession. Your willingness to embark on this intimate, open-ended, creative journey called action research will be rewarded with the knowledge that our students are the benefactors of our search for excellence in education.

Summary

This appendix provided a case study of Jonathan Stewart, a fifth-grade teacher at Curtis Elementary School. This case study captured much of what Jonathan did during his study of the effects of an "altered curriculum" on student achievement in reading. The case study also included a critique of the study using criteria for evaluating action research from Chapter 9. This case also exemplified how action research can be embedded into the culture of a Professional Development School (PDS) through cooperative work between public school and university faculty.

Tasks

1. What did you learn from Jonathan Stewart's case study that can help with your own action research?
2. How would you apply the criteria for judging the quality of action research to Jonathan Stewart's case?
3. How can you develop a collaborative action research network that involves your school's principal and teachers with other educators (such as preservice teachers, university faculty, etc.)?

Standard Deviation and Action Research

In this appendix I will briefly discuss standard deviation as a measure of variability, having already discussed measures of central tendency (mean, mode, and median) in Chapter 6. For a more detailed explanation of the appropriate use of these statistics, I recommend Gay, Mills, and Airasian (2009). Many readily available computer programs, such as SPSS 14.0 Student Version and Excel, may be accessible for computing statistics at your school or university. Remember, there are many excellent math specialists in your school or district, so don't hesitate to call on those resources with questions.

Measure of Variability: Standard Deviation

As a teacher, you may have been exposed to standard deviation (SD) but perhaps did not fully understand its meaning. For example, following the administration of a standardized test, you may have received test scores for your class, including individual scores, a class average, and a standard deviation. For our purposes, it is not important to see and memorize the formula for the standard deviation or even to know its origins. It is more important to understand the concepts of variability and standard deviation, to know what they mean, and to recognize when they would be appropriate to use.

A measure of variability tells us "how spread out a group of scores are" (Gay et al., 2009, p. 308). The standard deviation is the most important measure of variability for our action research purposes. Whereas the mean is a measure of a position in a distribution of scores, the standard deviation is a measure of distance from that mean (Witte, 1985, pp. 53–56). In essence, the standard deviation helps us to understand approximately how much a particular score deviates from the average score.

As a teacher researcher, I might also be puzzled about whether a relatively large or small standard deviation is "good" or "bad." Perhaps a better way to think of a standard deviation as it relates to our mathematics test scores is in terms of equity. Take the example from Chapter 6 for a mathematics test administered to 30 students with the following scores: 95, 95, 92, 92, 90, 90, 90, 88, 88, 85, 85, 85, 82, 82, 82, 82, 79, 79, 75, 75, 75, 75, 75, 72, 72, 72, 69, 69, 69, and 65. In this case, the mean is 80.8 and the standard deviation is 8.59. (I calculated the standard deviation using SPSS Student Version 14.0 for Windows. If you have a larger data set, however, this is not the kind of calculation you want to do by hand, although for a small data set you can calculate the standard deviation by hand—something we will tackle later in this appendix!) If the data set is too large to calculate by hand and you don't have access to SPSS, you can use computer programs such as Excel or a calculator with a statistics function to calculate the standard deviation.

In this example, where the mean is 80.8 and the SD is 8.59, the majority (68% to be precise) of the children scored (roughly) between 72 and 89 (±1 SD from the mean). In short, most of them probably succeeded on the test, if in fact scoring between this range of scores suggests some kind of mastery of the content. Now, let's compare the standard deviation of 8.59 to a standard deviation of, say, 16. If this were the case, we might conclude that the majority of children scored between 64 and 97. Again the question is one of mastery and whether or not a score of 64 suggests mastery of the content. The larger

Descriptive Statistics

DEFINITION OF MEASURE	TYPE USED IN ACTION RESEARCH
A **measure of central tendency** is a single number that gives us information about an entire group of numbers.	• Mean (the average) • Mode (the most frequently occurring score/s) • Median (the middle score)
A **measure of variability** tells us how spread out a group of scores are.	• Standard deviation (a measure of distance from the mean that helps us understand approximately how much a *particular* score deviates from the *average* score)

standard deviation suggests that the children's scores on the math test are more spread out and, hence, leaves us to question the degree to which the children have achieved mastery on the test. For the classroom teacher seeking mastery of subject matter on a criterion-referenced test (teacher-made test), a higher mean and smaller standard deviation would be a desirable outcome.

All of this leads us to the question, "So how does this help me understand my students' mathematics test scores?" Armed with the knowledge that the average score for the 30 students in your class is 80.8 and the standard deviation of this distribution of scores is 8.59, you can make the following statements:

- On average the children in the class scored 80 on the test.
- Approximately two-thirds of the children in the class scored between 72 and 89 on the test.
- The relatively small standard deviation and mean of 80 suggest that approximately two-thirds of the children achieved mastery of the content that the test covered.

Used in conjunction, the mean and standard deviation can provide you and your colleagues with a great deal of information about the data you have collected if you have determined that it is data that can be counted. See Key Concepts Box B–1 for some of the uses of descriptive statistics.

An Illustration

In my study of change in the McKenzie School District (Mills, 1988), I administered a survey to classroom teachers. One of the items on the survey focused on the teachers' perceptions of how the district's at-risk program had changed classroom practices. Specifically, teachers were asked to respond to the following question: "To what degree has the at-risk program changed your classroom practice?" The survey included an item that required teachers to circle a number between 1 and 5 (1 = no change, 5 = large change). A total of 52 teachers responded to the survey item with the following frequency:

Impact of At-Risk Program on Classroom Practices

	No Change				Large Change
	1	2	3	4	5
Number of Respondents	7(13%)	18(37%)	17(35%)	10(15%)	0(0%)

I used the following descriptive statistics to describe the distribution of teachers' responses:
4,4,4,4,4,4,4,4,4,4,3,3,3,3,3,3,3,3,3,3,3,3,3,3,3,3,3,2,2,2,2,2,2,2,2,2,2,2,2,2,2,2,2,2,1,1,1,1,1,1,1

$$\text{Mean } (\bar{x}) = \frac{\Sigma x}{n}$$

$$= \frac{134}{52}$$

$$= 2.58$$

Mode = 2.0 (most frequently occurring score—it occurred 18 times)

Median = 3.0 (the middle score in this distribution of 52 responses)

Standard Deviation = 1.02

For fun, let's calculate a standard deviation by hand so we have a good understanding of what was involved in arriving at a SD of 1.02! Since we are doing this example "for fun," let's use the following data set of student test scores. Although sample sizes of 5 are hardly ever considered acceptable, I will use this number of participants for illustration purposes.

To summarize, symbols commonly used in statistical formulas are as follows:

	X	X^2
Iggie	1	1
Hermie	2	4
Fifi	3	9
Teenie	4	16
Tiny	5	25
	$\Sigma X = 15$	$\Sigma X^2 = 55$
	$(\Sigma X)^2 = 225$	

X = any score

Σ = the sum of; add them up

ΣX = the sum of all the scores

$\overline{X}$ = the mean, or arithmetic average, of the scores

N = total number of subjects

n = number of subjects in a particular group

ΣX^2 = the sum of the squares; square each score and add up all the squares

$(\Sigma X)^2$ = the square of the sum; add up the scores and square the sum, or total

If you approach each statistic in an orderly fashion, it makes your statistical life easier. A suggested procedure is as follows:

1. Make the columns required by the formula (e.g., X, X^2), as just shown, and find the sum of each column.
2. Label the sum of each column; in the previous example, the label for the sum of the X column is ΣX, and the label for the sum of the X^2 column is ΣX^2.
3. Write the formula.
4. Write the arithmetic equivalent of the formula [e.g., $(\Sigma X)^2 = (15)^2$].
5. Solve the arithmetic problem [e.g., $(15)^2 = 225$].

The Standard Deviation

The standard deviation is the square root of the variance, which is based on the distance of each score from the mean. To calculate the standard deviation (SD), however, we do not have to calculate variance scores; we can use a raw score formula that gives us the same answer with less grief. Now, before you look at the formula, remember that no matter how bad it looks, it is going to turn into an easy arithmetic problem. Ready?

$$SD = \sqrt{\frac{SS}{N-1}}, \text{ where } SS = \Sigma X^2 - \frac{(\Sigma X)^2}{N}$$

or

$$SD = \sqrt{\frac{\Sigma X^2 - \frac{(\Sigma X)^2}{N}}{N-1}}$$

In other words, the SD is equal to the square root of the sum of squares (SS) divided by $N-1$.

If the standard deviation of a *population* is being calculated, the formula is exactly the same, except we divide the sum of squares by N, instead of $N-1$. The reason is that a sample standard deviation is considered to be a biased estimate of the population standard deviation. When we select a sample, especially a small sample, the probability is that participants will come from the middle of the distribution and that extreme scores will not be represented. Thus, the range of sample scores will be smaller than the population range, as will be the sample standard deviation. As the sample size increases, so do the chances of getting extreme scores; thus, the smaller the sample, the more important it is to correct for the downward bias. By dividing by $N-1$ instead of N, we make the denominator (bottom part!) smaller, and thus $\frac{SS}{N-1}$ is larger, closer to the population SD than $\frac{SS}{N}$. For example, if $SS = 18$ and $N = 10$, then

$$\frac{SS}{N-1} = \frac{18}{9} = 2.00 \quad \text{and} \quad \frac{SS}{N} = \frac{18}{10} = 1.80$$

Now just relax and look at each piece of the formula; you already know what each piece means. Starting with the easy one, N refers to what? Right—the number of subjects. How about (ΣX)? Right—the sum of the scores. And $(\Sigma X)^2$? Right—the square of the sum of the scores. That leaves ΣX^2, which means the sum of what? Fantastic. The sum of the squares. OK, let's use the same scores we used to calculate the mean. The first thing we need to do is to square each score and then add those squares up. While we are at it, we can also go ahead and add up all the scores.

	X	X^2	
Iggie	1	1	
Hermie	2	4	$\Sigma X = 15$
Fifi	3	9	$\Sigma X^2 = 55$
Teenie	4	16	$N = 5$
Tiny	5	25	$N - 1 = 4$
	$\Sigma X = 15$	$\Sigma X^2 = 55$	

Do we have everything we need? Yes. Does the formula ask for anything else? No. We are in business. Substituting each symbol with its numerical equivalent, we get

$$SS = \Sigma X^2 - \frac{(\Sigma X)^2}{N} = 55 - \frac{(15)^2}{5}$$

Now what do we have? A statistic? No! An arithmetic problem? Yes! A hard arithmetic problem? No! It is harder than $\frac{15}{5}$ but it is not hard. If we just do what the formula tells us to do, we will have no problem at all. The first thing it tells us to do is to square 15:

$$SS = \Sigma X^2 - \frac{(\Sigma X)^2}{N} = 55 - \frac{(15)^2}{5} = 55 - \frac{225}{5}$$

So far so good. The next thing the formula tells us to do is divide 225 by 5, which equals 45. It is looking a lot better; now it is really an easy arithmetic problem. Next, we substract 45 from 55 and get a sum of squares (*SS*) equal to 10.00. Mere child's play.

Think you can figure out the next step? Terrific! Now that we have *SS*, we simply substitute it into the *SD* formula as follows:

$$SD = \sqrt{\frac{SS}{N-1}} = \sqrt{\frac{10}{4}} = \sqrt{2.5}$$

To find the square root of 2.5, simply enter 2.5 into your calculator and hit the square root button ($\sqrt{}$); the square root of 2.5 is 1.58. Substituting in our square root, we have

$$SD = \sqrt{2.5} = 1.58$$

The standard deviation is 1.58. Now you know how to do two useful descriptive statistics.

However, numbers alone do not tell a complete story. They inform the reader about how a sample responded to a particular item. For example, the analysis of the earlier illustration related to classroom teachers' perceptions of how the district's at-risk program had changed classroom practices is incomplete using only descriptive statistics. To complete my reporting on this item, I included the following comments that were representative of the remarks that accompanied the question, "To what extent do you think that the at-risk program changed your classroom practices?" The responses were grouped under the categories of "Positive Impact" and "No Impact."

Positive Impact

"Reminded me and reinforced the concepts of learning styles and how to provide for them in my classroom."

"Having insight to these kids has allowed me to be more sensitive and caring toward them and to act more compassionately."

"I am more aware of needs of the "total child" as well as the student."

No Impact

"No time to plan and implement all of those ideas!"

"I feel that the services needed for at-risk students are not available."

"I was already using many of the skills."

"Have been dealing with at-risk students since becoming a resource teacher so was already aware of the problem."

"I believe that I have always been aware of the problem. It's only new at the district level."

The statistical analysis combined with the quotes from the teachers who responded provided me with a good understanding of the teachers' perceptions of the impact the at-risk program had on their classroom practices.

Displaying Data Visually

Appendix C includes examples taken from action research projects where the teacher researcher has displayed data visually for ease of data analysis and data sharing with other teacher researchers who wish to "see for themselves." Visual displays of data help the researcher to summarize information that in any other format may be clumsy and difficult to reduce to a manageable format. For the most part, the data collected, using the data collection techniques outlined in Chapter 4, have been recorded as narrative in fieldnotes. However, as we will see in this appendix, there are other ways to think about data reduction so that the teacher researcher can work with the data in a way that leads to a trustworthy analysis. As Miles and Huberman (1994) assert:

> Valid analysis requires, and is driven by, displays that are focused enough to permit a viewing of a full data set in the same location, and are arranged systematically to answer the research questions at hand. (pp. 91–92)

The examples provided in this appendix are intended to be illustrative of the ways in which teacher researchers can display their data visually in order to assist with analysis of the data, as well as sharing the data with their audiences.

Example 1: Writers' Workshop and ESL Students' Written Work and Attitudes

The following visual displays have been taken from a teacher researcher's study of the impact of a writing intervention (Writers' Workshop) on the quality of seventh- and eighth-grade ESL students' written work and their attitudes toward writing. Students' writing was assessed using a scoring rubric that measured "voice" and "ownership" in their writing (adapted from the Oregon Department of Education Writing Scoring Guide).

The teacher researcher's use of bar graphs to summarize and represent the pre-, mid-, and post-assessments for all ESL students is a helpful way of sharing the kinds of numerical data that would have been recorded in a grade book. These graphs also allow the teacher researcher to work with the data in a manageable way and to draw conclusions about individual student performance over the course of the writing intervention. Similarly, it provides the reader of the study with access to the same data—a powerful way of providing an "audit" for the outcomes of the study. (See Figures C–1 and C–2.)

Also this teacher researcher utilized a summary table of students' responses on a post-assessment questionnaire to the questions: Do you like to write? Why or why not? This summary of data, once again, allows the teacher researcher to provide illustrative examples of how the ESL students felt about writing in support of the themes "Likes to write" and "Does not like to write." (See Table C–1.)

In addition, this teacher researcher used a similar format to summarize student responses to the questions: Do you think your writing has improved this term? How? What have you learned? (See Table C–2.) This visual display of data allows the teacher researcher to reduce the students' responses to a manageable level while at the same time capturing the essence of the students' comments. This activity also

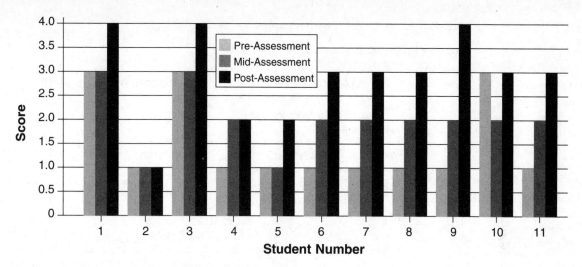

Figure C–1 *Overall Student Performance Gains—VOICE*

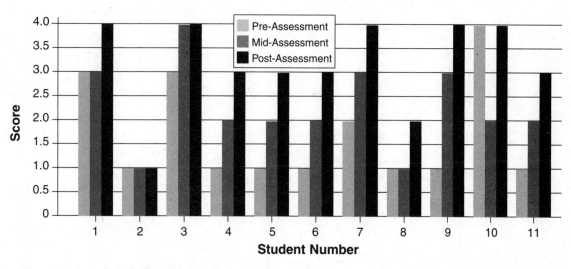

Figure C–2 *Overall Student Performance Gains—OWNERSHIP*

assists the teacher researcher's efforts to find themes that emerged from the students' comments. For example, all the students in this study believed that their writing had improved as a result of their participation in the Writers' Workshop intervention—even though the overall student performance gains graphs indicated that at least two of the students did not improve—as measured by the rubric.

Example 2: Teaching Mathematics Using Manipulatives

This example is taken from a second-grade teacher researcher's project that focused on the impact of math manipulatives on students' learning and "on-task" behavior. This project also involved five other

TABLE C–1 Post-Assessment Questionnaire

Question 1: Do you like to write? Why, or why not?

STUDENT NUMBER	LIKES TO WRITE	DOES NOT LIKE TO WRITE
1	Yes, 'cause that's how I let out my expressions.	
2	Yes, because I just like it.	
3	I like to write a little bit, not much. The reason I like to write is because you can express your feelings.	
4		No, because I do not like to write a lot.
5	Yes, I do.	
6	Sometimes, I like writing when I'm bored.	
7	Yes, because it expresses.	
8		No, because we have to write a lot at school and I get tired to write all day and to think about all different topics to write about. After a while you run out of topics to write about.
9	Yes, because I can express myself.	
10	Yes, because it expresses my feelings.	
11	Yes, because I can tell about myself.	

teachers' perceptions (six in all) of the impact of math manipulative use on student on-task behavior. Figure C–3 summarizes the six teachers' perceptions of the impact of the use of math manipulatives on student learning and on-task behavior. It is interesting to note that the teacher of classroom 4 indicated that while there was no change in student learning, there was a decrease in on-task behavior. This anomaly is evident in the visual representation of the data.

The following figures also use bar graphs to display the data that compares on-task behavior (Figure C–4), strategy/process (Figure C–5), and completion/accuracy (Figure C–6) for six students in a second-grade math class over the course of a "Math Mystery" series of lessons that were taught with and without manipulatives. Again, the use of the visual display allows the teacher researcher to reduce all of the data for the six students to a manageable format for analysis. In this case, the teacher researcher concluded that while most students' abilities to develop problem-solving strategies and processes improved with the use of manipulatives, only two students' completion and accuracy improved with the use of manipulatives.

TABLE C–2   Post-Assessment Questionnaire

Question 3: Do you think your writing has improved this term? How? What have you learned?

STUDENT NUMBER	WRITING HAS IMPROVED	WRITING HAS NOT IMPROVED
1	I've learned that it's better to make your own stories because you got more ideas.	
2	Yes, I learned to write better.	
3	I think my writing has improved a little bit, but not much.	
4	Yes, I have improved because every day I learn something new at school. I learned how to spell better.	
5	Yes, my writing is better because I wrote about what I wanted.	
6	Yes, by writing it longer.	
7	Yes, because I know how to spell more better.	
8	Yes, on spelling and commas, periods and more. I have learned where to put in my commas and periods.	
9	When I write about me or someone else I know, I learn a lot more things like writing everyday or express more myself.	

Example 3: The Impact of Book Sharing on Student Motivation to Read

This example is taken from a first-grade teacher's study of the impact of a "book sharing" intervention on students' motivation to read. This teacher researcher used a matrix to summarize the 15 students' responses to a series of questions that were given as a pre- and post-assessment and allowed the teacher to classify the responses as either a "positive change" or "no change" in attitude (see Table C–3). The teacher researcher was able to use this data display (along with bar graphs showing positive changes in student attitude toward reading) to support concluding statements such as "More students enjoyed reading during play time than before the intervention."

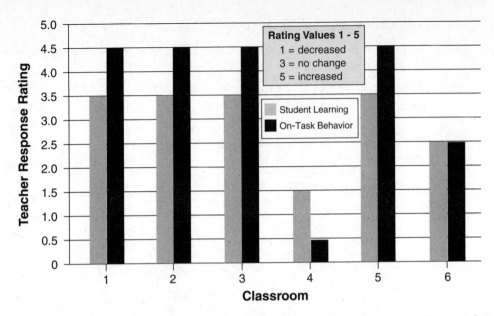

Figure C–3 *Results of Teacher Questionnaire: Effects of Math Manipulative Use on Student Learning and On-Task Behavior*

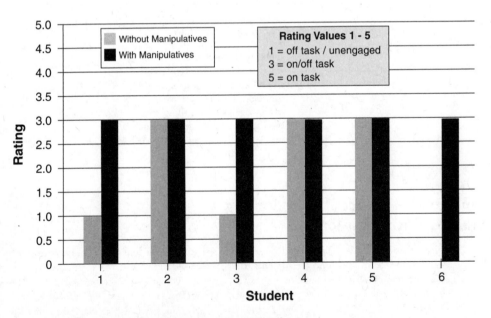

Figure C–4 *Math Mystery Format—On-Task Behavior*

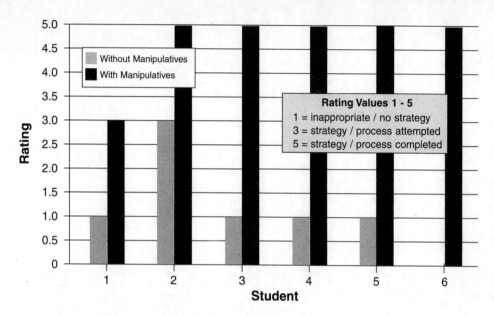

Figure C–5   *Math Mystery Format—Strategy/Process*

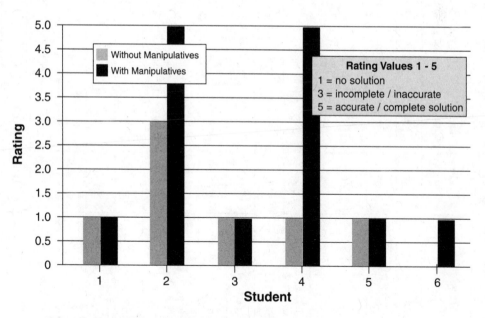

Figure C–6   *Math Mystery Format—Completion/Accuracy*

TABLE C–3 Comparison of Student Responses from Pre- to Post-Assessment Survey

STUDENT	Do you like to read?		Do you like to be read to?		Do you read every day?		Do you like going to the library?		Do you like to read during free time at school?		Do you like to read instead of play?	
	PRE	POST	PRE	POST	PRE	POST	PRE	POST	PRE	POST	PRE	POST
1	Yes	Sometimes	Yes	Yes	Sometimes	Sometimes	Yes	Yes	Sometimes	Sometimes	Sometimes	Yes
2	Yes	Sometimes	Yes	Yes	No	No	Yes	Yes	Sometimes	Sometimes	No	No
3	Sometimes	Sometimes	Yes	Yes	No	Sometimes	Yes	Yes	Sometimes	Sometimes	No	Sometimes
4	Sometimes	Yes	Sometimes	Yes	Yes	Yes	Sometimes	Sometimes	No	Sometimes	Sometimes	Sometimes
5	Sometimes	Sometimes	Yes	Yes	Sometimes	Sometimes	No	Sometimes	Sometimes	Sometimes	No	Sometimes
6	Yes	Sometimes	Yes	Yes	Sometimes	Yes	Yes	Sometimes	Yes	Yes	No	No
7	Sometimes	Sometimes	Sometimes	Sometimes	No	Sometimes	Yes	Yes	Sometimes	Sometimes	No	Sometimes
8	Sometimes	No	Yes	Yes	No	No	Yes	Yes	No	No	No	No
9	Yes	Sometimes	Sometimes	No	No	Yes	No	Yes	Sometimes	Yes	No	Yes
10	Yes	Yes	Sometimes	No	Yes	Yes	Yes	Yes	Yes	Yes	No	Yes
11	Sometimes	Yes	Yes	Yes	Yes	No	No	Sometimes	Sometimes	Yes	Yes	Yes
12	Yes	Sometimes	Yes	Yes	Yes	Yes	Yes	Yes	Yes	Sometimes	Sometimes	Sometimes
13	Sometimes	Sometimes	Yes	Yes	No	Yes	No	Sometimes	No	No	No	No
14	Yes	Sometimes	Yes	Sometimes	Sometimes	Yes	Yes	Yes	Yes	Yes	Sometimes	No
15	Yes	Yes	Yes	Yes	Sometimes	Yes	Sometimes	Yes	Sometimes	Sometimes	Yes	Sometimes

Dark—Positive Change in Attitude; White—No Change in Attitude; Light—Negative Change

Example 4: Mapping Teacher's "Locus of Control" and "Movement"

Sometimes, teachers may want to track their "locus of control," that is, whether a particular individual child or group of children in a classroom demand a majority of the teacher's time and effort. This kind of data collection is greatly enhanced by the use of a visual display that records the frequency of student-teacher interactions during a lesson. In this particular example, the teacher researcher would ask a colleague to record the frequency of interactions between the teacher and the students and to keep a tally (see Figure C–7). Similarly, the privileged observer can keep track of the teacher's movement around the classroom (lines connected to numbers). From this visual display of data the teacher researcher may conclude, for this particular teaching episode, that most of the teacher's time and energy was focused on a few children seated in a group at the rear of the classroom. This kind of data would challenge the teacher to consider other questions such as "Why?" and "What was happening to cause this lopsided attention to a few children?" Again, this visual display provides the teacher researcher with a powerful way of capturing data that would not otherwise be easily recorded.

Example 5: Concept Map

In Chapter 6 (Data Analysis and Interpretation) you will find another visual representation that is a useful tool to aid data analysis and interpretation—a concept map. In this example I have used a map to outline the factors that affected absenteeism in Eastview's study. Again, this display provides the teacher researcher and reader with a conceptual view of all the factors that might affect absenteeism at the school (see Figure C–8).

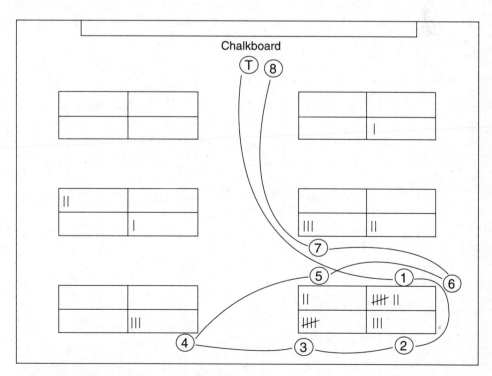

Figure C–7   Locus of Control/Teacher Movement

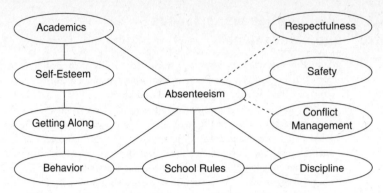

Figure C–8 *Eastview's Concept Map of the Factors Affecting Absenteeism*

Summary

The examples in this appendix have been extracted from preservice teachers' action research projects and are simple illustrations of how displaying data visually can enhance teacher researchers' data collection, data analysis, and sharing efforts. However, for the ultimate statement on the kinds of data displays that can be used to enhance data analysis, I would urge the reader to consult Miles and Huberman (1994), who provide concrete examples of visual displays such as a context chart, checklist matrix, time-ordered display, critical incident chart, causal network, and partially ordered meta-matrix—to name a few!

Clearly, there are perhaps as many ways to display data visually as there are teacher researchers. The challenge for each of us is to "think display" so as to enhance our ability to work effectively and efficiently with the mountains of data that emerge from our qualitatively oriented research efforts.

References

Adelman, C. (1993). Kurt Lewin and the origins of action research. *Educational Action Researcher, 1*(1), 7–25.

Agar, M. H. (1980). *The professional stranger: An informal introduction to ethnography.* Orlando, FL: Academic.

American Psychological Association. (2009). *Publication manual of the American Psychological Association* (6th ed.). Washington, DC: Author.

Anderson, G. L., Herr, K., & Nihlen, A. S. (1994). *Studying your own school: An educator's guide to qualitative practitioner research.* Thousand Oaks, CA: Corwin.

Becker, H. S. (1986). *Writing for the social scientists: How to start and finish your thesis, book, or article.* Chicago: The University of Chicago Press.

Calhoun, E. F. (1994). *How to use action research in the self-renewing school.* Alexandria, VA: ASCD.

Christians, C. G. (2000). Ethics and politics in qualitative research. In N. K. Denzin & Y. S. Lincoln (Eds.), *Handbook of qualitative research* (2nd ed., pp. 133–155). Thousand Oaks, CA: Sage.

Cochran-Smith, M., & Lytle, S. L. (1993). *Inside outside: Teacher research and knowledge.* New York: Teachers College Press.

Conley, S. (1991). Review of research on teacher participation in school decision making. *Review of Research in Education, 17,* 225–266.

Creswell, J. W. (2002). *Educational research: Planning, conducting, and evaluating quantitative and qualitative research.* Upper Saddle River, NJ: Merrill/Prentice Hall.

Creswell, J. W. (2005). *Educational research: Planning, conducting, and evaluating quantitative and qualitative research* (2nd ed.). Upper Saddle River, NJ: Merrill/ Prentice Hall.

Creswell, J. W. (2008). *Educational research: Planning, conducting, and evaluating quantitative and qualitative research* (3rd ed.). Upper Saddle River, NJ: Merrill/ Prentice Hall.

Cronbach, L. J., & Meehl, P. E. (1955). Construct validity in psychological tests. *Psychological Bulletin, 52* (4), 281–302.

Cunningham, J. B. (1983). Gathering data in a changing organization. *Human Relations, 36* (5), 403–420.

Deal, T. (1987). The culture of schools. In L. T. Sheive & M. B. Schoenheit (Eds.), *Leadership: Examining the elusive* (pp. 3–15). Alexandria, VA: ASCD.

Eisner, E. W. (1991). *The enlightened eye: Qualitative inquiry and the enhancement of educational practice.* New York: Macmillan.

Elliott, J. (1991). *Action research for educational change.* Bristol, PA: Open University Press.

Flinders, D. J. (1992). In search of ethical guidance: Constructing a basis for dialogue. *Qualitative Studies in Education, 5*(2), 101–115.

Fueyo, V., & Koorland, M. A. (1997). Teacher as researcher: A synonym for professionalism. *Journal of Teacher Education, 48*(5), 336–344.

Fullan, M. (1993). *Change forces: Probing the depths of educational reform.* New York: Falmer.

Fullan, M. (1997). Emotion and hope: Constructive concepts for complex times. In A. Hargreaves (Ed.), *Rethinking educational change with heart and mind* (pp. 216–233). Alexandria, VA: ASCD.

Gay, L. R., Mills, G. E., & Airasian, P. (2009). *Educational research: Competencies for analysis and application* (9th ed.). Upper Saddle River, NJ: Merrill/ Prentice Hall.

Greenwood, D. J., & Levin, M. (2000). Reconstructing the relationships between universities and society through action research. In N. K. Denzin & Y. S. Lincoln (Eds.), *Handbook of qualitative research* (2nd ed., pp. 85–106). Thousand Oaks, CA: Sage.

Guba, E. G. (1981). Criteria for assessing the trustworthiness of naturalistic inquiries. *Educational Communication and Technology, 29* (2), 75–91.

Gunz, J. (1996). Jacob L. Moreno and the origins of action research. *Educational Action Research, 4* (1), 145–148.

Hammersley, M. (1993). On the teacher as researcher. *Educational Action Research, 1*(3), 425–441.

Hendricks, C. (2006). *Improving schools through action research: A comprehensive guide for educators.* Boston, MA: Allyn and Bacon.

Holmes Group. (1986). *Tomorrow's schools of education.* East Lansing, MI: Author.

Hord, S., Rutherford, W. L., Huling-Austin, L., & Hall, G. E. (1987). *Taking charge of change.* Alexandria, VA: ASCD.

Imig, D. (2001). Back-to-school questions. *AACTE Briefs, 22*(9). Washington, DC: AACTE.

Jackson, P. (1968). *Life in classrooms.* New York: Holt, Rinehart & Winston.

Jones, J. H. (1998). *The Tuskegee syphilis experiment.* New York: Free Press.

Joyce, B. R., Hersh, R. H., & McKibben, M. (1983). *The structure of school improvement.* New York: Longman.

Juenemann, P. (2004). 'Let's Talk': Discussion in a Biology Classroom: An Action Research Project. *AR Expeditions,* http://arexpeditions.montana.edu.

Kemmis, S. (1988). Action research in retrospect and prospect. In S. Kemmis & R. McTaggart (Eds.), *The action research reader.* Geelong, Victoria, Australia: Deakin University Press.

Kennedy, M. M. (1997). The connection between research and practice. *Educational Researcher, 26*(7), 4–12.

Kincheloe, J. (1991). *Teachers as researchers: Qualitative inquiry as a path to empowerment.* Philadelphia: Falmer.

Krathwohl, D. R. (1998). *Methods of educational and social science research: An integrated approach* (2nd ed.). Reading, MA: Addison-Wesley.

Lewin, K. (1952). Group decision and social change. In G. E. Swanson, T. M. Newcomb, & E. L. Hartley (Eds.), *Readings in social psychology.* New York: Holt.

Lortie, D. C. (1975). *Schoolteacher.* Chicago: The University of Chicago Press.

Lytle, S. (1997). *Action research keynote address.* Kansas City, MO: The Learning Exchange.

Maxwell, J. A. (1992). Understanding and validity in qualitative research. *Harvard Educational Review, 62*(3), 279–300.

McMillan, J. H. (1996). *Educational research: Fundamentals for the consumer* (2nd ed.). New York: Harper Collins.

Miles, M. B., & Huberman A. M. (1994). *Qualitative data analysis: An expanded sourcebook* (2nd ed.). Thousand Oaks, CA: Sage.

Milgram, S. (1964). Group pressure and action against a person. *Journal of Abnormal and Social Psychology, 69,* 137–143.

Miller, L., & Lieberman, A. (1988). School improvement in the United States: Nuance and numbers. *International Journal of Qualitative Studies in Education, 1*(1), 3–19.

Mills, G. E. (1985). Transient children. Unpublished M.Ed. Thesis. Perth, Australia: Western Australian Institute of Technology.

Mills, G. E. (1988). *Managing and coping with multiple educational change: A case study and analysis.* Unpublished doctoral dissertation. Eugene, OR: University of Oregon.

Mills, G. E. (1993). Levels of abstraction in a case study of educational change. In D. J. Flinders & G. E. Mills (Eds.), *Theory and concepts in qualitative research: Perspectives from the field* (pp. 103–116). New York: Teachers College Press.

National Council of Teachers of Mathematics. (1991). *Professional standards for teaching mathematics.* Reston, VA: National Council of Teachers of Mathematics.

Noffke, S. (1994). Action research: Towards the next generation. *Educational Action Research, 2*(1), 9–18.

Nolen, A. L., & Vander Putten, J. (2007). Action Research in Education: Addressing Gaps in Ethical Principles and Practices. *Educational Researcher, 36*(7), 401–407.

Osterman, K. F., & Kottkamp, R. B. (1993). *Reflective practice for educators: Improving schooling through professional development.* Newbury Park, CA: Corwin.

Patton, M. Q. (1990). *Qualitative evaluation and research methods* (2nd ed.). Newbury Park, CA: Sage.

Pelto, P. J., & Pelto, G. H. (1978). *Anthropological research: The structure of inquiry.* Cambridge, MA: Cambridge University Press.

Sagor, R. (1992). *How to conduct collaborative action research.* Alexandria, VA: ASCD.

Sagor, R. (2000). *Guiding school improvement with action research.* Alexandria, VA: ASCD.

Sagor, R. (2005). The Action Research Guidebook: *A Four-Step Process for Educators and School Teams.* Thousand Oaks, CA: Corwin Press.

Sarason, S. B. (1990). *The predictable failure of educational reform: Can we change course before it's too late?* San Francisco: Jossey-Bass.

Smith, L. M. (1990). Ethics in qualitative field research: An individual perspective. In E. W. Eisner & A. P. Peshkin (Eds.), *Qualitative inquiry in education: The continuing debate* (pp. 258–276). New York: Teachers College Press.

Soltis, J. (1990). The ethics of qualitative research. In E. W. Eisner & A. P. Peshkin (Eds.), *Qualitative inquiry in education: The continuing debate* (pp. 247–257). New York: Teachers College Press.

Spradley, J. (1980). *Participant observation.* New York: Holt, Rinehart & Winston.

Stringer, E. T. (1993). Socially responsive educational research: Linking theory and practice. In D. Flinders & G. E. Mills (Eds.), *Theory and concepts in qualitative research: Perspectives from the field* (pp. 141–162). New York: Teachers College Press.

Stringer, E. T. (1996). *Action research: A handbook for practitioners.* Thousand Oaks, CA: Sage.

Stringer, E. T. (2004). *Action research in education.* Upper Saddle River, NJ: Merrill/Prentice Hall.

Tickle, L. (1993). Testing for quality in educational action research: A terrifying taxonomy? *Educational Action Research, 3*(2), 233–236.

U.S. National Research Center. (1996). Third international mathematics and science study. Report No. 7. Washington, DC: Author.

Van de Walle, J. A. (2003). *Elementary school mathematics: Teaching developmentally.* New York: Longman.

Vockell, E. L., & Asher, J. W. (1996). *Educational research.* Upper Saddle River, NJ: Merrill/Prentice Hall.

Wells, G. (Ed.). (1994). *Changing schools from within: Creating communities of inquiry.* Portsmouth, NH: Heinemann.

Witte, R. S. (1985). *Statistics.* New York: Holt, Rinehart & Winston.

Wolcott, H. F. (1982). Differing styles of on-site research, or "If it isn't ethnography, what is it?" *Review Journal of Philosophy and Social Science, 7*, 154–169.

Wolcott, H. F. (1988). Ethnographic research in education. In R. M. Jaeger (Ed.), *Complementary methods for research in education* (pp. 187–210). Washington, DC: American Educational Research Association.

Wolcott, H. F. (1989). *Kwakiutl village and school.* Prospect Heights, IL: Waveland Press.

Wolcott, H. F. (1990). On seeking—and rejecting—validity in qualitative research. In E. W. Eisner & A. Peshkin (Eds.), *Qualitative inquiry in education: The continuing debate* (pp. 121–152). New York: Teachers College Press.

Wolcott, H. F. (1992). Posturing in qualitative inquiry. In M. LeCompte, W. L. Millroy, & J. Preissle (Eds.), *Handbook of qualitative research in education* (pp. 3–52). San Diego: Academic.

Wolcott, H. F. (1994). *Transforming qualitative data: Description, analysis, and interpretation.* Thousand Oaks, CA: Sage.

Wolcott, H. F. (1997). Ethnographic research in education. In R. M. Jaeger (Ed.), *Complementary methods for research in education* (2nd ed., pp. 325–398). Washington, DC: American Educational Research Association.

Wolcott, H. F. (2001). *Writing up qualitative research* (2nd ed.). Thousand Oaks, CA: Sage.

AUTHOR INDEX

SUBJECT INDEX

Process validity, 109
Professional development, 8–9, 161
Professional development days, 189
Professional development schools, 215–224
Professional disposition, 8–9
Professional model of education, 164
Professional organizations, 50, 52
Promising practices, 44, 45
Proofreading, 83
Propositions, 115
Protection from harm, 30–31
Psychological Abstracts, 47–48
PsycINFO, 47–48
Publication Manual of the American Psychological Association (APA), 55, 56, 172, 186–187
Punctuation, 186
Purpose, 16–17

Qualitative data
    analysis and interpretation of, 128–139, 144–147
    antecedent and consequences analysis with, 134–135
    from archival documents, 85–86
    asking key questions about, 131–132
    collection, 73–89
    concept maps with, 134
    from direct observation, 74–78
    displaying findings from, 135–136
    identifying themes in, 129
    from interviews and questionnaires, 78–85
    from journals, 86
    from maps, recordings, and artifacts, 86–89
    organization of, 126–128
    organization reviews of, 134
    sample analysis of, 137–139
    stating what's missing in, 136
    from surveys, 84–85
    triangulation with, 92–93
    validity in, 103–112
Qualitative research, 4
    validity in, 103–112
Quantitative data
    analysis and interpretation of, 126, 139–144
    from attitude scales, 91–92
    central tendency measures for, 140–141
    claims about, 143–144
    collection, 73, 89–92
    descriptive statistics with, 139–140
    from report cards, 90–91

from standardized tests, 90
from teacher-made tests, 89–90
triangulation with, 92–93
variability measures for, 141–142
Quantitative research, 4
    validity in, 102–103
Questionnaires, 78, 83–84
    coding, 129–131
    post-assessment, 232, 233
Questions
    convergent and divergent, 79–80
    developing research, 61
    evaluating research, 209, 210
    pilot, 79
Quick-fix strategies, 125
Quotations, indicating in research, 55

Random assignment, 3, 89
Readers' Guide to Periodical Literature, 49
Reading data, 127
Reciprocity, 216
Reconnaissance, 42–44
Refereed journals, 53, 184
References, 179. *See also* Literature reviews
    APA style for, 186–187
    credibility of, 104
Reflection
    in action planning, 155, 160–161
    on area of focus, 42–43
    data analysis and, 124–125
    in school culture, 161–162
Reflective practice, 8, 162–163
    developing, 13–14
    power roles and, 165
Reflective Practice, 184
Reflective stance, 9
    evaluating, 209, 211–212, 223
Reflexivity, 105
Reform, educational, 12
Relevance, 11, 45–46
Reliability, 103, 112–113
Reliability coefficients, 112–113
Report cards, 90–91
Reporting of research results, 170–195
    APA style for, 186–187
    editing, 180–181, 192
    establishing routines in, 180–182
    feedback on, 190–191
    format and style in, 172
    full, 111
    journal submission guidelines for, 183–194
    length of, 190
    outlines for, 181, 182
    reasons for writing, 171–172

sample action research article, 173–179
sample of, 197–207
selecting a style for, 185–186
self-assessment of, 187–188
stating what's missing in, 136
titles for, 191–192
writing rituals and, 179–182
Research. *See also* Action research
    bias in, 114–115
    criteria for, 208–209
    ethics in, 22–37
    evaluating sources in, 49, 53–54
    gap between practice and, 10–13
    generalizability of, 113–114
    insider, 27
    literature review in, 44–60
    mixed-methods, 4–5
    overview of educational, 2–5
    qualitative, 4
    quantitative, 4
    stating limitations of, 208
    teacher access to findings in, 12
Researcher's Guide to the Department of Education, A, 50
Resistance, 161–162
Resources
    hopefulness, 166–167
    lack of for teacher researchers, 161
Resources, statement of, 62
Reward systems, 182
Rights of research participants, 26, 27–28
Routine, seeing in new ways, 77

Schoolteacher (Lortie), 11
Schoolwide action research, 157, 160
Search engines, 49, 50
Self-assessment, 187–188
Self-renewing schools, 161–162
Semantic differentials, 92
Shareholders, engaging, 167
Sharing, data, 163
Social principles, 34
Social responsiveness, 7, 8
Software. *See* Computer software
Sources, evaluating, 49, 53–54
Spelling, 186
SPSS, 85, 139
Standard deviation (SD), 139, 141–142, 225–229
Standardized tests, 86, 90
    reliability of, 112–113
Statements of resources, 62
Statistical significance, 3
Statistics
    descriptive, 139–140, 226